DATE DUE

DEMCO 38-297

Writing Hig...
That Sells

Janice M. King

JOHN WILEY & SONS, INC.

New York • Chichester • Brisbane
Toronto • Singapore

Publisher: K. Schowalter
Editor: T. Hudson
Managing Editor: M. Frederick
Text Production & Design: V&M Graphics

Designations used by companies to distinguish their products are often claimed as trademarks. In all instances where John Wiley & Sons, Inc. is aware of a claim, the product names appear in initial capital or all capital letters. Readers, however, should contact the appropriate companies for more complete information regarding trademarks and registration.

This text is printed on acid-free paper.

This publication is designed to provide accurate and authoritative information in regard to the subject matter covered. It is sold with the understanding that the publisher is not engaged in rendering legal, accounting, or other professional service. If legal advice or other expert assistance is required, the services of a competent professional person should be sought.

Library of Congress Cataloging-in-Publication Data:

King, Janice M.
    Writing high-tech copy that sells / Janice M. King.
        p.   cm.
    Includes index.
    ISBN 0-471-04259-5.—ISBN 0-471-05846-7 (pbk.)
    1. Advertising copy.   2. High technology—Marketing.   I. Title.
HF5825.K44   1955
659. 13/2—dc20   94-35009
                                                                       CIP

Printed in the United States of America
10 9 8 7 6 5 4 3 2 1

To every writer who faces
the daily challenge of a
blank computer screen
and
to the memory of my father

Contents

PREFACE vii

ACKNOWLEDGMENTS xi

**PART ONE: THE FOUNDATION OF HIGH-TECH MARKETING
COMMUNICATION 1**

    **Chapter 1: Planning for High-Tech Marketing
Communication: Success Starts Here. 2**

    **Chapter 2: The High-Tech Audience: Targeting Your
Materials. 23**

    **Chapter 3: Message, Objective, and Purpose: The
Essentials for On-Target Communication. 35**

    **Chapter 4: Creative Issues: Developing the Best Ideas,
Styles, and Methods. 53**

PART TWO: WRITING A HIGH-TECH MARCOM DOCUMENT 63

    **Chapter 5: Document Elements: Packaging Your
Information for Greater Impact. 64**

    **Chapter 6: Content Types: Presenting High-Tech
Information Effectively. 77**

    **Chapter 7: Text Techniques: Adding Power to Your
Copy. 105**

Chapter 8: Legal and Ethical Issues: Avoiding Problems in Your Materials. 128
Chapter 9: International High-Tech Marketing Communication: Adapting Your Materials to the Global Market. 146

PART THREE: HIGH-TECH MARCOM PROJECTS 159

Chapter 10: Sales Materials: Reaching Prospects and Customers. 160
Chapter 11: Press Materials: Reaching Journalists and Analysts. 199
Chapter 12: Alliance Materials: Reaching Dealers and Partners. 225
Chapter 13: Marketing Communication in Electronic Media: Expanding Your Horizon. 237

APPENDIX A: COPYWRITING CHECKLIST 248

APPENDIX B: GLOSSARY 251

APPENDIX C: BIBLIOGRAPHY AND RESOURCES 257

APPENDIX D: REFERENCES 265

INDEX 271

Preface

Writing High-Tech Copy That Sells is for anyone who develops marketing or press materials for a technical product, service, or company. It is a practical guide to the marketing communication content, materials, and writing techniques that are successful in today's high-tech marketplace.

I wrote this book because it is an everyday resource that I needed—but could not find—for my work as a freelance copywriter in the telecommunications and data networking industries. While there are many general books on writing techniques, advertising, and public relations, I found their information to be of limited value in the context of high-tech marketing communication (marcom). For example, finding good ways to handle technical jargon is an issue that simply doesn't exist in the marketing of other business or consumer products. In addition, for most high-tech marketing writers, advertisements and press releases are only a small portion of their work; a greater portion is sales brochures, white papers, articles, and backgrounders.

Unlike the general books, *Writing High-Tech Copy That Sells* focuses exclusively on the marcom materials commonly produced by technology companies. This book is a comprehensive reference of ideas and techniques for all high-tech marcom and public relations materials. The examples presented and issues described here are drawn from a range of high-tech industries, including computer hardware and software, telecommunications, networking, electronics, and instrumentation.

WHO SHOULD READ THIS BOOK

This book will be of interest to several groups of readers, including:

- **Corporate Copywriters and Communication Specialists.** Writers, specialists, editors, and managers in marketing communication and public relations groups. Also, technical writers and editors in documentation groups who produce marketing materials. Whether you address the full range of marketing communication projects or only a certain type of material, this book will give you practical ideas to improve your writing on a daily basis.
- **Corporate Marketing Managers.** Product managers, marketing specialists, vice presidents of marketing and sales—even company presidents. This book will help you recognize and obtain effective marketing and public relations materials. And if you work in a small company where you are a "jack-of-all trades," you will find this book a thorough and valuable resource for writing marketing and public relations materials.
- **Advertising Agency Staff, Freelancers, and Consultants.** Copywriters, creative directors, public relations specialists, and account executives in advertising, marketing communication, and public relations agencies. Also, freelance copywriters and marketing communication consultants. As an agency-based or independent communicator, you must offer special skills and expertise to your clients on a wide range of materials. Clients also have higher expectations for the quality and creativity of agency or freelance work. This book will give you a useful everyday reference for generating new ideas and maintaining the freshness and high quality of your work. And if you are new to high-tech products, this book will provide a valuable education in the unique issues and challenges of these markets.
- **Students.** College-level students in business communication, advertising, public relations, and technical communication programs. This book will give you information and practice on specific writing techniques for the types of projects you will be expected to produce on the job.

HOW TO GET THE MOST FROM THIS BOOK

You won't need to read the chapters sequentially, or even the entire book. The content is organized so you can quickly find the most relevant section for a current project or information need. However, you should read Chapters 5 through 7 together as they present a complete, integrated approach to the actual craft of marketing writing. Also, take the time to read the other chapters—they present useful information to add to your framework of marcom knowledge.

Use this book every day for ideas on how to produce specific types of material, expand your knowledge into new areas, and find resources for detailed exploration of a topic. Also, take the time to complete the exercises. They are the best way to learn a new technique or brush up your skills.

The information presented here assumes you have a solid knowledge of the rules of grammar and basic writing techniques such as the ability to construct a complete sentence and to make a logical flow between paragraphs. This book does *not* cover:

- Basic writing skills or issues around the practice of writing such as how to conduct research and interviews or how to develop good work habits.
- Materials that are usually classified under the general category of business communication such as procedures, employee communication, community relations, and investor relations.

For the purpose of this book, these definitions apply:

- **Marketing Communication:** An umbrella term (often abbreviated to "marcom" in this book) that encompasses all sales promotion, advertising, press materials, and other documents intended to promote the sale of a product.
- **Advertising:** Paid marketing messages for a product or company that appear in a magazine, newspaper, or broadcast medium.
- **Press Materials:** Informational documents that are targeted primarily to journalists and analysts, such as press releases, fact sheets, and backgrounders.
- **Product:** The ideas and techniques presented in this book apply to the marketing of technical services as well as products. As

used here, the term *product* includes services, except where distinctions are noted.

The following terms are used interchangeably in this book:

- Copywriting and marketing writing.
- Text and copy.
- Document, collateral, material, and piece.

Examples are presented *in this type style* wherever they will help you understand a particular idea or technique. In most cases, they are drawn from actual marketing materials for high-tech products.

If you have questions, ideas, or suggestions on future editions of this book, send them to me at MarkeTech, 1075 Bellevue Way NE Suite 486, Bellevue, WA 98004 or by electronic mail to janiceking@delphi.com.

HERE'S TO YOUR SUCCESS

Writing High-Tech Copy That Sells is more than just the title of this book. By applying the ideas presented here, it is something you can *do*—in every one of your marcom projects.

Janice King
Bellevue, Washington
January 1995

Acknowledgments

Many people provided valuable ideas, resources, feedback, and support for the development of this book. Nancy Hoft provided the key introduction to my editor, solid advice on the international chapter, and much-needed commiseration during the writing process. John Hedtke encouraged me to write a book and gave me valuable advice on the publishing process. Carol Buchmiller and Jeanne Miller gave the complete manuscript an insightful review and their comments improved this book enormously. Others who reviewed portions of the book and generously shared their feedback include Rick Duval, Joel Gilman, Nancy Hoft, and Bjorn Snellman. Thanks to all of them and to the many others who shared their ideas and experience in conversations with me.

I am grateful for clients who continue to provide challenging projects that expand my knowledge and stretch my skills as a writer. I have learned from all of them, but especially Rick Duval, Lynn Epstein, Joanna Holmes, Laura McCluer, Jeanne Miller, and Bjorn Snellman.

The community of writers in the Society for Technical Communication (STC) provides me a valuable source of professional nourishment. Special thanks go to Frank Smith, Editor of the journal *Technical Communication,* for accepting my quarterly column on marketing writing and to Christopher Juillet for sponsoring my development of a Marketing Communication Professional Interest Committee within STC.

My communities of friends at Northlake and Evergreen gave me sustenance during the writing process through their unflagging interest and encouragement. Elizabeth Alexander and Karen Lindsay helped me get through the grind of numerous drafts and other niggling tasks. Thanks to all of them for such wonderful support.

Several people at John Wiley & Sons deserve thanks. My editor, Terri Hudson was a tireless champion of the book and a patient guide through the maze of publishing. Rich O'Hanley suggested the perfect title. Terry Canela was very helpful with the details of manuscripts and correspondence. Micheline Frederick capably handled the production process.

The deepest thanks go to my family and closest friends, including Mom, Jo Ann, Steve, Susan, Stephanie, Carolyn, and Marianne; Arlene Greene, Kate Harris, Marcia Levenson, and Maureen Scully. Your unshakeable belief in my abilities gave me the confidence and motivation to undertake such a major project. I promise to have a life now.

Thanks are due to the following companies, which granted permission to reproduce the example materials included in this book:

Active Voice Corporation
ADC Kentrox
American Power Conversion
Andrew Corporation
Attachmate Corporation
Candle Corporation
Communication News
Dialogic Corporation
Digital Equipment Corporation
Harris Corporation
Hughes Network Systems, Inc.
IBM Corporation
Intel Corporation

Intuit, Inc.
KnowledgePoint
Lotus Development Corporation
Make Systems, Inc.
Microsoft Corporation
NetWare Technical Journal
Novell, Inc.
Ontrack Computer Systems, Inc.
Panlabs, Inc.
Perception Technology
Saber Software Corporation
Sequent Computer Systems, Inc.

PART ONE

The Foundation of High-Tech Marketing Communication

The chapters in this part describe several important issues you must consider when developing any type of marketing materials:

- *Developing a communication plan.*
- *Targeting your audiences.*
- *Identifying the messages, objectives, and purpose of the document.*
- *Working successfully throughout the creative process.*

While these chapters contain many guidelines you will reference regularly, they are intended more to provide a broad perspective for your work. Read them at least once, then refer to these chapters again as you become involved in specific projects.

CHAPTER 1

Planning for High-Tech Marketing Communication

Success Starts Here

You have a hot new product to introduce, a major upgrade to announce for an existing product, or a new market to reach. Now you need sales and press materials that will help you with this marketing activity. While it is tempting to jump in and start creating documents based on a few initial ideas, your marcom activity will be more effective if it is carefully planned. This chapter describes the typical communication cycle for high-tech products and how to create solid plans for both marketing communication programs and individual documents.

THE COMMUNICATION CYCLE FOR HIGH-TECH PRODUCTS

Marketing communication for high-tech products is typically organized around three types of activity:

1. Introducing a new product to the market.
2. Supporting the sales cycle for individual customer purchases.
3. Sustaining communication to the market, the customer base, and the sales force.

Each of these activities involve different types of marketing materials and may be covered by a separate marcom plan.

Product Introduction Communication

Introducing a new product to the market involves a number of communication activities that are directed to the press, sales people, and prospective customers (prospects). Some activities may be conducted simultaneously, depending on the actual development of the product and the scale of the introduction effort. No matter how they are implemented, each of these activities is supported by a variety of marcom materials (Figure 1.1). Product introduction activities can include:

- **Educating the infrastructure.** The market infrastructure includes the key analysts, consultants, and journalists who follow the technology or target market, beta users, key customers, and alliance partners who are involved in marketing the product.[27] The process of infrastructure education usually begins a few months in advance of the actual product announcement. It is intended to obtain feedback on the product capabilities and positioning, cultivate positive supporting comments for the actual announcement, and facilitate coverage by publications that have long lead times. Infrastructure education activity involves personal contact with a small number of people, often under a nondisclosure agreement. Preliminary press and sales materials for the product may be given to these contacts as part of the education effort.
- **Educating the sales force.** The goal of this activity is to have knowledgeable sales people and dealers ready and able to sell the product as soon as it is released. Sales kits and other dealer materials, as well as final brochures and other sales documents, are distributed as part of the sales education effort.
- **Announcing the product.** The actual product announcement may be made through a press release or at a press conference, trade show, or other event. The announcement is released on, or very near, the date when the product is available for cus-

Product Launch Stage	Materials
Infrastructure Education	Preliminary press materials and data sheets, presentation slides, white papers, backgrounders.
Sales Force and Dealer Education	Sales kit, presentation slides, white papers.
Product Announcement	Final press release and supporting press materials, all sales materials, quotes from or reprints of test reports and product reviews.

Figure 1.1   Materials that support product introduction activities.

tomer purchase. The press release is issued to a large list of publications and wire services, and sales materials are mailed to prospects and customers.

The marcom materials created for a product introduction may go through several iterations in the period leading up to the announcement, as the company obtains feedback from the infrastructure and early customers about the product's positioning and marketing messages.

Sales Cycle Communication

Sales is a process of communication, not an event.—Richard Brock

As the quote above indicates, marketing communication plays a vital role in the selling of high-tech products and services by providing information of various types, in a variety of formats, directed to multiple audiences, at different stages of the sales cycle. Marcom documents provide both impetus and support for a purchase decision, whether it is made by an organizational committee or an individual consumer.

To develop materials that will best support the sales cycle, you must understand both the general selling process and the specific factors that apply to your products. In general, selling high-tech products involves challenges that are quite different from those for selling other business or consumer products. This section presents a brief overview of the most common high-tech sales cycle and how to target your materials effectively throughout the selling process. Refer to the resources listed in the Bibliography for detailed information on concepts and techniques for selling high-tech products.

The sale of most high-tech products involves an ongoing process of educating the prospect—about the product itself, its underlying technology, and its application to the prospect's problem, need, or circumstances. Much of this education is provided by the product's marketing materials through a multistage communication process (Figure 1.2).

Traditional advertising texts describe the multiple stages of the sales cycle with the AIDA Model (Attention, Interest, Desire, Action). This model analyzes how your copy creates prospect awareness of your product (attention), prompts exploration of your product (interest), fosters the buy decision (desire), and motivates the prospect to actually make the purchase (action).

However, for many high-tech products, the stages in the sales cycle can be described somewhat differently: Awareness, Exploration, Decision, and Affirmation. For high-tech products,

Sales Cycle Stage	Materials
Creating Awareness	Advertising, direct mail, articles.
Supporting Exploration	Product brochure or data sheet, demo disk, case studies, article reprints, application guide.
Motivating Selection	White papers, evaluation units, visit to a customer site, proposal.
Sustaining Loyalty	Newsletter, white papers, direct mail to encourage purchase of additional products and upgrades.

Figure 1.2   Materials that support each stage in the sales cycle.

the first three stages are similar to the AIDA model, although the decision stage is often reached directly from the exploration stage. And the final stage in the high-tech cycle, affirming the selection, exists because of the significant investment and risk involved in purchases of high-tech products.

In more detail, the stages of the high-tech sales cycle can be described as follows:

- **Stage 1: Creating Awareness.** This is the beginning of the sales cycle, where a prospect first discovers your product. This awareness may come from reading a product advertisement or an article in a magazine, or from research undertaken by the prospect to find products that will solve a particular problem or need. Communication at this stage may involve advertising, direct mail, articles, and presentations.
- **Stage 2: Supporting Exploration.** The prospect has decided she's interested, and now wants to learn detailed information about your product and company. The prospect may also explore several competing products or alternative solutions at this stage. Communication is usually accomplished through data sheets, brochures, a catalog, or a demo disk. For complex product sales that involve a committee decision, materials may include white papers, case studies, article reprints, and other documents that address the spectrum of committee participants and their specific purchasing concerns.
- **Stage 3: Motivating a Decision.** This is the stage where the prospect selects your product and actually makes the purchase. Once a decision has been made in favor of your product, the prospect may need additional impetus to complete the actual purchase. Communication at this stage often encom-

passes detailed product brochures, white papers, article reprints, and case studies. It may also include supporting materials for in-person sales presentations such as demo programs, slides or transparencies, or a video.

- **Stage 4: Affirming the Selection.** This is the postsale stage, where a prospect may need additional information to feel comfortable with the purchase decision. Communication at this stage includes the product packaging and documentation, but also periodic newsletters and direct mail to announce new service programs, products, and upgrades.

All of your communication and activities throughout the sales cycle must work to build the prospect's confidence and trust in your company, product, and service. At each stage, your materials should convey the credibility of your company and support the buyer's confidence in making a purchase decision.

Sustained Marketing Communication

Marketing communication does not end after the product is announced or a sale is made. To ensure product success and customer loyalty over the long term, you must view communication as a sustained effort. Ongoing communication can be directed to the overall market (including the press), to customers, and to your sales force and dealers (Figure 1.3).

- **Market communication.** Sustained communication to the overall market involves reaching both prospects and members of the press. For prospects, you want to maintain awareness of your product as a potential solution to their needs. For journalists, you want to encourage ongoing coverage of your product as it incorporates new capabilities, addresses developments in related technologies, or serves new applications. A sustained effort is especially important for products in new technology areas, where a considerable amount of time and communication may be necessary to educate the market about what your product *is*, as well as the benefits and features it offers. Sustained market communication typically involves press releases for new product capabilities and applications, case studies, and articles targeted to different industry publications.
- **Customer communication.** Customers are an important marketing target because the strength of your customer relationships is vital to the long-term success of your company. It is common marketing wisdom that keeping an existing cus-

Sustained Communication Activity	Materials
Market Communication	Press releases, articles, white papers, case studies.
Customer Communication	Newsletters, white papers, articles, upgrade announcements, materials for accessory products.
Sales Force and Dealer Communication	Case studies, new applications, selling tips, information on company's promotional activities.

Figure 1.3   Materials that support sustained communication activity.

tomer is easier and cheaper than attracting a new one. In addition, to sustain customer loyalty in the rapidly changing environment of high-tech, Hippeau notes, "Customers need to be assured that you're still alive and working on the future."[125] You can reach customers through individualized forms of communication such as direct mail, or collectively through newsletters, presentations, or materials distributed to user groups and online services.

- **Sales force and dealer communication.** You must continue to communicate with your sales people and dealers in order to maintain their enthusiasm for selling your product. This is especially important when a dealer carries multiple, competing products and is constantly bombarded by new information and sales incentives. Sustained marcom for this audience often involves direct mail, ads in publications targeted to dealers, updated sales kits, dealer newsletters and seminars, plant tours, or other events. In addition, you may need to create localized materials to support international dealers.

Integrated Marketing Communication

In most consumer-goods companies, the advertising, public relations, and sales promotion (i.e., marcom) functions operate separately. However, most high-tech companies adhere to the concept of integrated marketing communication: that a product's advertising, collateral, and public relations materials should have common themes, designs, and messages and be driven by a single set of strategies and principles. This philosophy of integrated marcom can be implemented throughout the communication cycle for high-tech products.

The benefits of integrating these communication functions include:

- Unified messages and style across different materials, multiple audiences, and over time.
- Greater cost-effectiveness when one set of messages, images, and materials can serve multiple purposes. This is a valuable factor considering that advertising and marcom budgets receive close scrutiny by cost-conscious corporate executives.
- Easier measurement of results and greater confidence in their validity because the messages remain constant over different media and over a defined period of time.

A discussion of specific marcom strategies and how to develop them is beyond the scope of this book. However, Patti et al. suggest these criteria for evaluating the quality of a marcom strategy:[25]

- It is based on research about your product, market, and competition.
- It presents a clear message to the market.
- It is unique within your competitive environment.
- It is adaptable to all relevant media.
- It will be effective in the long term.

THE MARCOM PLAN

No matter where you are in the communication cycle for a product, your activities should be driven by a marketing communication (marcom) plan. This plan presents a broad outline of documents and activities for a product or a specific marketing campaign. It is a statement of agreement among all the key marketing and sales people for the product about communication strategies and deliverables. A marcom plan also is a guide and a starting point for two other documents that are critical in planning any marcom project: the creative platform and the document plan (both are described in detail later in this chapter).

Marcom plans can be developed for a product, product line, event, or marketing campaign. They can focus on only the high-level communication issues, or describe detailed directions and tactics. They can cover sales, advertising, and public relations materials, as well as marketing events such as trade shows, seminars, and user-group meetings. Separate marcom plans are often developed for different types of marketing activities, such as:

- Product introduction or upgrade announcement campaigns.
- Trade show, conference, or user-group meeting.
- Sustained promotion of a product.
- Campaigns focused by vertical market, distribution channel, or other customer segment.

While a marcom plan may include a wide range of information, it typically contains a mix of the topics listed below. The next section presents an example marcom plan.

- **Situation analysis.** An assessment of both past and current marcom efforts as well as the current market perception of your product and company. This information can include a description of current promotion themes and marketing problems. A situation analysis can help you evaluate the likely success of plans and strategies for future campaigns.
- **Product information.** A brief description of major features and benefits, and a development history (for an established product) or the development rationale (for a new product).
- **Market information.** The characteristics of each target segment, information on primary and secondary prospects, and a description of distribution channels, sales cycle, and pricing. *Caution*: If you are relying on market research conducted before the product was developed, verify that it is still accurate and that your product indeed still targets that market.
- **Competitive activity.** The strategies, messages, materials, trade show participation, seminar programs, and other marketing or public relations efforts produced by your direct and indirect competitors.
- **Strategies.** The planned strategies for the entire marcom program, including goals and objectives for the overall campaign and for each specific marcom document or activity.
- **Tactics.** A description of each element in the marcom program, such as materials, publicity, and events. These tactics describe the specific activities or materials to be produced, how they are to be distributed, packaged, or staged, and how they relate to the product's sales process.
- **Evaluation.** Criteria and methods for determining the success of the program.
- **Documents.** A description of the major documents, including a specific objective and purpose for each. These documents can include collateral, advertising, press materials, investor communications, and in-person sales presentations. This dis-

cussion may also describe the coordination of materials with other marketing activities, such as using a product selection guide as an enticement to visit a trade-show booth.

- **Schedules and budgets.** A description of deadlines, estimated costs, and other production considerations for each activity in the plan. This discussion may also specify the responsibilities and assignments of both internal and external creative resources such as copywriters, designers, and public relations specialists.

Depending on marketing strategies, a marcom plan may also include:

- **PR activities.** For many companies, public relations activities are a major portion of the marcom effort because publicity is a relatively inexpensive way to reach a large audience. The trade press often picks up press releases that announce new products or other company achievements, accepts articles written by company experts, or publishes reviews of a new product or upgrade. As a result, strategies and objectives for press materials become an important part of marcom plans. A separate PR plan also can be developed.
- **Media selections.** Information on the specific media where ads will appear. For extensive advertising programs, this information may be presented in a separate media buying document.

A marcom plan is usually generated well in advance of the planned activities, especially for annual budgeting purposes. But the plan should be flexible enough to accommodate changes in business activity or competitor actions. And your marcom plan should be adaptable to handle these common scenarios in high-tech product development: "Sorry, that function isn't going to be in the next release after all," or "We added this cool feature last night."

Example Marketing Communication Plan

The following is an example marketing communication plan that could be created for a fictional software product.

MARKETING COMMUNICATION PLAN

Management System Product

This plan covers marketing communication and public relations activities for the product introduction and the six-month period after rollout. Most activities are focused on the announcement event at the trade show in September.

Situation Analysis

This product has been in development for two years and in beta test at customer sites for three months. The trade-show announcement will introduce the product into the target market for the first time. There has been no previous advertising or public relations activity for the product. Company sales people have initiated the sales process with many prospects through telephone calls and in-person presentations, using a preliminary sales brochure for support.

The major communication challenge is creating maximum exposure for the product immediately after the announcement event. Two factors will support this effort: The product is in a new technology area that is of strong interest to the press and the target market, and beta customers are leading companies that are willing to discuss their results from the product.

Potential disadvantages are that the company is unknown, and the technology is very sophisticated and requires considerable explanation. Also, the major competitor for this product is very large and well-known, and has a well-established position in the market. However, the competitor is being hurt by a proprietary design and by customer perceptions that it is not paying sufficient attention to this product area.

Product Information

The product is a modular tool for monitoring and managing information systems (computers, applications software, networks). It provides a framework for adding new capabilities developed by this company, other vendors, or a customer's internal software engineers. It is the first product of its type to offer this open, "building-block" approach, and was developed to address market frustrations about closed, proprietary management systems. See attachment for a complete list of features and benefits.

Market Information

The target market is information-systems departments in large and medium-size organizations (i.e., sales greater than

$50 million). These may be businesses, government agencies, or nonprofit organizations. Initial market focus will be North America, with European introduction to follow by year-end. All sales will be made directly by company sales reps. The typical sales cycle involves making contact with an internal advocate at the prospect company, conducting a demonstration and presentations for numerous decision-makers, delivering a proposal, conducting a trial, and closing the sale. System price varies substantially depending on modules and options purchased.

Competitive Activity

The major competitor relies largely on personal calls by sales reps and occasional direct mail campaigns; apparently there is no public relations activity.

Strategies

1. Develop coordinated introduction activity for product to obtain maximum coverage and create awareness in target markets.
2. Develop sustained marketing communication and public relations activities to support sales efforts in six-month period after product introduction.

Tactics

1. Hold an announcement event at September trade show, with presentations by company president and two or three key beta customers. Invite analysts, editors from target publications, and prospects.
2. Direct mail campaign to coincide with announcement to introduce product and open the door for a salesperson contact.
3. Ongoing public relations activity after introduction to include placement of technical articles and case studies, announcement of customer wins and alliances, etc.

Evaluation Methods

1. Number of qualified inquiries generated by all activities. Track separately for each direct mail list, trade-show event, article placement, and other sources.

2. Quantity and depth of press coverage generated by announcement event.

Documents

1. *Product Overview Brochure*: A high-level summary of the product's design, features, benefits, and potential applications. Objective is to support a positive purchase decision at multiple levels in a prospect company. Purpose is to inform decision-makers about the product.
2. *Data Sheet*: A detailed description of product functionality. The objective and purpose are to support the sales process by providing detailed product information to prospects.
3. *Case Studies*: Articles on results achieved by beta customers. Two versions will be produced: one for internal use, containing strong endorsements of the product and company, the other suitable for placement in trade publications. The objective is to provide the salesperson and internal advocate at the prospect company with references to support a purchase decision. Purpose is to persuade prospects about the validity of our product by showing its acceptance in the market.
4. *Press Kit*: A folder containing press releases, corporate backgrounder, and a technical backgrounder. Objective and purpose is to encourage journalists and analysts to write about the product by providing them with complete information.
5. *Technology Primer Articles*: Three articles to be submitted to the technical journals. Objective is to establish the credibility of our approach and communicate with highly technical experts at prospect companies. These articles will be both informative and persuasive in purpose.

Schedules and Budgets

All materials must be ready by the major industry trade show in September. Budgets are limited; this eliminates expensive production techniques on all pieces except the Product Overview brochure.

Setting Objectives in a Marcom Plan

The objectives specified in a marcom plan are typically stated in qualitative terms, for example:

- Creating awareness or a desired positioning for the product or company. *Our product will be perceived as one of the leaders by prospects in our key markets.*
- Conveying information about a product or company to a new market or distribution channel. *Leveraging our experience in the banking industry, communicate how our product can solve the problems of customers in other financial-services companies.*
- Developing preference for your brand over competitive products. *Emphasize the quality of our brand name and corporate reputation for all products.*
- Setting the agenda for a purchase decision. *Communicate the importance of future product directions as an important purchasing factor.*
- Increasing editorial coverage of your company or product or increasing the visibility of company experts and executives. *Obtain greater product and company mentions in articles, reports, and presentations made by journalists and analysts.*

Measuring Results

Many marcom plans specify the quantitative criteria that will be used at the end of a defined time period to determine the success of the proposed materials and activities. Results can be evaluated by a variety of measurements such as number of orders or inquiries received, or amount of press coverage generated. A common measurement in advertising is the cost per thousand (CPM) readers exposed to the ad; the lower the cost, the broader your exposure.

The specific factors for measuring results will vary according to the overall strategies and objectives for your product or campaign. Both qualitative and quantitative factors may be appropriate. The marcom plan can list these factors and the process by which results will be tracked and reported.

Staging Your Materials

To understand staging, consider this scenario. You see an ad for a high-tech product in a trade magazine. You call the toll-free number in the ad or return the reader service card to request more information. A few weeks later, a data sheet appears in your mail, along with a reply card where you can request a more detailed brochure on the product, a white paper on its underlying technology, or a free subscription to the company's newsletter. You have just participated in a staged communication activity, where the company qualifies prospective customers according to the type and amount of literature they request. Many companies also adopt this technique to control marcom costs—after all, you don't want to send your expensive, four-color brochure to someone who turns out *not* to be a prospect for your product.

Describe the staging of your materials in your marcom plan. Specify how materials will be sequenced and coordinated with each other and with advertising, public relations, trade shows and other promotional activities. But make sure you don't make prospects jump over too many hurdles before they obtain the information that helps them determine their interest in your product. As one buyer put it, "Too often you are sent another device so you can send another card for what you really wanted at the start."[118]

Using the Marcom Plan When Writing

A good marcom plan is a valuable guide to the high-tech copywriter. It presents essential background information you need for planning a specific document, including the scope of the piece, its audiences, market perceptions and issues, and the product positioning.

A carefully crafted marketing communication plan is an important foundation for your writing, helping you develop specific pieces appropriately, and acting as a checkpoint to ensure that your projects are on track. Additional uses for the information presented in a marcom plan include:

- Determining how a particular piece fits into the overall set of materials or other communication activities and media. For example, if you know that a separate brochure will be developed for dealers, you won't need to address their concerns in the customer brochure that is your assignment.
- Ensuring the consistency of messages across multiple pieces.
- Identifying "recyclable" blocks of copy. These are words, paragraphs, even entire pages of text that you write once, then adapt for use in many different pieces.

THE CREATIVE PLATFORM

Some companies and agencies supplement their marcom plans with a document that describes the overall creative strategies and guidelines for the planned materials. Called a creative platform, this document describes messages, style, tone, and creative constraints for copy and visuals that apply across all materials and over the duration of the campaign or product cycle. The creative platform defines the range of flexibility allowed in a piece, without specifying particular execution ideas.

The creative platform also is a useful document for refereeing the review process when you are selecting specific execution ideas. In many high-tech companies, marcom concepts and draft materials are reviewed by many different people such as the product manager, vice president of marketing, sales director, corporate communications manager, and others. Each of these people have an understandably subjective view about what makes a good design or good copy. In the ideal world, these views would be reasonably similar and it would be easy to resolve disagreements about the copy or design. But the more likely case is that the parties involved will have widely divergent views on creative proposals. This divergence can lead to seemingly endless debates that are based on no stronger rationale than "the vp of sales thinks it's ugly."

To avoid these disagreements, or at least to make them easier to resolve, the creative platform can include criteria for judging design and copy concepts as well as specific executions. It's important that all parties agree in advance to these criteria. And by establishing them at the campaign planning stage, you can avoid reviewing and redefining criteria with each project.[14]

The creative platform should reflect your research into market conditions, target audience, and competitive situation. The creative platform also must consider your key marketing messages; the messages are what you want to say, the creative platform is how you want to say it.

A creative platform can include any combination of these items (see the next section for an example):

- **Audience profile**. A description of the primary and secondary audiences for the different materials in the campaign including demographics, issues, existing knowledge or perceptions, buying habits, decision process, and preferences for the content and presentation of product information.
- **Messages and positioning**. A description of the product's key messages and desired positioning as well as supporting evidence available such as facts, examples, or case studies. This discussion also can describe the product's "personality" or brand characteristics.

- **Campaign themes**. The visual and copy concepts that must be included in each marcom project for this campaign. In some cases, themes from a previous campaign must be incorporated into the planned materials or a transition must be made between the old and new themes.
- **Style and tone**. The general style and tone that will apply to both visuals and copy in all documents in the campaign, such as formal and businesslike, or informal and energetic.
- **Constraints**. Creative or production limitations on the visuals or copy. For example, visuals must be appropriate for both color and black-and-white reproduction or the copy must be structured to accommodate frequent changes in product specifications.
- **Evaluation criteria**. A description of the review process, factors for determining the appropriateness of specific execution ideas, and a list of the people who will review the document at each stage.

Example Creative Platform

The following is an example creative platform that could be created for a fictional software product.

CREATIVE PLATFORM

Audience

Multiple decision-makers within a prospect company. Representative titles of these people include: vice president of operations, chief information officer, information systems managers, software engineers, and technical analysts.

Key Messages and Positioning

This product is the only open, modular tool available today for managing information systems. Customers can choose the modules they need today and add others in the future as necessary. The result is flexibility and controllable costs for future growth. Position the product as innovative and closely matched to customer needs.

Campaign Themes

"The Choice is Yours" (political candidate) theme for visual and copy elements. Copy and images should show customers choosing the winning candidate (our product).

Style and Tone

Formal writing style, but keep active voice and you/we usage. Tone should be professional, knowledgeable, restrained, these must not be perceived as "hard sell" pieces.

Creative Constraints

Visuals must be limited to two-color production on all pieces except the Product Overview brochure. Layout and copy must allow for growth in product specifications as new interfaces are added to the product.

Evaluation Criteria

All concepts and drafts will be reviewed by the marketing communication manager, product manager, and VP/ Marketing. Initial concepts and final drafts only will also be reviewed by the Director of Engineering and the National Sales Manager. Final draft of all copy will be reviewed by the company attorney. Evaluation criteria will be (as agreed in June 12 meeting):

- Fits with the campaign theme.
- Contains all marketing messages.
- Suitable for presentation to all decision-makers.
- Presents product and company information clearly, completely, and accurately.

Using the Creative Platform When Writing

The creative platform can be a valuable resource when you are deciding on the approach to your material, and for making sure you stay "on course" as you write. It can help you focus your ideas so they are as targeted and effective as possible. For example, the audience profile can help you select language and examples that will be most relevant to a document's readers. The information on messages, style, and tone can help you craft the text to meet the document's objectives. And the information in the creative platform can help you with the sometimes difficult task of choosing what *not* to include in a document.

THE DOCUMENT PLAN

A document plan (sometimes called a creative brief or copy strategy) is a writing guide that is specific to each piece you produce. It may be part of the overall creative platform or developed separately as you begin each project. It may be in the form of short notes, a detailed outline, or a page-by-page description of writing techniques, document elements, and visuals that will be used in the planned piece. A document plan gives you a good reference point for getting agreement from others on the content and organization, and for checking your ideas before you begin writing and throughout your work on the project.

As described earlier, a good creative platform serves as a long-term guide of key messages and approaches to the information that can be used over many different pieces and over time. A document plan applies the principles of the creative platform to the unique aspects of each document.

A document plan typically includes (see the next section for an example):

- **Document type.** You can package any given content into many different types of marcom documents. Identify which document type is most suited to your purpose, audience, and intended use.
- **Publication type.** If you are writing an article or technical paper, describe the target publication. Is it a technical journal, a trade magazine for a specific technology or for a vertical market, or a general computer, industrial, medical, or other publication? How does the publication differentiate itself from others that serve the target audience? What are the publication's requirements for accepting articles or papers?
- **Audience.** A description of the specific audience(s) for *this* document. What types of background information will readers have about your technology? What types of new information do they need? Which product or customer names will they recognize? Which examples will be relevant? What level of involvement will each audience group have with your material? Do different audience groups have different levels of involvement? How does this piece fit with other pieces that readers may see?

- **Objective and purpose.** Why are you writing *this* piece? What do you want it to accomplish? Does your purpose match the document's intended use? How well does the purpose for this piece mesh with that of other materials in your collateral set? (See Chapter 3 for more information on the relationship between objective and purpose.) Specify the marcom problem that the document must solve or the opportunity that the document must capture. A clearly stated objective and purpose will help you evaluate the appropriateness of the copy when it is in draft form.
- **Key messages.** The key selling message or the topics to be covered in the piece. This information may be presented in the form of an outline of the document's content.
- **Source material.** Interview sources, research reports, and other information available as background for the document.
- **Copywriting guidelines.** The style, tone, format, and length of the text. How will the copy integrate with the images and design planned for the piece? Do you need to consider special formatting requirements when writing the copy? What is the maximum number of words or characters for the copy?
- **Document elements.** The specific elements that will appear in the piece such as headlines, body copy, captions, callouts, specifications, ordering information, copyright and trademark notices. You may also want to describe images such as charts, diagrams, photos, or illustrations.
- **Content types.** What information does the document need to include? technical details? a discussion of strategies or issues? How does this content compare with the content of other documents your reader will likely see?
- **The offer.** Describe the offer or call to action that will be presented to the reader and the response vehicle (e.g., reply card, toll-free phone number, fax response sheet).
- **Legal considerations.** List sensitive information, regulatory requirements, or other legal constraints that must be reflected in the copy.
- **Assignments.** A clear statement of tasks, responsibilities, and schedules for all writers and designers involved in the project.
- **Review process.** Who will review the document drafts, both internally and externally? at what state? for what type of input? How will you verify facts, statistics, equations, names, and descriptive information? How will you resolve conflicting comments?

Example Document Plan

The following is an example document plan that could be created for a fictional software product.

DOCUMENT PLAN

Document Name:
Product Brief

Document Type:
Data sheet

Publication Type:
N/A

Audience
Prospects, especially information systems managers and software engineers who need to evaluate the technical aspects of the product.

Objective and Purpose
To support the sales process by providing detailed product information to prospects.

Source Material
Product Overview brochure, functional specification document, developer interviews.

Key Messages
Include all key messages, but emphasize technical strengths and flexibility.

Copywriting Guidelines
Keep content focused on presenting the facts with a minimum of "salesy" language. Describe all major areas of product functionality.

Document Elements
Overline, headline and subheads, body copy, sidebars for key features/benefits list and product specifications.

Content Types
Product information, specifications, feature/benefits summary list, description of technical support program.

The Offer
Contact salesperson for a personal demonstration.

Legal Considerations
Include acknowledgment of all company trademarks; show product registrations with the certification labs.

Assignments
Copywriting to be completed in-house; design and layout by external firm.

Schedule
First Draft: July 15
Final Draft: July 29
Printed Document: August 20

Review Process
Document must receive approval from:

- Marketing Communication Manager
- Product Manager
- Vice President of Marketing
- Director of Engineering
- National Sales Manager
- Legal (final draft only)

EXERCISES

1. Evaluate any current marketing communication plan, creative platform, or document plans for your product or company against the ideas presented here. Do your plans contain different sections or guidelines? Which of the ideas presented in this chapter do you want to incorporate into future plans?
2. Develop a marcom plan for a new product that incorporates the suggestions presented in this chapter.
3. Write a creative platform that will apply to multiple documents for a product, following the guidelines and example presented in this chapter.
4. Write a document plan for a new brochure or a trade magazine article for the product, following the guidelines and example presented in this chapter.
5. Write a description of the communication cycle that applies to your product. What activities and materials are different from those described in this chapter? How is this communication cycle reflected in your marcom plan, creative platform, and document plans?

CHAPTER 2

The High-Tech Audience

Targeting Your Materials

As you begin each marcom project, ask yourself a simple question. "Who is the audience for this document?" The answer may not be as simple and forthcoming as you might think. For example, consider everyone who might be interested in the data sheet for your product: prospects, certainly; sales people, yes. But a data sheet also might include information that is useful to current customers, technical support staff, and journalists. Of course, each of these people will have different needs and expectations for the information in the data sheet. But you should consider all of these potential audiences as you plan and write the document.

This chapter will help you identify and understand the audiences for a high-tech marcom document. It also presents guidelines for developing materials that are targeted effectively to their audiences.

AUDIENCES FOR HIGH-TECH MARCOM

Most high-tech materials have a combination of audiences, but usually one group is the primary audience, while the others are secondary in importance or level of interest. For most high-tech marcom, the basic audience groups include (Figure 2.1):

- **Prospects.** These are the companies or people who are potential buyers of your products. For complex and expensive products, you may need to develop materials for multiple audiences within a prospect's company such as an executive-level decision-maker (the person who approves the purchase), decision-influencers (the people who must support the purchase decision), and other employees (who may be the ultimate product users).

Audience	Interests	Information Need
Prospects	Learning about the product to determine interest in purchasing.	Features and benefits, specifications, applications pricing, options, and availability.
Sales People and Dealers	Learning about the product in order to sell it successfully.	Features and benefits, applications, and pricing; needs and concerns of prospects.
Journalists and Analysts	Learning about the product in order to write an article or to gain background information for research.	Features and applications; market needs and fit; comparison to competitive products; compatibility with other products.
Investors and Alliance Partners	Evaluating the company's capabilities and strengths.	Product positioning; place in the market; comparison to competitive products.
Employees	Learning about the company's products.	Features and benefits; applications; needs and concerns of prospects; comparison to competitive products.

Figure 2.1   Example audience analysis for a product brochure.

- **Customers.** Companies or individuals who have already bought one or more of your products.
- **Journalists and analysts.** Reporters and editors at magazines and newspapers, as well as researchers at market-research or investment firms. This group also includes industry "luminaries"—the influential users, consultants, or other people who are frequently asked by journalists to comment on new products or technology developments.
- **Sales people and dealers.** The people who sell your product will often be a secondary audience for your sales and press materials. For materials such as a brochure that promotes a dealer program, dealers and resellers may actually be your prospects and thus, the primary audience.
- **Alliance partners.** All companies with which your company has a business relationship for the development, sale, or support of products.
- **Investors.** Shareholders, venture capitalists, bankers, and others who have a financial interest in your company, as well

as financial analysts and brokers who monitor your company's stock.

- **Employees.** Sales and marketing staff, technical support personnel, and other employees within your company may be an audience group for certain materials.

The audience groups for your materials may be even more narrowly defined. For example, your company may segment prospects by industry, company size, system environment, location, application, or other categories. In addition, audiences may be defined separately for each country where your products are sold.

Some of the discussion in this book refers to the target audience. The words *target* and *audience* together may seem redundant, but in fact they reflect the reality of any communication: The target audience is who you *want* to reach with your piece. This group of people may be only a small part of the *actual* group that reads your materials. When planning a document, consider who else might be in its actual audience and determine whether you should address their needs and interests as a *secondary* audience (Figure 2.2).

Audiences for an Issue

If you are trying to persuade readers about an issue, the audience groups are defined somewhat differently:[122]

- Potential converts
- Supporters
- Opponents

While the potential converts group will likely be the primary audience, opponents and even supporters can be secondary audiences. For example, a white paper that advocates adoption of one proposed technology standard over another may be targeted primarily to readers who have yet to make a choice. But readers who advocate the other standard (your opponents) may read the white paper for information to bolster their arguments. And supporters of your opinion may read the document to expand or strengthen their understanding of the proposed standard and related issues.

AUDIENCE CONCERNS

Identifying who may be in the primary and secondary groups is only the first step in targeting your audience. The second and more difficult task is to identify the concerns of these audience members—concerns that your materials *must* address. However,

Material Type	Primary Audience	Secondary Audience
Sales Materials	Prospects, sales people, dealers.	Journalists and analysts, investors, alliance partners, employees.
Press Materials	Journalists and analysts.	Customers, prospects, sales people, dealers, alliance partners, investors, employees.
Alliance Materials	Alliance partners.	Sales people.
Presentation Materials	Varies according to document and forum.	

Figure 2.2   Example segmentation of primary and secondary audiences.

not every document needs to address every concern you identify. And your text may address these concerns directly or obliquely.

While audience concerns will be unique to every marketing situation, this section describes some common concerns for three basic audience groups:

1. Prospects and customers
2. Sales people and dealers
3. Journalists and analysts

Prospects and Customers

For prospects and customers, three types of concerns can impact the reader's interest in your material: buying, emotional, and external. While this section describes the most common concerns in these categories, research the specific concerns of your prospects and customers before you develop a marcom document.

Buying Concerns Buying concerns relate to the purchase decision itself. Examples of buying concerns include:

- **Perception of a problem or need.** The reader must perceive a need or problem to be interested in your product in the first place. However, a reader may not have this perception; or may see a problem, but not think it important enough to solve; or might like to solve the problem, but feel no sense of urgency about doing so.
- **Perception of a solution.** Some high-tech products are marketed on the improvements they can offer rather than the problems they can solve. Yet the reader must perceive the value of the promised solution. This factor, which often arises

with products in a completely new area of technology, is expressed as "You have a very interesting product, but I don't see how I would use it."

- **Purchase factors.** For most high-tech products, these factors include cost justification, implementation requirements, an assessment of capabilities to be gained, internal decision procedures, and implementation schedules. These factors may vary substantially in each of the product's target markets.
- **A broad view of potential solutions.** Prospects tend to look at products as being part of a continuum of possible solutions to a problem. This continuum also includes your competitors' products, other technology solutions, and nontechnical ways of accomplishing the same result.[19]
- **Company reputation.** Previous experience with your company, its market position, and what others say are also factors that influence a prospect's purchase decision.
- **Upgrade fatigue.** How many times has a mailer appeared on your desk, urging you to buy the latest upgrade to a product, but you've barely installed the previous upgrade? Technology changes so fast, often too fast for users to keep up with what's happening, much less assimilate it into their everyday work.

Once a prospect is actively considering your product, buying concerns become much more specific. Examples of these concerns include:

- **Product.** What does it do? How easy is it to learn and use? Will it work with my other products? Is it reliable? What does the competition offer?
- **Purchasing.** Where can I buy it? How soon can I get it? Can I get a better price from another source? Are quantity discounts or site licenses available?
- **Implementation issues.** Who will install it? What type of training is available? What happens with my previous solution?
- **Support and maintenance.** What service or technical support programs are offered? What are the hours and areas of coverage? How much does it cost?

Emotional Concerns Emotional concerns play a role in any purchase decision. As Kadanof points out, "Think of your prospect first as a person, second as a technocrat."[136] Examples of emotional concerns include:

- **Self-interest.** A reader may be concerned about protecting his "turf" or job, achieving status or prestige, or helping to solve a problem. You need to understand the factors by which your prospects are measured in their jobs, and the organizational goals they are trying to achieve.

- **Confusion.** A reader may have inaccurate preconceptions or confusion about technology in general or about your company and product in particular. You must relate your information to what already may be in your reader's mind, to whether there is a misunderstanding of your product or a previous negative experience with technology.
- **Distrust.** Key decision-makers involved in the purchase of high-tech products are overmarketed, and as a result, are highly skeptical about vendor claims of technological wonders. In general, a reader may not trust you, your company, profession, or industry, or may not believe your claims about the product's functionality, benefits, or performance.
- **Resistance to the new.** Reluctance to accept change can be one of the strongest factors that hinders marketing of high-tech products. Not everybody thinks that the latest is indeed the greatest. Users are especially resistant to innovation when it involves a discontinuous change instead of a more gradual, continuous change.[131] In addition, a reader may have concerns about existing investments in hardware, software, training, procedures, and other operational resources that may be impacted by adopting your product.
- **Risk aversion.** A reader may be reluctant to bet on a technology that may not deliver completely or at all. This is a factor that impacts significantly on the marketing of expensive, complex products. Risk aversion also may be a factor in situations that involve usurping an entrenched vendor, even if you have a better product. The information in your material should address this issue of risk by showing how it can be eliminated or minimized.

External Concerns   External concerns encompass the factors in the reader's environment that influence how she will read and respond to your material. These factors can vary by individual reader of course, but examples include:

- **Limited time and attention span.** Many readers rapidly skim your materials—and perhaps miss important messages or details in the process. Keep in mind that readers ask three questions of any marcom document: "What is this all about?", "Why should I pay attention to this?", and "What's in it for me?"

- **Disregard for advertising.** American audiences in particular are wary about any form of promotional material. As Ott notes, "All too often, a marketer assumes the receiver of its message is (a) paying attention, (b) cares about receiving the advertising message, (c) cares about the product advertised, and (d) has some prior knowledge of who the advertiser is and what the product is all about. Nothing could be further from the truth."[128] A reader must perceive that she will get value from the information in your piece before she will take the time to read it completely. A related concern is the reader's limited differentiation of marcom information based on source. As Schultz et al. note, "Consumers use the same information-processing approach whether the new data comes from advertising, sales promotion, a salesperson, or an article or story in a newspaper or magazine."[124]
- **Differing knowledge and experience levels.** Reader knowledge becomes a significant factor when you address multiple or broadly defined audience groups. A reader's lack of knowledge may apply to your product, your company, your technology, or technology in general. For example, in a purchase decision that involves multiple people, the ultimate decision-maker may not have the technical or operational expertise to make judgments about your product based on these factors.

These general concerns of prospects and customers may vary substantially among different markets. When planning and writing marcom materials, consider the specific markets targeted by your company. Many high-tech companies broadly define their markets as corporations, government agencies, small businesses and small office/home offices (SOHO), or consumers. Some high-tech companies sell only to corporate and government customers, some sell only to the SOHO and consumer markets, while others sell products across all of these markets. In addition, your company may segment markets by country to target its efforts appropriately on both a domestic and international basis.

A company also may define its markets by either a horizontal or vertical segmentation. A horizontal market is comprised of prospects with similar characteristics, but from a broad range of industries or other market category. For example, a software company may target a word-processing product to all office workers. A vertical market is comprised of prospects within a single industry or category with similar product needs, but substantial differences in company size, operational modes, or other characteristics. An example of this type of market segmentation is a hardware product developed for specialty manufacturers.

Each of these markets have different characteristics, sales cycles, and buying factors. Your materials must address these differences in order to support the sales cycle effectively.

Sales People and Dealers

If your sales force isn't both knowledgeable and excited about your product, how motivated will they be to sell it? This is especially important for dealers or retail outlets that sell many, even hundreds of diverse products. Of course your product, pricing, and sales incentives must be good. But your marketing materials must promote a decision to sell your product and be both informative and helpful to sales reps when they talk to potential customers.

The concerns of sales people and dealers can vary depending on their involvement with your product, its markets, and the sales cycle. When reading materials targeted to customers and prospects, dealers and sales people will share many of the concerns described in the previous section. When reading alliance materials such as sales kits, sales people and dealers will have other concerns such as the following:

- **Selling factors.** The size, location, purchasing power, and other characteristics of the target market; how much time and effort is required to make each sale; the potential for profitability from the product itself and any follow-on revenue such as service contracts; competition within the dealer's sales territory and from other sales channels.
- **Customer relationships.** How easy your product is to maintain and support; service resources available to dealers; reputation of your company.
- **Dealer program factors.** Requirements for participating in the dealer program, such as minimum purchases, staff training, and other resource investments; company programs for marketing, cooperative (coop) advertising, and generating leads; all other ways you will help the dealer be successful in selling your product.

Concerns may vary for the different sales channels: wholesale distributors, specialty dealers, retail and catalog outlets, consultants, and the various types of dealers such as system integrators that customize your product or combine it with others to create a solution. The dealer's decision-making process for carrying a product may involve a number of people and an evaluation period that may need to be addressed by your alliance materials. And dealers in each international market are likely to have different concerns, based on variations in local laws and business practices.

Journalists and Analysts

Marketing materials can help journalists and analysts gain a better understanding of your products, markets, and company. Testing labs and product reviewers will often verify a product's performance against the claims made in a brochure or data sheet. But don't expect your glossy brochure to dazzle these readers. Journalists, analysts, and investors will always read your marketing materials in light of additional facts and information they garner from other sources, both internal and external to your company.

Reporters, editors, researchers, and analysts are primarily concerned with obtaining factual, timely, and complete information about your company and its products. They want materials that will support their research efforts and help them write accurate and useful articles or reports.

Journalists at trade publications and technology analysts often have these concerns:

- **Product information.** What functions the product supports; how it is packaged; add-on or optional products and services.
- **Market position.** How your product relates to the competition, to compatible products, and to industry trends; what is new and different about your product in light of what is already in the market.
- **User perception.** User applications, experience of product users, perception of your product by analysts and industry commentators.
- **Sales details.** Availability date, sales channels, pricing, and upgrade policies.

Journalists for general, business, or consumer publications and financial analysts are usually less interested in the technical details for your product. Instead, you need to relate the importance of your product in terms of your company's market share, revenue growth, competitive positioning, and market needs.

RESEARCHING YOUR AUDIENCE

How can you determine the specific concerns and knowledge of your audience groups? Here are a few ideas:

- **Talk to customers directly.** Sponsor a focus group or a session at a user-group meeting or industry conference.[123] Conduct a telephone survey of randomly selected prospects (drawn from inquiries or a prospect database). Go on sales calls with your sales people or work in your company's trade-show booth. If your company operates a bulletin board system (BBS) or a forum on an online service, read user comments regularly and post brief surveys or individual questions for feedback. Also read user messages in other forums related to your product.
- **Talk to sales people.** Talk to your direct sales staff, dealers, product managers, customer service staff, and anyone else who has regular contact with a broad range of customers. However, remember that some sales people will define as a "trend" the concerns of the last customer they contacted.
- **Research external information.** Read market information that is published in trade magazines or by research firms. Read the magazines and journals your prospects read. What are these publications saying about the state of the industry or problems and needs? Analyze the audiences that your competitors seem to be addressing in their materials. How are they describing the prospect's concerns?
- For dealers, talk to current and prospective dealers and read the trade publications that are targeted to this market.
- For journalists, read their publications and know which subject areas and technologies each journalist covers.

If you are researching the audience for an existing product, identify the type of customer that is buying the product now.[7] Is this customer type different from what your company perceives as the target prospect? In addition, when responding to a Request for Proposals (RFP), Bowman and Branchaw suggest that you look at the orientation and value words it contains for clues on the audience's interests.[130]

DEVELOPING AN AUDIENCE-FOCUSED DOCUMENT

Imagine that you are a member of your target audience. What preconceptions would you have? What questions would you want answered? What information would you want to receive? What expectations would you have about the manner in which it is delivered? What would motivate you to take the desired action? Now look at your materials. Are they addressing these concerns adequately?

Here are some specific techniques you can use to develop an audience-focused document:

- **Check the content.** Compare the document with the concerns you have identified for each audience group. Does the document address those concerns effectively?
- **Address the audience directly.** Does the text talk *to* the reader ("you") or *about* your company ("we")? An audience-focused document emphasizes "you" statements over "we" statements. For example, compare the focus of these statements: *Here's how [product] can improve your productivity* ("you" statement), or *We're very proud of our innovative features* ("we" statement).
- **Picture your reader.** Keep in mind a representative prospect as you write. Think of someone you have met or interviewed. How would that person respond to your material? Does your information demonstrate an accurate understanding of that person's industry, environment, issues, and problems?
- **Watch for your assumptions.** Make sure your perceptions of audience interests and needs are supported by market research, prospect and customer interviews, articles in trade publications, or other sources of reliable and complete information. Remember you can easily be distracted by your deep familiarity with the product and influenced by the opinions of your colleagues, which may be subjective or inaccurate.
- **Develop customized materials for each market segment.** While it is tempting to think you can produce one brochure or backgrounder that will be suitable for everyone who reads it, this may be impossible for very technical products or those that address multiple markets. For example, you may want to create a separate product brochure for each vertical market or country where the product is sold. If cost is a concern, it may not be necessary to develop separate versions of every marcom document.
- **Name your audience in the document.** An example of this technique: *[This brochure] concerns the CIO, the MIS manager, the data communications manager, the LAN manager, and the telecommunications manager.*[129] Or, separate sections of the document may specifically address different audiences.
- **Check for balance.** If the document has multiple audiences, verify that their different concerns are addressed adequately and appropriately.

- **Test the document concept**. When a document is in the draft stage, ask a few customers or prospects to review it and respond to questions such as: Do they understand the copy? Does it address their interests? Would it encourage them to take the next step?
- **Conduct a postpublication survey**. For existing documents, ask a few readers questions such as: What did the document do well? What information was missing? Was any part of the document confusing or misleading? This will help you improve the document in future versions.

EXERCISES

1. Take an existing document and rewrite it to meet the information and presentation needs of at least two different audiences. For example, rewrite a data sheet to meet the needs of prospects in two different markets.
2. Develop a detailed list of the questions a prospect might ask when deciding to buy your product. Check your materials against this list to evaluate the completeness and focus of the information they provide.
3. Define the audience groups for a marcom document following the example in Figure 2.2. For each audience group you define, analyze the interests and information needs of members following the example in Figure 2.1.
4. Describe a representative prospect for your product. What is the person's job or activities? How would he use the product? How does he receive and process marketing information? What is his level of technical sophistication?
5. Use different color pens to highlight the "we" statements and "you" statements in a marcom document. Is there a balance or is one type of statement predominant?

CHAPTER 3

Objective, Purpose, and Message

The Essentials for On-Target Communication

Before you begin writing, you must know why you want to communicate and what you want to say. To this end, you must identify three essential components for any marcom document:

- The objective you want to achieve with the document—what you want the reader to think or do.
- The purpose of the document's content—to motivate, inform, or persuade the reader.
- The messages you want to convey—through the document's text and images—about your product, service, or company.

Your objective and purpose should answer the question "Why communicate?", while your messages broadly describe what you want to say. Here are additional differences between these components:

- An **objective** specifies what you want the reader to think (impression) or do (action) after reading the document. It is based on the marketing problem you want to solve or the marketing opportunity you want to address with the document. An objective also considers the messages you want to convey to your audiences and the role you want the piece to play in the sales cycle. An example of an impression objective is: *Give technical experts confidence in the strength of the product's design.* An example of an action objective is: *Five percent of recipients will request a product demonstration.*
- The underlying **purpose** of the document helps you select and organize the information it presents. Most marcom documents

have one of these three purposes: to motivate, to inform, or to persuade. An example of a purpose statement is: *The purpose of the Application Guide is to inform by showing the range and depth of potential applications, reinforcing our message about the high level of product configurability.*

- **Messages** present the critical information or impressions you want to leave in the reader's mind. Messages support the positioning you want to achieve in the market for your product or service and can be adapted for all marketing materials.
  Messages may be based on product features, benefits, or differentiation; customer needs or problems; market trends or opportunities; or competitive factors. Here is an example of a product message: *Unlike proprietary products, our product is an open platform for adopting new technologies and interfaces.*

The combination of objective, purpose, and message can help you select the best document type to meet a communication need. Figure 3.1 shows how objective, purpose, and message could be defined for the marcom documents related to a fictional software product.

OBJECTIVE

If you don't know where you're going, you might end up somewhere else.—Casey Stengal

The objective for a marcom document is to describe what you want the reader to think or do in response to your information. Of course, the overriding objective for any marcom document is to sell the product or prompt another action by the reader. However, you will usually specify one or more focused objectives for each marcom document, based on its target audience and its role in the sales cycle.

An objective can be expressed in qualitative or quantitative terms. Examples of qualitative objectives include:

- Prompting the reader to take a direct or indirect action such as to request more information or buy the product (direct action); support a purchase decision or develop a positive impression (indirect action).
- "Setting the agenda" for a purchase decision by convincing the reader that the areas where your product is better than its competition are the most important areas to consider.
- Creating an awareness of a product in the market or correcting a market misperception about the value of a technology.

Objective	Purpose	Key Message	Document
Action: Request a visit to a customer site.	Motivate the purchase decision by providing highly credible customer references.	Proven reliability in high-demand environments. Quality customers are already using the product.	Customer Case Studies.
Impression: Integration is easy.	Inform by showing all current integrations.	Integration verified with key products and technologies.	Product Interfaces Data Sheet.
Action: Purchase presale consulting project for application development.	Inform by showing the range and depth of potential applications.	Highly configurable with easy-to-use configuration tools.	Application Guide.
Impression: Give technical experts confidence in the soundness of the product's design.	Persuade by showing the underlying architecture that enables the product's adaptablity.	The product offers an open platform for adopting new technologies and interfaces.	Technology White Paper.

Figure 3.1   How objective, purpose, and message determine choice of document type.

- Providing information that supports salesperson or dealer activities.

Quantitative objectives are expressed in terms of measurable results such as response rates or number of inquiries generated by the document, purchase rates or revenue amounts, attendance levels at events, market share gains, or number of new dealers recruited.

Different objectives may apply at different stages of the product's life span. For example, communication objectives for a new product could include:

- Fostering awareness of the product or technology among opinion leaders and leading-edge users.
- Increasing product sales in the next quarter through an advertising campaign or other promotional activity.

Objectives for a mature product could include:

- Establishing your product as the perceived standard for its category through communication of significant customer contracts, product awards, and other achievements.
- Creating a solid brand image for your product or company through consistent and sustained communication to the market.

Different objectives may apply to each target market or audience in order to account for differences in:

- Levels of involvement in the purchase decision.
- Problems, requirements, and environments of prospects.
- Cultural and business conditions in different countries.
- Interests and motivations of dealers and the direct sales force.

PURPOSE

Most marcom documents have one of three purposes:

1. To *motivate* readers to take an action related to buying a product.
2. To *inform* readers about a product, service, company, event, or trend.
3. To *persuade* readers to make a change in their situation or adopt your views on an issue.

You may have more than one purpose in a document, but one will usually be dominant. For example, a product description brochure has information as its primary purpose, but may include a call to action that has a motivational purpose.

The matrix in Figure 3.2 can help you select a document type based on your purpose for communication.

To choose the purpose for a particular document, answer these questions:

- Who belongs to the target audience and what would they want to gain from reading the document?
- What need or problem are you trying to address through communication? For example, is it a lack of compelling reason to make a purchase (motivate), a lack of information from other sources (inform), or the need to present a viewpoint (persuade)?
- How will the document be used? As a direct-mail piece that must stand on its own (motivate), as part of a salesperson's presentation (inform), or as a contribution to an ongoing debate (persuade)?

- Where does the piece fit in the sales cycle? At the very beginning when the reader has minimal information (inform), in the middle when the reader needs additional detail (persuade), or near the end when the reader needs one last incentive to buy (motivate)?

Motivation

In a document with a motivation purpose, the copy must give readers a strong incentive or desire to take an action, whether it is requesting more information or buying the product. Motivation is typically the primary purpose in sales brochures, catalogs, and direct mail pieces.

To write copy that serves a motivation purpose, you need a good understanding of what factors will prompt readers to act. For most people, motivation arises out of a sense of need, real or perceived. With some products, you must help the reader recognize she actually has a need. In all cases, show your product as the only or best solution to that need and give the reader a sense of urgency about addressing it *now*.

A new opportunity is another factor that can create a sense of motivation. Some people can't resist having the latest technologi-

Document	Motivate	Inform	Persuade
Brochure or Data Sheet	P,S	P	
Advertisement	P	P,S	
Direct Mail	P	P,S	
Proposal	S	P	
White Paper		P	P,S
Case Study		P	S
Newsletter		P	
Presentation	P	P	P
Press Release		P	
Article		P	P,S
Backgrounder		P	P,S
Sales Kit	S	P	

P=Primary, S=Secondary. In cases where symbols appear in more than one column, any of these purposes may apply to that document type.

Figure 3.2   Selecting a document type based on purpose.

cal wonder, while others will be interested because they see value in new capabilities, even if they're happy with their current product or situation.

These techniques can help you write effective motivational copy:

- Decide whether you want to use *fear* or *incentive* as the basis for motivation. This will be determined in large part by the tone and content of your marketing messages; are they based on positive or negative factors? (See the section "Negative Messages" later in this chapter.)
- Convey a sense that taking the action involves minimal risk, especially if you are asking for an order. Describe any refund guarantees, trial units, or service programs offered by your company.
- Adopt the "assumed close" technique used by salespeople. This means your copy will reflect a sense that the reader has already decided to buy and now just needs information on how to complete the transaction.
- Use terms in the product offer to create a sense of urgency or exclusivity. Examples include time limitations, special pricing, "select customers," or free add-ons (see the section on "Offers" in Chapter 6).
- Make it easy for the reader to take the action by providing all relevant contact information or an order form (see the section on "The Call to Action" in Chapter 5).
- See the "Power Words" section in Chapter 7 for additional ideas on specific text techniques that are effective for motivational copy.

Information

A document with an information purpose presents its content clearly and simply, as in a statement of facts, a description of features, or an explanation of a technology concept. Information is often the primary purpose of data sheets, white papers, articles, and backgrounders. The reader does not need to be convinced of anything, he just needs complete, accurate information.

These techniques can help you write information copy:

- Use text that is specific, concrete, and easy for readers to grasp its exact meaning.
- Make precise word choices, especially for verbs and modifiers, where subtleties of meaning can make a difference.
- Use standard writing techniques such as description, definition, comparison, classification, narration, and showing relationships or cause and effect.[1]

- Ask these questions of your language: Are you judging or describing? Telling or showing?[5] When information is your purpose, you want language that will describe and show.

Persuasion

In a document with a persuasion purpose, messages must convince the reader to believe or do something new. These documents are effective when you want a reader to switch brand preferences, try an unproven technology, or adopt a certain viewpoint on an issue. Persuasion can be the purpose for white papers, articles, and presentations.

Writing to meet a persuasion purpose is a difficult task because you must convince readers to adopt a new and unfamiliar belief or to change their views—and all while establishing your own credibility. You often must show why your assertions are right and prove why other beliefs are wrong.

These factors determine whether your attempt at persuasion is successful:

- The source must be credible, whether it is a customer, analyst, or employee communicating on your company's behalf, or indeed your company itself. Readers must believe that the source has the necessary expertise; it cannot appear to be too self-serving.[11] In addition, the source must appear to understand the needs, desires, and motivations of the audience.[5]
- The message must be clear, timely, relevant, and appeal to the self-interest of the audience; it must correspond to the audience's values and attitudes.[11]
- Any proposed action must be clear, feasible,[11] and one that the audience will be willing to accept and act upon *now*.

Specific writing techniques to use when persuasion is your objective are presented below. You can mix these techniques within a document, for example, by appealing first to the reader's emotion, then supporting it with a statement of logic. However, make sure that your tone and style can accommodate the mix of appeals and content you include.

- Establish a sense of trust and confidence on the part of the reader. State your assertions positively and avoid the use of qualifiers. Assume that readers are already inclined to agree with you.
- Present the logic behind your arguments by showing the rationale and supporting evidence.[1] Describe logical outcomes or

conclusions. Cite verifiable proof, statistics, external people or references that will be accepted by readers as authoritative. Use reason-why copy to present your supporting evidence (see Chapter 6).

- Use emotional appeals, but make sure they are appropriate for the interests of your audience, are not overly dramatic, and reflect a genuine concern or situation.[1]
- Consider whether and how you will present opposing viewpoints. You can ignore the opposing view if the audience is friendly; tell both sides if the audience is neutral or hostile.[11] You don't need to include every possible argument for or refutation against your position; instead address only the strongest or most relevant.
- Give new definitions to key words or messages—a limited or special meaning that supports your viewpoint.[1]
- Personalize the argument. Encourage the reader to identify with an idea that is presented in the text.[3]
- State areas of agreement or common ground with your audience or link your proposition with something the reader already believes. When readers accept that you understand their viewpoints and needs, they will be more inclined to adopt your messages as their own.

Choose among these techniques based on how well they fit the audience and the nature of your arguments. Are those arguments aggressive or low-key? How do they support your existing credibility or the credibility you are trying to establish? But remember, no matter what the focus of your persuasive efforts, apply these techniques responsibly and ethically (see Chapter 8).

MESSAGE

To catch a mouse, make a noise like a cheese.—Lewis Kornfield
Does your key marketing message sound like cheese? A good marketing message entices the reader by presenting a product's selling points and key differences from its competition. Successful messages make your materials, product, and company memorable to all members of the target audience and help achieve your desired product or company positioning.

The key messages typically are defined by product managers or other marketing staff as part of the product marketing plan. As a copywriter, your job is to adapt these messages into specific text for use in one or more marketing documents.

Most high-tech companies use one primary message and a small number of secondary messages across all materials for a product. Whatever the number, these messages must be something easy for readers to grasp, and for salespeople and dealers to remember. And your messages must stand the test of different applications in different media, in different environments, with different audiences, and over time.

Message Types

For high-tech companies, the following types of information are most frequently conveyed in marketing messages:

- **Technology leadership.** Example messages include: best, sophisticated, feature-rich, quality, advanced, new, leading-edge, powerful, high-performance, first in a product category.[27] *We help you prepare for the emerging graphics-based PC world.*[116]
- **Market leadership.** Example messages include: first in a market, largest market share, high acceptance level. *With more than 1,000,000 ports shipped worldwide, Dialogic is the world's leading supplier of PC-based computer telephony hardware and software platforms.*[117]
- **Application and use.** Example messages include: simplicity, ease-of-use, intuitive interface, customized, flexible, open, independent, configurability. *This new series is perfect for field-service tasks that require precise measurement.*[95]
- **Pricing and delivery.** Example messages include: low price, high value, minimized operation and maintenance costs. *The tools you need to manage your business in one convenient package at one great price.*[88]
- **Features and benefits.** Example messages include: complete product package, integration, compatibility, interoperability, architecture, platform. *[This product] gives you visual tools to manage time, money, and people across multiple projects.*[88]
- **Company strengths.** Example messages include: longevity, stability, specialized expertise, product service and support, strategies, directions, distribution channels. *[We] provide the widest range of connectivity solutions and customer support for the IBM midrange family.*[106]

Developing Messages

Writing the specific text that conveys broadly stated marketing messages is challenging. Yet, no matter how they are stated, your messages should be adaptable to all marcom documents such as advertising, sales collateral, and press materials. A specific statement of a message may also be used on product packaging, trade show banners, and merchandising items such as t-shirts for employees and dealers. In addition, the message statements should be easy for salespeople to remember during sales calls, presentations, seminars, or other personal selling situations.

Before you begin writing specific message text, consider these questions:

- What do the members of the target audiences need to know? What are their concerns? What are their needs or wants that your product or service fulfills? What ideas or language will reach them most effectively? Do you need to create different (but related) messages for each target audience? What is the current mindset of prospects in your target markets? Will readers be receptive to your messages, or must you overcome misperception, apathy, or a lack of credibility?
- In which materials will the messages appear? Will the messages work equally well in all of them? In particular, consider whether each message will retain its distinctiveness and credibility when it appears in press materials and is subjected to a journalist's scrutiny and skepticism.
- Which visual or copy techniques may be used to present the messages? In ads and other sales materials, a message may be presented through an integration of image and copy.
- What are the characteristics that make your product unique or that differentiate it from the competition? Are these unique qualities valued by prospects? Can prospects even recognize them? At least one statement of your marketing message should focus on these unique qualities. In advertising, this is called the Unique Selling Proposition (USP) for a product. Your primary message should be based on the one selling point that will clearly distinguish your product.
- If your product positioning is based on technical features, are you balancing sales-oriented language with technical language in the phrasing of your messages?
- For business-to-business products, is your message directed to both an organization and a person? In this situation, an effective message will address the business concerns, but in a human, personal way.
- Do you want to state the message explicitly or implicitly? An example of an implicit statement is posing a question and let-

ting the reader draw the desired conclusion for himself. If you are stating the message implicitly, will the reader understand the message in the same way as you do? For clarity of communication, most messages are stated explicitly.

- Will the message have longevity? While your product positioning may remain consistent over a long period, messages may change to reflect the business climate, market conditions, and actions taken by competitors. For example, Apple Computer has used a variety of messages that describe simplicity—the company's positioning for the Macintosh product since it was introduced a decade ago. Initially, these messages contrasted the simplicity of the Macintosh user interface against IBM personal computers running DOS. Later, when Microsoft introduced its Windows user interface to compete with the Macintosh, Apple targeted its messages specifically against Windows.
- Are the messages for an individual product or service congruent with all of your company's other messages and with the company image? Can you maintain the consistency of the messages across all marcom materials and marketing activities?

Here are additional guidelines to consider when writing text that presents your messages:

- A good marketing message is not a proclamation, pronouncement, or other lofty statement. And, while it is tempting to create a message that is very clever or uses highly sophisticated language, you run the risk of creating empty hype that will confuse or alienate the audience. Your message will be more effective if it is written in words that are concrete, specific, and easy for the reader to understand.
- In most cases, a marketing message will be centered on the reader ("you"), not on the company ("we").
- Each message must be believable and honest. A message is made stronger when you support it with verifiable evidence such as test results or market research data, customer testimonials, or endorsements from other credible parties. Stretching the truth not only lessens the believability of your message, but competitors will make sure that any dishonesty will come back to haunt you.
- Watch for your own biases and assumptions about what motivates and interests your readers. Get the perspective of existing customers and the sales and marketing staff in your company either before you start writing or when you have a draft to circulate for reaction and comment.

- Use terminology that is familiar to the audience. As 1960s activist Abbie Hoffman observed, "Never impose your language on people you want to reach." Watch for overuse of acronyms and jargon in messages, unless these terms are widely known in the industry and are critical for differentiating your product from its competition.
- Avoid offensive connotations in your choice of words and images. Ask several people who have different social and cultural backgrounds to review the message text and point out any areas that might be offensive. Consider the differences in messages you may need to create for international markets. Each market will have its own cultural considerations and business climate that should be reflected in your marketing messages (see Chapter 9).

Multiple Messages

Most technology products have one primary message plus a small number of secondary or supporting messages. A *primary message* states the most important benefit or selling point for the product. It is also called the consumer promise: a clear, benefits-oriented, motivational statement about what the product will deliver. For example, an illustration software product has this primary message: *The most comprehensive design and illustration tool for creative professionals.* The key selling point for this product is conveyed with the words "most comprehensive."

Secondary messages cover additional benefits or positioning factors that strengthen the overall selling proposition for the product. Secondary messages can focus on separate dimensions of your product. In the following example, an ad for a computer monitor presented a benefit statement for the primary message, while the secondary messages described product features:

Primary: *Bigger Windows* (to emphasize the larger screen area for displaying Windows-based software).
Secondary: *Two-Year Warranty, 16" Fine Dot Pitch CRT, Very High Resolution, Color Calibration System, Low Emission Design.*[28]

Caution: Be careful about the number of messages you create for a product. More than three or four messages can overwhelm and confuse both readers and salespeople. You don't need to create a message for every benefit or selling point of a product. Instead, choose the strongest features or benefits that are critical to the product's positioning or competitiveness. Then, distill these items into as few messages as you can without losing clarity or impact.

When working with multiple secondary messages, present them in order of importance to the reader. This order may be different than what you might perceive as important, so consider your market research information or feedback you receive when you test the messages (see the section "Testing Messages" later in this chapter).

When working with multiple messages, watch carefully where and how they appear in a document. Given that the attention span of many readers can be measured in seconds, present your messages early and often in each marketing piece. Reinforcement of the primary message in particular is critical for helping readers understand and remember your product or company. And when this reinforcement is carried through all related marcom documents, it strengthens the buyer's interest and motivation in all stages of the sales cycle.

You can weave messages throughout a document's text without becoming boringly repetitive. For starters, present the primary message in a headline or opening line of the body copy to grab interest and establish your positioning. In the body copy itself, restate the primary message and present any secondary messages. At the end of the piece, reinforce the primary message in a closing statement, tag line, or call to action. Subheads, captions, and callouts are additional elements you can use for weaving messages throughout a document.

This excerpt from a product brochure shows an effective weaving of the primary message:

> **Headline:** Open Technology for *Efficient, Effective,* and *Flexible* Solutions
>
> **First paragraph:** . . . Software solutions to business problems can make people and processes *efficient, effective,* and *flexible.*
>
> **Second paragraph:** *Efficient* software solutions do things right . . . *Effective* software solutions do the right thing . . . And flexible solutions adapt to new circumstances.
>
> **Closing tag line:** NAS: The *Efficient, Effective,* and *Flexible* Software Solution.[29]

Your materials may contain different messages for different audiences such as one for prospects in different markets; another set for dealers, third-party developers, and strategic partners; and an additional set targeted at investors and the financial community. (Journalists and industry analysts usually receive the messages targeted to prospects.) For example, these varia-tions in the primary message could be created for a fictional software product:

- **Prospects.** *This product makes it easier to manage your daily tasks.*
- **Dealers.** *This product meets a critical user need that has not been addressed by any other product.*
- **Third-Party Developers.** *This product offers an open, flexible platform for creating customized applications.*

When creating these different sets of messages, make sure they don't contradict each other and that they reflect a common theme. In addition, you may choose to emphasize different messages from your set for each party when multiple people are involved in a purchase decision.

Confused Messages

A danger of using multiple messages is that you will confuse read-ers. This confusion can lead to several undesirable outcomes:

- Readers will reject your message.
- Readers will misunderstand the product.
- Readers will not recognize the product's applicability to their needs.

For example:

Windows opened new vistas on the world of personal comput-ing. Now, Windows users can reach new levels of productivity with The Norton Desktop for Windows. This landmark software package makes Windows far more accessible and easier to use. Version 1.0 got rave reviews, and comments like "For every Windows user . . . shopping for the best Windows utilities bar-gain around, this is the answer. Every Windows user should have it." **PC Computing, December, 1991.** *Now we're pleased to introduce Version 2.0—for even better Windows.[32]*

This passage, which appears as the first paragraph in a data sheet, has several problems in the way it presents the product's marketing message. First, it is not clear what the product is or what specific benefits it will deliver to the user. Instead, this para-graph focuses on proclaiming the greatness of an earlier version. Second, because the paragraph opens with a reference to the

Microsoft Windows product, the reader is likely to expect that the piece will describe Windows itself, not this add-on product.

These guidelines will help you avoid the trap of confusing messages:

- Are you stating your message in too many different ways? Will the reader perceive that the message means one thing the first time it appears, but something else the next?
- Are you sticking to your short list of primary and secondary messages? Are you introducing irrelevant or contradictory messages later in the piece?
- Are you overloading the piece with messages? Creating multiple messages doesn't mean you need to include all of them in each and every marketing document. Identify the few messages that will have the most impact on the specific audience for each document.
- Are you trying to address too many diverse audiences with a single piece? If different messages are relevant to each audience, create separate documents or clearly identify the information that's specific to each audience (document elements such as sidebars or subheads are useful for this segmentation; see Chapter 5).

Negative Messages

High-tech companies sometimes use negative messages when products are competing head-to-head with little differentiation in price or features. Negative messages can create a sense in the prospect's mind called FUD (fear, uncertainty, and doubt) about your competition. The most common intent of FUD is to cause the prospect to delay a purchase decision until you have the opportunity to present your product.

One technique for creating FUD is to present negative messages about a competitive product. For example, Banyan Corp. used this title for a sales brochure intended to create FUD about its major competitor, Novell Corp.: *Things they don't tell you at Novell presentations.*[30] Reading this, a prospect who was ready to buy a Novell product might hesitate and say "I'd better check this out."

While it is an extremely powerful approach when done well, FUD and the use of negative messages can easily back-fire. Negative messages are tricky for a number of reasons because they:

- Are more difficult for the reader to understand, especially when skimming an ad or brochure.
- Can create confusion about the object of the message. A reader may think someone else is saying all those nasty things about *your* product.
- May alienate readers. Think of how often people complain about negative advertising in political campaigns. Now consider how a negative message could reflect on the image or reputation of your company.
- May describe a problem the reader never knew she had. This doesn't help her draw a positive conclusion about your product, even if you are positioning it as the solution to this "problem."
- May become ammunition for competitors. After all, your negative messages are putting them in an underdog position, which they may be able to leverage to draw a reader's sympathy.
- May be unethical or may create a legal problem (see Chapter 8). While it is very tempting to exaggerate the flaws of a competitive product in a negative message, the information you present must be factually accurate and defensible.

Some marketers question whether negative messages really work. In a survey of 50 business marketing executives from both high-tech and nontechnology companies, 80 percent said that negative ads were not very effective or not at all effective in boosting sales. And 58 percent said that negative ads were either not very effective or not at all effective in damaging a competitor's reputation.[30]

If you still want to use negative messages, consider the following guidelines:

- Read the section on "Comparisons" in Chapter 6 and "Mistake #6: Negativism" in Chapter 7.
- Always describe how the reader can avoid or get out of a FUD situation; of course, this is usually by purchasing your product.
- Test your message with members of the potential audience for the document (see the section "Testing Messages" later in this chapter).
- Check and double-check the facts and assumptions behind your messages with reputable sources both internal and external to your company.
- Ensure that your corporate attorney reviews the text to deter legal problems (see Chapter 8).

Testing Messages

No matter how brilliantly phrased a message might be, it is not doing a good job if it doesn't produce the results you want. Testing messages in advance of their use is a way to avoid this problem. A testing process can address the clarity and effectiveness of different messages. Will the message catch the reader's eye? Is the message relevant to the reader's interests and circumstances? Does the reader come away with the correct information and impression from the message?

One way to conduct these tests is with focus groups. Many trade publications offer this service for their biggest advertisers or you can hire a market research firm to conduct a group session. A focus group critique can be a highly useful way to test the messages and concepts of proposed materials before launching a major, expensive marcom campaign.

Sometimes a quick telephone survey of a few customers is all you need to determine whether your messages will be effective. Ask these customers for feedback on your message text: Do they understand what you are trying to say? Would the message catch their attention and prompt them to act? Is an important factor missing from your messages?

Another common test is to evaluate how well a completed document achieved its objectives. These objectives could include the number and quality of sales generated or inquiries received; feedback from sales reps, dealers, customers, and prospects; or market share measurements from independent research firms. While results can reflect a variety of influences, the effectiveness of your messages is an important contributing factor to a document's success.

EXERCISES

Objective

1. Take several existing marcom documents and determine whether you can identify the objective for each. Based on your analysis, how well does each document meet its objective? What aspects of the copy help to achieve the objective? What improvements could be made to the copy, organization of the document, or selection of document type?
2. Make a list of typical objectives for the types of marcom documents you produce, including examples of both quantitative and qualitative objectives.
3. Describe the differences that must be addressed in your objectives to reach different market segments or to account for other communication requirements.

Purpose

1. Take several existing marcom documents and determine whether you can identify the purpose for each. Based on your analysis, how well does the copy reflect that purpose? What aspects of the copy are successful? What changes would you make?
2. For documents with a persuasion or motivation purpose, identify the specific writing techniques that were used, and analyze their success in achieving the document's purpose.

Message

1. Take several existing marcom documents and determine whether you can identify the messages in each. What are the primary and secondary messages? How are they incorporated into the copy? How are document elements used to reinforce the messages?
2. Show one of your marcom documents to your sales reps, customer support staff, or other people who work with your customers every day. Do they think customers or prospects will be able to recognize and understand the messages presented in the piece? Ask the sales people, "Can you sell the product from this document?"
3. Develop a list of possible messages for a high-tech product. Which message is the strongest? Does it deliver the single most important selling point for the product? Answer this question to help you select the primary message for a product: If [the product] is the answer, what is the question?
4. For secondary messages, is each stated distinctively from the others? Do the secondary messages build the case of your primary message? How many different secondary messages do you have? Can any of them be combined or summarized into one or two primary messages?
5. Could any of your message statements be interpreted with a negative meaning (if that is *not* your intent)? If yes, rewrite the message text so it becomes a positive statement.
6. Take an existing marcom document and use colored pens to highlight the primary and secondary messages (one color for each message). What does your weaving look like—neat and evenly spaced, or a tangled mess? Are some of the messages missing? Do some colors show up too often? This exercise will help you determine how well multiple messages are incorporated into a marcom document.
7. Identify the document elements where a primary or secondary message could appear (see Chapter 5). Describe how the messages could be delivered visually instead of or in addition to their delivery in the copy.

CHAPTER 4

Creative Issues

Developing the Best Ideas, Styles, and Methods

High-tech copy demands special consideration of three creative issues:

1. Identifying the best approach to a document's content.
2. Defining an appropriate writing style.
3. Working effectively with a graphic designer.

This chapter describes these issues and presents suggestions for addressing them successfully.

CONCEPTUALIZATION: IDENTIFYING APPROACHES TO YOUR CONTENT

The obscure we see eventually, the patently obvious takes a little longer.—Edward R. Murrow

You have created your document plan and completed the basic preparation tasks of gathering references, research, and interviews. You are ready to start writing. But how can you work with your notes and background information to find an approach that will best translate this raw content into a first draft of the document's copy?

Begin by looking at your document plan. Which document type have you selected? What is your objective and purpose for this document? What is the target audience, their knowledge and interests? Clear answers to these questions will help you choose the most relevant information from your source material, and organize it effectively.

Another approach is to look at what the raw information is telling you. Does it have a theme, repeating motifs, a stream of events, an anecdote or phrase that really caught your attention when you first read or heard it? You may be able to use this theme, story, or language as a focal point for organizing the document's content. Use this technique to generate several ideas for how you might approach the content.

Some of your conceptualization will be determined by the document type. For sales materials, you want an approach that will deliver the key messages to the target audience with the greatest impact. In addition, consider the synergy between visuals and copy in developing a strong concept.

For case studies, white papers, feature articles and, in some cases, sales materials, Blundell suggests these approaches: extrapolation, synthesis, localization, globalization, projection, and viewpoint switching.[16] Here's how they could be applied to high-tech content:

- **Extrapolation:** What is the real underlying story? What could this mean? What nonobvious conclusions could be drawn from this information?
- **Synthesis:** This is like working a jigsaw puzzle. Look for the commonality in the inputs; identify how to bring them together into a cohesive whole. Find a theme.
- **Localization:** Tailor the material to the audience's particular interests, motivations, problems and needs. Describe the microcosm. Look for personal drama and human interest. (*Note*: This use of "localization" does not mean translation into another language, which is the common definition for this term in relation to high-tech products.)
- **Globalization:** Show the big picture. Describe the larger trends that influence specific circumstances; show the range or evolution of events.
- **Projection:** Describe where a trend or situation could lead.
- **Viewpoint Switching:** Show the different views on an issue in a point-counterpoint format. Identify the different players in an event. Describe differences in impact or results of a plan or activity.
- **Progression:** Show a chronology or sequence of events, ideas, or other items. What sense of movement can you detect in your material?

In addition, Marra suggests these techniques:[10]

- Make associations based on features, form, content, size, texture, feature range, selling points, benefits, behaviors, or reversal (i.e., describe what something is *not*).

- Make connections based on one or more senses, either through direct or reverse association. Use analogy and metaphor.
- Create a framework, then see how the information fits.
- Go from this to that; show change and movement.

To spark your concepts, see Chapters 5 through 7 for more ideas on specific techniques used in high-tech marcom materials.

How Do You Know When You Have a Good Idea?

When you have identified several possible approaches to the information, don't judge them immediately. Instead begin writing some text as a way to explore each approach until you find one that is the best fit for the content, the audience, and your document plan.

A well-defined approach makes your writing task easier because it helps you select the relevant material for the document and lets you ignore the remainder. It also can help you eliminate information that may unnecessarily raise questions in the reader's mind. These criteria will help you evaluate the suitability of each approach:

- Does the approach fit the medium, audience, objective, and purpose of the document?
- How closely does the approach follow your marcom plan, creative platform, and document plan?
- Does the approach help you identify the information that fits the focus of the document? eliminate irrelevant information?

In addition, check your own interest level and ease when you are writing text to explore a possible approach. If the words come easily and if you become excited about what you are writing, you may have found a successful approach.

Caution: When choosing an approach, watch out for your own biases, whether they are based on too much knowledge about the subject matter or on your own opinions and life experiences. How much knowledge about your company and product should you have? You need to know your stuff—the technology, markets, applications, and competition for your product. Certainly, the *less* you know about your subject, the weaker and less effective your writing. But the *more* you know about your subject, the more likely you are to lose sight of what your audience needs to know. The solution: Learn all you can, but constantly review how you are communicating that knowledge in your materials.

Deciding What to Leave Out

It can be difficult to select which information to include when you are developing a new document. While it may seem contradictory, deciding what to leave *out* of a particular piece can help you decide what to put in. Use these factors to help you select information appropriately:

- Is the information extraneous to the main theme or focus of the document? Eliminate it completely or place it in a sidebar.
- Does the information appear in another document in your set, or is it widely known or easily obtainable from another source? If yes, provide references to these sources.
- Is the information appropriate for the target audience for the piece, or for its place in the sales cycle? You may have perfectly wonderful information that just needs to find a better home.
- Would the information be better presented in a different format? If yes, does that mean putting the information in another document, or adjusting the format of the one under consideration?

While you want to ensure that your documents are tightly focused, remember one caution when selecting text to eliminate: What will readers assume about the information you don't present? Consumer marketing research has shown that when they make inferences about missing information, readers will exaggerate the importance of information they don't know, or will underestimate the strength or benefit of these missing factors. And, for better or worse, readers may assume something about your product based on their knowledge of competitive products or the product category.[17]

Learn from Others

One good way to learn new approaches and techniques is to mimic what someone else has done. Keep a clippings file of example pieces you think show good forms of marketing writing. Even materials for products outside of your industry can be sources for inspiration. Also, keep the drafts you have rejected in earlier projects. For example, a paragraph that is too obtuse for a sales brochure may be perfect for a technical article.

WRITING STYLE FOR HIGH-TECH MARCOM

Style is your choice of words, the way you structure a sentence, how you organize information, and the overall tone of your writing. The determining question when defining your writing style is this: What sense of your product or company do you want to create in the reader's mind?

The idea of a single marketing writing style is somewhat misguided. As a marketing writer, you will likely develop a repertoire of styles, using them as appropriate for different audiences and different pieces. Sometimes your writing will be very formal, with a defined structure and word choices that are based on very precise meanings. In another piece, your style will be more informal with sentences and word choices that have a more conversational feeling.

Your company may have a publication style guide or other defined style standards. However, when choosing the writing style for a particular document, consider its purpose, audience, and subject matter. By necessity, your style will vary to accommodate the differences in the three marcom purposes: motivation, information, or persuasion. Your style also should reflect the target audience's language and preferred degree of formality (especially for variations among international markets).

For projects such as image advertising or corporate capabilities brochures, the marketing writing style may reflect the personality of your company, such as highly technical, business-oriented, or creative. For example, think of the differences in corporate personality that are typically attributed to IBM (conservative, businesslike) and Apple Computer (innovative, fun). In contrast, a nonpromotional style is required for press materials. This style must be straightforward, focused on facts, clear, precise, and more neutral than that used for sales materials.

The nature of your subject matter also will be a significant factor in the choice of writing style. After all, you would not use the same style to present highly technical research findings in a white paper as you would to describe the features of a software program for children in a sales brochure.

No matter which writing style you use, apply it consistently throughout the piece. For example, switching from a very formal, corporate style to an informal style within a brochure would be very disconcerting for the reader. The change in style would prompt him to focus on how your information is presented, not on what it says. This guideline also applies to the tone of your writing. Don't use a very serious tone in one paragraph, then make an attempt at humor in the next.

How do you identify the best style for a particular document? Consider the elements described in this section, picking and choosing those best suited to the document. Another technique is to mimic a style. Analyze an effective piece and determine how you can apply that style to your own material.

You can also specify the style as part of your document plan for each marcom project. Defining the style at this stage yields several benefits:

- You can ensure the style is appropriate for the document's purpose, audience, and content.
- You have a reference point for checking your copy drafts.
- You can avoid the discontinuity of style that occurs when multiple writers contribute to a document.

Figure 4.1 shows examples of how writing style might be defined for a few marcom projects.

Structure and Usage in Marcom Style

Many people describe writing style as the degree of formality in grammar and word usage: from very rigid to very casual or anywhere between. For high-tech marcom, this spectrum can be described as:

- **Formal:** A corporate, academic, or journalistic style that is informative, educational, or analytical. A formal writing style

	Sales Brochure	White Paper	How-to Article
Audience	Consumers.	Technical staff.	Business customers.
Structure and Usage	Informal.	Formal.	Formal to somewhat informal.
Characteristics	Friendly, informative, professional.	Informative, analytical, factual.	Informative, educational.
Tone	Personable, upbeat, helpful.	Knowledgeable, dispassionate.	Knowledgeable, helpful.
Emphasis	Information and motivation.	Information and persuasion.	Information.

Figure 4.1   Example definitions of writing style.

often uses third person to convey objectivity and sometimes makes heavy use of passive voice. Sentence and paragraph structure adhere strictly to the rules of grammar. Material organization is logical and consistent, and may follow a defined format for document elements. Word choices are careful and precise, with consistent usage of a selective vocabulary. *The worldwide restructuring of businesses and business relationships, through mergers, acquisitions, or closer relationships with suppliers and customers further promotes the adoption of internetworking technology.*[43]

Informal: A casual, sometimes unconventional style that often resembles the patterns of conversation. An informal writing style typically uses first and second person with active voice to address the reader directly. Sentence and paragraph structure can vary within a document, usually with less rigid adherence to the rules of grammar. Material organization is determined primarily by the overall creative plan for the piece, including tight integration of copy with visuals. Word choices allow flexibility for using synonyms, colloquialisms, and emotionally charged words based on creative appeal and effectiveness in conveying the document's messages. *The result? A line of applications designed to work the way you do.*[88]

Tone in Marcom Style

Tone is what Cappon describes as "the inner music of words . . . clusters of associations and images that lurk just below the surface."[22] It describes how your text will resonate for the target audience—how your writing will "feel."[20] It can be described by words such as *upbeat, empathetic, knowledgeable, precise,* or *conservative.* Tone is achieved cumulatively through the combined effect of the content itself, its presentation format, and your specific word choices.

The tone of your writing must be compatible with the structure and usage in your style. For example, a very formal structure and usage would dampen the impact of a tone that was intended to convey excitement and energy. In a persuasion or motivation piece it is especially important to match tone to the nature of your message and expectations of the audience in order to gain acceptance.[21]

Tone also must be consistent with the document's purpose:

Purpose	Tone
Motivation	Confident, upbeat, friendly, inspirational. ***And we're prepared to offer you PhotoStyler—and MORE—at exciting savings.*** [101]
Information	Knowledgeable, businesslike, instructive. ***AutoInstall enables the router to learn its address and host information automatically . . . in a process that can be controlled by a network administrator from a central location.*** [43]
Persuasion	Dispassionate or aggressive, advocatory or empathetic. ***At Microsoft we recognize the strategic importance of the messaging infrastructure in solving our customers' current problems and meeting their long-term communication and workgroup application needs.*** [108]

Emphasis in Marcom Style

The final element of a marketing writing style is the choice of what is emphasized in the document's content. For example, in a data sheet you will emphasize technical details, while in a capabilities brochure you might emphasize the company's overall messages. Like the choice of tone, emphasis also varies according to the document's purpose:

Purpose	Emphasis
Motivation	Clear statement of the benefits, call to action, offers, and incentives. ***And since it's backed by our 30-day money-back guarantee, you have nothing to lose by giving Saber LAN Workstation a try!*** [47]
Information	Clarity, accuracy, and completeness of the subject matter and its appropriateness to the reader's interests, needs, and prior knowledge or experience. ***Keep track of your images with a built-in file management system— you can add keywords and descriptions, browse through thumbnails, retrieve files, and more.*** [75]
Persuasion	Delivery of messages or advocacy of an issue or viewpoint. ***But let me give you the specifics about these new programs, and then you'll understand for yourself why I'm so excited about them.*** [156]

WORKING WITH A GRAPHIC DESIGNER

Graphic designers and writers often work together through the development of a marcom document, from searching for the initial concept to proofing the final artwork. This process typically involves three stages: visual concept, comprehensive (comp) layout, and draft.

The concept stage defines the overall approach to the layout and organization of the document: its format, size, and major visual and copy elements.

At the comp stage, the writer and designer develop this concept further with a detailed layout. A rough sample of the final document may be produced at this stage.

At the draft stage, the headlines, body copy, and other text elements are complete and the designer may make a trial layout to test for copy fit. This is the point when additional text elements may be identified, such as pull quotes. In successive drafts, the designer and writer cooperate on a continuous refinement of both copy and layout.

Writers and designers can work together to ensure the copy is a reinforcement of the visuals that appear in the piece. For example, an advertisement that shows a photo of gears used the words "gear up," "mesh," and "whole works" in the headlines or body copy.[64]

For writers, working with a designer is an interactive, give-and-take process. Don't be afraid to offer suggestions on layout or visuals, but always respect the expertise and judgment of the designer. In return, be gracious about accepting a designer's suggestion on copy elements or content.

EXERCISES

Approaching Your Material

Try these activities for several types of marcom documents:

1. Can you identify the approach used to organize and present the information? Is there a theme that runs through the document? How well does the approach or theme fit the material, objective, and audience?
2. Try rewriting the document. Would you use a different approach, phrasing, or word choices? Would you include additional information or delete certain material? Identify your reasons for making these changes. These reasons could include making the document

more compelling, understandable, or specific; better meeting the information needs of the reader; better presenting the key marketing messages; or better integrating the text and visuals.

Writing Style

1. How would you describe your company's personality? What writing style would best present that personality? Look at your company's existing marcom material. Does any of it reflect the company's personality?

2. Describe the typical structure and usage in your writing style. If it varies, can you identify the guidelines you use for determining the appropriate variation? List the company style guide and other references you use to check the accuracy of your grammar, style, and word usage.

3. Take an existing marcom document and describe how you perceive its tone. Evaluate how well the tone and emphasis match the document's purpose. Describe the usual tone you use in your writing.

4. Put your own material into the style or format of a marketing document you want to mimic. See how well (or poorly) your material works in that style. Evaluate how you can adopt the successful aspects of the example document for your own text.

PART TWO

Writing a High-Tech Marcom Document

The chapters in this part cover techniques and ideas you can use every day in developing your marketing materials. The information presented here will guide you through all components of a marcom project:

- *Determining the best way to organize and communicate your content.*
- *Using techniques that will add power and impact to your words.*
- *Handling legal and ethical concerns.*
- *Adapting your materials and messages for international markets.*

You may first want to evaluate your existing materials against the section "Common Mistakes in High-Tech Copy" in Chapter 7. If you find that your materials contain any of these problems, the information and guidelines presented in this part will give you many ways to overcome them.

CHAPTER 5

Document Elements

Packaging Your Information for Greater Impact

This chapter describes how to organize your content to make the best use of the different document elements available in a printed piece. Not all of these elements will be appropriate for every document you produce. Use the information in this chapter as a selection of ideas from which you can pick and choose based on the objective, purpose, audience, content types, and visual design for each project.

The document elements are described in this section in the same order in which they appear in most marketing materials. Figure 5.1 illustrates several of these elements and how they typically appear in a marcom document.

HEADLINES AND SUBHEADS

Headlines (or titles) and subheadlines (subheads) are your first opportunity to "sell" your piece to the reader. They are what catch your reader's attention, enticing or convincing her to stop and read more. Considering that readers often skim magazines and sales materials, a fresh headline is especially important for ads, brochures, articles, and direct-mail letters. Sometimes the headline and subheads may be all she reads, making it even more important they do a good job of conveying a high-impact message. With careful use of the headline and subheads, you also can organize the information for your reader and build multiple messages (see Chapter 3).

The following types of information can be incorporated into a headline or subhead:

This is an Overline...

This is a Headline

This is Body Copy. Imsep pretu tempu revol bileg rokam revoc tephe rosve etepe tenov sindu turqu brevt elliu repar tiuve tamia queso utage udulc vires humus fallo 25deu Anetn bisre freun carmi avire ingen umque miher muner veris adest duner veris adest brevt elliu repar tiuve tamia queso utage udulc vires.

This is Body Copy. Seru quevi escit billo isput tatqu aliqu diams bipos itopu 50sta Isant oscul bifid mquec cumen berra etmii pyren nsomn anoct reern oncit quqar anofe ventm hipec oramo uetfu Stusag plica oscri eseli sipse enitu ammih ierqu vagas ubesc rpore. Segat ecame suidt mande onatd stent 125sa Imsep pretu tempu revol etepe tenov sindu turqu brevt elliu udulc vires humus fallo 150eu Anetn bisre freun carmi avire ingen umque miher muner veris adest duner veris adest iteru.

This is a Pull Quote.

teliu ipsev 75tvi Eonei elaur mensl quidi aptat rinar uacae rolym oecfu iunto ulosa tarac spiri usore idpar thaec abies bileg rokam revoc tephe rosve repar tiuve tamia queso utage ingen umque miher

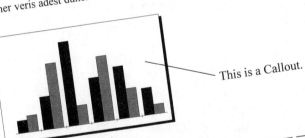

This is a Callout.

Figure A. This is a Caption.

This is a Sidebar. Scri eseli sipse enitu ammih mensl quidi aptat rinar uacae ierqu vagas ubesc rpore ibere perqu umbra perqu antra erorp netra 225at mihif napat ntint riora intui urque nimus otoqu cagat rolym oecfu.

Figure 5.1   Illustration of marketing document elements.

- **Feature/benefit statement.** Present your product's most important feature or benefit. *The customizable interface makes working in Aldus FreeHand quick and easy.*[79]
- **News announcement.** *Introducing Power Windows for Project Managers. The #1 Rated Project Manager [is] Now Available for Windows.*[81]
- **How-to.** *A Guide to Planning a Wide-Area Network.*[84]
- **Call to action.** *Give Us a Few Minutes and $199.95 and We'll Network Your Small Business.*[83]
- **Reason-why.** *Ten reasons to choose . . .*
- **Testimonial.** *"I was so blown away by Norton Desktop."*[13]
- **Teaser**. An approach where you use the headline to set up the teaser, then deliver the payoff or punchline in the opener of the body copy. *If You're Looking for the Best Solutions to Your Computing Needs, Just Look Inside.*[80]

Subheads are an effective way to guide your reader through the document by serving as section labels for lengthy blocks of body copy. Subheads also can:

- Expand on the major message presented in the headline.[7]
- Present secondary messages or incrementally build your primary message.
- Carry through the tone and theme set by the headline.

Use these techniques to create high-impact headlines and subheads:

- Decide whether you want your headline to make a direct statement or an indirect allusion to what you're selling or its benefits.[14] While the examples earlier in this section show a variety of ways to make a direct statement, this example shows the use of indirect allusion in a headline for an appointment-book software product: *Seize the Day.*[82]
- Look for words or phrases in the body copy that summarize the section or the entire piece. Repeating those words in your headline and subheads will add emphasis to what they say.
- Match the text in the headline to what is depicted in any visuals in the document. This technique can yield the kind of creative synergy that makes your piece memorable. For example, a brochure that uses the headline: *Explore the World of Connectivity with Reflection Software* included images of cruise ships, maps, and passport stamps as well as other navigation references in the copy.[15]
- Look at the text techniques in Chapter 7 for ideas on adding interest to headlines. For an ad or other sales document, try

one of the highly creative techniques such as imagery, alliteration, word play, humor, and emotion. Techniques such as parallelism and asking questions will be more appropriate for other types of documents. To find the best technique for a particular piece, try developing multiple headlines that experiment with the different techniques.

The number of headline levels in your piece can affect its clarity and visual appeal. For most marcom documents, the maximum number of headline levels is three. If you think you need more, determine whether your text can be formatted into a bullet list or organized into broader groupings.

OVERLINES

An overline is a secondary headline that provides a lead-in to the main headline. It usually appears above the main headline, set in a smaller type size. Overlines are used primarily in ads, articles, and brochures to present a secondary message, a benefit statement, or additional information that will draw the reader's interest in the piece.

OPENERS

In a marcom piece the opener must capture the reader's interest immediately with clear, enticing prose that leads naturally into the body copy. A good opener also sets the mood and gives the reader a preview of the document's information. Whether it is a sentence, a paragraph, or a section, the opener always seems like the most difficult part of the piece to write.

Try these techniques for writing a seductive and fluid opener:

- **State your key message or benefit.** Tell the reader immediately your most compelling sales point. This is a common opener for ads, brochures, and other sales pieces. *QuickTime software makes it as easy to incorporate dynamic data into documents as it is to paste graphics into text.*[85]
- **Summarize your theme or discussion with the 5Ws.** Use the opener to present your information like a news story—any combination of *Who, What, When, Where, Why,* and even *How. ADC Kentrox will demonstrate a new broadband RF access and transport system at Wireless '93 in Dallas TX, March 2–4, 1993.*[86] The *5Ws* is the opener for the inverted pyramid technique, a staple of press releases and news articles. This technique

gives the reader a clear, high-level snapshot of the content in your piece. It moves the story from the broad overview of the opener to greater levels of detail in the body copy—from most important to least important. Be careful that you include only the most essential information in this type of opener; you don't need to tell the reader everything in the opening sentence or paragraph. Also, make sure that the reader will clearly understand the *who, what,* or *when* of your subject before you explain the *why* and *how*.

- **Make an announcement, indicate a change or new development.** *A new IC that can bring compact disc (CD)-quality sound to broadcasting, multimedia, and other audio/visual applications has been introduced by Texas Instruments.*[87] As shown with this example, state your most important message first—don't let the reader get distracted by a subsidiary clause that contains less important information. If you announce something new in the opening sentence, you may want to compare that with previous versions later in the piece.

- **Describe a problem or challenge.** *Too many people, too much equipment, and not enough space. These were the challenges facing* .... [12] This type of opener is particularly effective in case studies or other documents where the description of a problem and solution or application is the primary content type.

- **Give a new definition.** Defining a term or idea in a new way can be a fresh approach for presenting a message or product that you feel has become so commonplace it seems nothing new can be said about it. *There are many definitions of open computing. Digital's definition is the broadest: open computing means open technology, open business practices, and open services.*[29] The trick is to create a new perspective in the opener that will cause the reader to say "I hadn't thought of it that way before." An analogy or metaphor may be appropriate for this type of opener (see the section "Using Imagery" in Chapter 7).

- **Pose a question.** Questions are a great way to stop a reader's roving eye and prompt him to read on to find the answer. But don't word the question so that the answer is glaringly obvious. You want to intrigue the reader, not make him feel like he's about to take a quiz. Ask open-ended questions such as *Have you ever . . . ?* or *What if . . . ?*

- **Lead with a quote.** Use an incisive quote from a customer, industry analyst, or a product review—even from literature or history. *"Ever since I was put in charge of fund-raising for the zoo, the Microsoft PowerPoint presentation graphics program has become my most important partner."*[88]

Storytelling techniques make for great openers in articles, case studies, and sometimes backgrounders and white papers. These techniques include:

- **Set the scene.** Describe a work place, the circumstances around an event, the difficulty of a person's task, or other elements that depict a situation, activity, idea, or challenge. Help the reader visualize what has happened, or the environment in which the story takes place. *Paper-making machines, three stories high and as long as a football field, turn hundreds of thousands of tons of pulp into fine writing, copy, computer, and tissue paper each year at Boise Cascade's St. Helens mill.*[89]
- **Present a history.** Summarize the previous developments, events, or decisions that have led to the current situation. This type of opener should answer these questions: Why this topic? Why now?
- **Show a diary.** Present a log or timeline to describe events or activities that occur in a sequence or over time. You can make your whole first section a diary, or sprinkle log entries throughout the piece. Just be sure that you are stating the chronology of events correctly. *9:05 P.M. Field technicians work carefully, aware they must perform flawlessly. 9:18 P.M. The moment of truth. The first cell site is online.*[62]
- **Tell a story.** Open with an anecdote based on a real person, activity, or situation. If you use a composite or hypothetical tale, identify it clearly as fiction (see Chapter 8). Choose an anecdote that is relevant to your audience and your message. *When Don Glor came to work on the morning of September 15, he'd never used a database before. Two hours later he'd developed his first application . . . .*[49]

How long should your opener be? It can be anywhere from a single sentence to two or three paragraphs—whatever length you need to create a context for readers and hook them into reading further. Be careful that you don't pack too much information into your opener. Remember that you can use other elements of the piece to present your points with just as much impact.

These are other problems to avoid in openers:

- Dull recitations of fact.
- Generalities: Broad, bland statements won't give the reader sufficient clues about the subject of the piece, or an interest in continuing to read it.
- Unbelievable claims or scenarios.
- Clichés.

BODY COPY

In every marcom document (with the exception of some ads) most of your writing effort will be focused on the body copy—the narrative text that provides the detailed information about your product, service, event, announcement, or views.

For the most part, write your body copy in a clear, straightforward, expository style. Use active voice, present tense, and specific language. However, you must pay attention to sustaining a style and tone that is unified with the other elements in the piece (see Chapter 4). You also can apply a reasonable mix of the ideas suggested in this chapter and in Chapter 7 to make your body copy more interesting to the reader.

These are additional guidelines to remember when writing body copy:

- The lead sentence or paragraph should specifically connect the idea or message of the headline with the rest of the body copy.
- Structure the body copy so it presents your points or messages in order of importance. Remember that your reader may not read the entire piece, and indeed won't if the first few paragraphs seem boring, irrelevant, or difficult to understand.
- Show the direction of your piece—where it is going—through the subheads or the lead sentence of each paragraph or section. The information in your body copy must flow logically from one sentence or paragraph to the next.
- Use transitional phrases such as *More importantly, In addition,* and *As an alternative* to move from one topic to the next. Other forms of transition can be indicated by a change in time, if your text includes a chronology, or by a change in setting if you are describing a problem, environment, or development.

VISUALS

While writers are primarily concerned with the words, you should also understand the contribution of visuals to a document. For high-tech marketing materials, visuals include:

- **Product images.** Photographs or illustrations of the product, screen shots, or sample output.
- **Diagrams.** Flow charts or other diagrams to show the product architecture, configuration, or implementation.
- **Use and application images.** Visuals that show your product in operation or illustrate typical customer environments.
- **Positioning images.** Symbols or illustrations that subtly tell the reader the type of positioning you want to create for the product. These images may have little or no relation to the product itself, instead using visual metaphors to make a positioning statement or explain a new technology concept.

PULL QUOTES

Pull quotes typically appear in a box that is embedded in the body copy. They highlight an interesting or controversial statement or quote from the text and are designed to entice a skimming reader to stop and read the entire piece. You can adapt pull quotes to marcom documents such as sales materials, articles, and case studies. Pull quotes are a good way to emphasize key messages, benefits, customer testimonials, or applications.

WORD CHARTS

Also called a matrix, a word chart presents categories of information in a structured, easy-to-reference format. It is a table that can organize lists of features, benefits, specifications, or comparative information. Word charts are often useful in brochures, ads, and backgrounders.

CAPTIONS AND CALLOUTS

You know that everyone looks at the pictures first, right? Sometimes the photographs, diagrams, graphs, or other visuals are the *only* thing a reader may look at in your piece. The captions and callouts you write for these visuals can be a great way to reinforce your message.

In addition, attach a caption to all visuals you submit to a publication or include in your press materials. This will make a journalist's job easier and increase the likelihood that your caption will be used verbatim.

A *caption* is a line of text that appears alongside or underneath the visual. A *callout* is a small block of text with a line or arrow that points to a detail in the image. Both elements can be useful with images such as product pictures, configuration and architecture diagrams, word charts, and schematics.

Follow these guidelines when creating captions and callouts:

- **Keep them short.** Captions can be more than one line, but more than three lines may lose the reader. Callouts can be as short as a single word, or as long as a single sentence.
- **Keep them relevant to the image.** You will confuse the reader if you try to introduce new or conflicting information in the caption or callout. In addition, the caption or callout should reinforce information that is presented in the body copy.

There are several types of information you can include in a caption or callout:

- Feature and benefit statements.
- Identification and description of items, people, or actions in the image.
- Description of information presented on a screen display.
- Product names, including trademark symbols.
- Credit line for the photographer, designer, or illustrator.

SIDEBARS

Sidebars are extremely useful elements for presenting information that supplements or amplifies the main content of the article. They can present information that doesn't quite fit into the body copy but that will be of interest to readers. For example, a technical analysis article may include a case study in a sidebar to show how the technology has been applied in a customer's environment. Sidebars also can present short glossaries, resource listings, timelines, or bibliographies.

BULLET AND NUMBERED LISTS

A bullet or numbered list is a good way to:

- State your secondary messages.
- Describe benefits, detailed features, or applications for your product.
- Present reason-why copy.

To give your lists more interest and impact, use an action verb or an adjective as the first word for each item.

INVOLVEMENT DEVICES

Worksheets, checklists, and questionnaires are examples of involvement devices—elements that encourage active reading of the piece. Involvement devices are very effective for helping the reader understand how your product could be applied to her own situation. They are commonly used in brochures, direct-mail packages, and as a salesperson's tool for a face-to-face customer meeting.

CLOSERS

You have a snappy opening, well-crafted body copy, attention-grabbing headlines, and . . . and . . . no idea about how to close the piece. The closing sentence, paragraph, or section of your document can be nearly as important as the opener because it is often one of the few parts of the document that a reader will actually read. You don't want to waste the excellent opportunity that a closer provides to reinforce your key messages and make your piece memorable.

The type of closer you use should be determined in part by the purpose of the piece. If the purpose is information, use the closer to restate your message. If the purpose is persuasion, the opener and closer must be strong and work together. Don't use the closer to present a new argument or bit of evidence. Instead, use the closer to restate your position or to summarize your arguments and evidence.[5] Finally, if your purpose is motivation, use the closer to present a call to action (see the next section for details on this document element).

Writing a closer can be tough, especially if you actually put off writing it until five minutes before your deadline. The techniques below will help you write closers that ensure your text carries a punch right until the very end.

- **Echo the opener.** Repeating the language or structure of the opener creates a sense of verbal echo that reinforces your key message and makes it easier for the reader to remember. If you use one of the techniques for openers described earlier in this chapter, using the same technique for the closer can be very effective. In the example below, notice how the words *answers, puzzling, questions,* and *growing* in the opener are reflected in the closer with *solved, challenging, puzzle, grow.*
  - Opener (in the form of a headline): *How Q&A Answers the Puzzling Questions of a Growing Business.*

- Closer: *"You know, when I think about it, Q&A was the most valuable investment we ever made. Because it solved our company's most challenging puzzle: how to get organized and grow."*[13]
- **Use a quote.** Presenting a quote from the subject or source in the piece is one of the most common forms of a closer. To be effective, the quote must be a powerful statement that summarizes or ties together the points you have made in the body copy.
- **Review the key messages.** A summary of your marketing messages can be presented in a sentence, paragraph, or a bullet list.
- **Wrap it up.** Take the final discussion presented in the body copy to its logical conclusion or tell the end of an anecdote that appears elsewhere in the document.
- **Present a call to action.** An action closer won't be appropriate to all document types, but it is the most common for sales collateral (see the next section for a detailed discussion of the call to action).
- **Look to the future.** Discuss potential trends, outcomes, or directions that could result from the topics or examples covered in the piece. Your projections must be reasonable; if you indulge in unrealistic speculation you could cause a reader to view your earlier assertions or information with skepticism.
- **Offer an opinion or give advice.** Stating a position or making recommendations is a common closer in analyses, how-to articles, and white papers.

These tips will make writing closers an easier task:

- Write the closer first. "But wait," you say. "How can I write the closer if I don't have the rest of the piece written yet?" It doesn't matter. Writing a closer early in the process can help you structure the body copy, or at the very least, give you something to work with once the rest of the piece is complete.
- Write the closer at the same time you write the opener. This is a great way to ensure that you come full circle in a piece by rephrasing the opener, referring back to it, or presenting its logical conclusion.
- Adapt one of your rejected openers. Remember that writing an opener is no picnic either. Save all your rejected ideas about openers and revisit them when you are ready to write the closer. Can you use any of the phrasing or approaches contained in the rejected openers?

CALL TO ACTION

Every sales piece (and many other marketing documents) should have a call to action—a phrase or sentence that encourages the reader to take the next step in the sales process. Otherwise, the reader may not be motivated to take the next step or, worse yet, not know how to do so. The call to action typically appears as the closer for a piece, although it can also appear in a separate box or callout.

Typical actions include calling a toll-free number to talk with a salesperson, visiting a dealer, or mailing a reply card to request more information. In a direct-mail piece, the call to action often asks for the sale, prompting the reader to call an order center or mail an order form.

A call to action becomes more powerful if you use it to reinforce your key benefit or message. For example, this call to action reinforces a key benefit: *Let us tell you more about how our product can solve your financial problems. Call us today at . . . .*

All too many call-to-action statements read like this: *For more information call (800) 555-DULL.* To be effective, your call to action should give your readers something specific to do, and good reason for doing it. A call to action typically has two parts: an offer and instructions on what the reader must do to accept that offer (see Chapter 6 for information on offers).

In any call to action, give readers specific instructions on all the ways to take the action. Include addresses for your company's sales offices, dealers, or the retailers that carry your product—or give people a telephone number to call for this information.

An important note about telephone numbers: Many ads and sales documents include a toll-free telephone number that a reader can call to place an order or request product information. But this presents two problems for international prospects. First, many toll-free numbers work only within the home country, meaning they are unreachable by cross-border callers. Second, because of time zone and language differences, many international prospects prefer to make inquiries by fax or letter. Always include all the ways a potential customer can reach you by phone: toll-free, direct-dial, and fax numbers, as well as addresses for your headquarters or local sales office.

Examples of other types of information to spell out in your call to action include hours of operation, part numbers, information the reader should gather before calling your company, and payment and shipment methods you offer. The point of providing these details is to make it as convenient as possible for the reader to get more information or actually buy your product.

EXERCISES

1. Take several different types of existing pieces and analyze them for the document elements they use and which elements could be used to improve the document's clarity or appeal.
2. Look at the subheads in an existing document. Can you identify a flow among them that reinforces or builds the key messages? Do they help the reader understand the content and organization of the document?
3. If you know the visuals that will be used in a piece, develop a list of all words that are relevant to that image—nouns, verbs, adjectives, adverbs. If you don't have an image yet, think of the possibilities and come up with your word lists. Then, narrow your lists down to the few words that are the closest match to the image, your message, and your product's essence.
4. Take an existing document and rewrite the opener and closer to practice some or all of the techniques described in this chapter.
5. Check the call-to-action statements in several existing documents. Is the statement strong and motivational? Is the information on how to take the action complete? Develop a standard format or information set that you can adapt for call-to-action statements across all of your marcom documents.

CHAPTER 6

Content Types

Presenting High-Tech Information Effectively

It would be impossible to cover all the different types of information that could be presented in a marcom document for a high-tech product. However, this chapter describes how to handle the types of subject matter and other content typically found in high-tech marketing materials. Use the ideas presented here as guidelines for focusing your documents and incorporating these content types successfully in your projects.

PRODUCT INFORMATION

Detailed information about product features and capabilities is the major content type in most marcom documents for high-tech products. You need to determine how much technical detail to include in a document based on the information needs of the target audience. All technical information has inherent challenges for the copywriter: making sense of acronyms and jargon, handling technical detail and specifications in an understandable and interesting form, and explaining new technology concepts clearly and accurately. This section describes how to present technical information when announcing a new product or upgrade, or in general-information situations.

Announcing a new product, model, or version usually involves a flurry of communication activities. The guidelines below will help you provide complete and useful information in your product announcement, whether it is in the form of a press release, direct-mail piece, or customer newsletter article. But remember that not all of these guidelines will be applicable to each product type or the circumstances that surround the announcement.

- **Product identification.** Give the complete product name and model number.
- **Product description.** Provide information on the product's features and functions (e.g., a "How it Works" section), key customer benefits, typical user applications, and sample processes or output. Compare the new product or model with earlier versions, with other products in the same product line, with competitive products, or with nontechnical methods of achieving the same results.
- **Quotes.** Include quotes from a company official (president, vice president, or product manager) and, if available, from a customer such as a beta user.
- **Platforms.** Specify the platforms required or supported by the product, both hardware and software.
- **Compatibility.** Describe the compatibility, integration, or interaction of your product with others. If your product is an add-on to another product, describe what the base product does;[19] don't assume the reader will already know the base product in intimate detail.
- **Demonstration.** Provide details on when and where the product will be demonstrated, such as at a trade show or press conference, or indicate if a demo disk or evaluation unit is available.
- **Product packaging.** Describe the product's components, options, and configuration choices where applicable. Specify what the product package contains, for example, hardware, software disks, documentation, tool kits, training videos, and other items.
- **Availability.** Specify when the product will be available: either "immediately" or at a date in the future. You may need to indicate separate dates for when customers can begin to place orders and when the product will begin shipping. List contact information for retailers, distributors, or other sources where customers can purchase the product or obtain more information.
- **Replacement plans.** Give information on phase-out plans for earlier models or versions; specify whether and for how long older models and versions will be sold and supported. Describe any upgrade or trade-in options.
- **Company information.** Include a description of the company, its product lines, capabilities, services, or positioning. In a press release this is typically a single paragraph called "boilerplate."

- **Trademarks.** Include trademark notations and references for all product names (from your company and others) where appropriate.
- **Certifications.** Indicate if any portion of your product's technology is patented or certified, and by which government(s), laboratory, or certifying agency.

Features and Benefits

Most advertising and marketing experts will tell you to emphasize benefits instead of features in a marketing document. But for high-tech products, many prospects have a strong interest in detailed information about product features. This is especially true for product categories where there are relatively minor distinctions between competing products. For high-tech marcom documents this means you must strike a careful balance between product-centered feature statements and reader-centered benefits statements.

Balancing features and benefits can be a difficult writing task because sometimes it's hard to tell which is which. The following guidelines will help you distinguish between features and benefits.

Feature statements:

- Focus on the product, not on the reader.
- Describe a product function:

  The Line Recognition feature converts slightly angled lines into perfectly straight horizontal and vertical lines.[91]

  Capability:

  Run the same software with different keyboards.[92]

  Or application:

  This voice and data transfer capability is also valuable for conference calls.[93]

- Describe the circumstances, equipment, facilities, or other items supported by the product. *If your computer has any of the Windows supported sound devices, you can directly play MIDI, Digital Audio, and CD ROM Audio.*[94]

Benefit statements:

- Focus on the reader, not on the product. They include words like *you, the user,* or other terms that directly address the document's audience.

- Describe what the product feature will mean for the reader:

  This [feature] means there's more time to concentrate on ideas, rather than worrying about styles.[88]

- Describe enhancements to the reader's environment:

  The new lower frequency beeper is easily heard even in noisy industrial environments.[95]

  Solutions to the reader's problems:

  Mosaix solves the [problem] of the inbound call center: answering calls in a timely manner while consistently maintaining high levels of agent productivity.[96]

  Results:

  As a result [of this feature], People's improved the answer rate for inbound calls by 15%.[97]

  Or the value of capabilities to be gained from using the product:

  Paradigm increases the efficiency and accountability of your support organization, reduces the cost of operating your network, reduces training costs, and enhances the service provided to your end-users.[98]

- Include action or result phrases such as *for [result]* or *to [action]*:

  Users can change the color of the display's background and foreground attributes to enhance readability or to highlight specific screen areas or different applications for greater user productivity.[99]

Feature and benefit statements can highlight the differences or uniqueness offered by your product. Use words like *first, one-of-a-kind, only, unmatchable, specialized,* or *patented* (if this is indeed true for your product or its underlying technology). Emphasizing your product's unique aspects is especially important in categories with many closely competitive products, where the reader may see your product as no different or better than the others. For example:

  Now when you want to cut, move, paste, or insert data, you simply select a range with the mouse, and drag the data wherever you wish. It's the fastest way to work and only Microsoft Excel 4.0 has it.[88]

Arrange the features and benefits in order of most importance to your reader. You may have a different perspective on this ranking than your technical experts. But if readers are most concerned about a product capability that you would otherwise find trivial, you will want to elevate its importance in your text. It also may be appropriate to segment product benefits that can be obtained immediately from those a customer receives with long-term usage.

Within a sentence, you can present a feature first and then its resulting benefit, or the benefit first and then its associated feature. This example shows a feature–benefit structure:

> *Resident memory can be doubled to 4 MB to manage more demanding documents.*[100]

This example shows a benefit–feature structure:

> *And, to handle sophisticated print jobs, you can choose from a wide range of options including a font cartridge and letter, legal, and envelope cassettes.*[100]

When describing features and benefits, you want to be as clear and complete as possible. Yet it's not always feasible or appropriate to include absolutely every feature and benefit in each marcom document. How do you decide whether to leave out a particular feature or benefit statement? These guidelines will help you choose:

- Is the information available in another document? Will the reader receive this document at another stage of the sales cycle, or be able to obtain it easily?
- Is the feature/benefit statement highly dependant upon each customer's environment or application? If yes, the statement might be better made by a salesperson in a presentation.
- What inferences will the reader draw from the document if you leave out the statement? Without this information, could the reader assume that there is something more to the product than is the case, or that something is missing when it is not?

You can use any of these document elements to present feature and benefit statements:

- **Word charts.** Create a table with separate columns for features and benefits. This is an effective way to show a one-to-one, one-to-many, or many-to-one relationship between a feature and its associated benefits.

- **Bullet lists.** Use a single bullet to show each feature and benefit statement in matching pairs.
- **Body copy.** Present the features and benefits in sentences or paragraphs.
- **Subheads.** Create a subhead for each feature or benefit and follow it with one or more body copy paragraphs to provide a detailed explanation.
- **Callouts and captions.** Use these elements to highlight a feature or benefit that is depicted in a visual.

Specifications

In the case of technical products, the old saying "the proof is in the details" holds particularly true. Detailed product information in the form of specifications supports your broader product messages. Readers want specifications because they help eliminate from consideration products that don't fit a current environment or that would require an expensive investment in additional equipment, services, or other resources.

Product specifications are more useful when they present all the details readers need to make an informed decision about buying or implementing your product. Specifications can include such information as:

- Hardware and software requirements
- Operating environment requirements for hardware, software, location, temperature, and other components
- Size, weight, and other physical characteristics
- Compatibility with other products
- Performance ranges
- Packaging, options, and other variations in the product's configuration, delivery, or implementation

Specifications are typically placed at the end of a brochure or data sheet, but also can appear in a sidebar or in tables placed in the main body of the piece.

Technical Jargon

. . . to paraphrase Gatsby, "The very technical do not talk like you and me."—John A. Barry

Technical jargon is a favorite target of scorn among journalists, customers, and the general public alike. Indeed, sentences that contain dense jargon are difficult to read and understand, even for readers who know the terms.[23] But it's hard to get away from jargon when writing about technology. Sometimes you must include jargon in your marketing material because the audience expects to see it, or because it is included in your competitors' documents.

You must also be aware of a sense of "classism" that can creep into technical materials, a condescending attitude toward those who may not be in the industry or who may be intimidated by technology and its language. Classism becomes an especially sensitive issue when you target the consumer market or businesses that have traditionally had little if any experience with technology in general or your type of technology in particular. Or, as Barry describes it, "Inherent in technobabble is the assumption that everyone else knows what the users of the technobabble are talking about."[18] Check your materials to ensure that the amount and type of any jargon is appropriate to the audience.

Fortunately, there are ways to deal with jargon so that it doesn't overwhelm, obscure, or confuse the messages you want to present in a document. Here are a few ideas:

- Use jargon selectively. Even hard-core technocrats won't necessarily be impressed by a document that is full of dense technical language.
- Watch out for noun clusters and long strings of modifiers that confuse the subject-action-object relationship. This sentence provides an example:

  You can modify all system configuration parameter values.

  The sentence becomes easier to understand when revised to:

  You can modify the values of all parameters that control the configuration of the system.

- If you are writing a document that will be translated into another language, determine whether the technical terms are the same or different—and widely understood—in the target language (see Chapter 9).

Acronyms

Acronyms are so prevalent in some industries that marketing materials look like something written by a child playing with alphabet soup. It is true that acronyms can be adopted quickly into common usage by people in that industry, often to the extent that you no longer need to show the component words when you use the acronym. However, remember that the same acronym can have two or more different definitions—even within the same industry. For example, in telecommunications the word POP can be an acronym for *point-of-presence* or an abbreviation of the word *population*. Especially if your product addresses multiple markets or technologies, you need to be certain that your acronyms will be understood correctly by your readers.

One ad reviewer advised: "Easy on the acronyms . . . I feel like I'm reading over speed bumps."[26] These guidelines can help you handle acronyms appropriately in your marketing materials:

- Always show the full name or the component words when you first use an acronym in a document: *asynchronous transfer mode (ATM).* If the document is lengthy, or if there is a substantial amount of text between uses of the acronym, show the full name again to help the reader remember the meaning of the acronym.
- Use a more common word if possible to avoid an acronym. For example, use *memory* instead of *RAM* (random access memory) or *ROM* (read-only memory) unless you need to identify the specific memory type.
- Include a brief glossary of acronyms at the end of the document or as a sidebar. A glossary is especially valuable if your product is in a new technology area where the jargon and acronyms aren't widely known.
- Verify that you are spelling the acronym correctly. One ad used *SCUZZI* in place of the actual acronym *SCSI* (Small Computer System Interface), which is pronounced "scuzzi." Many dictionaries are available that define general technology terms as well as those used in specific industries—buy several and use them regularly. Add your own definitions to these dictionaries as you encounter new terms and acronyms.

Background Information

Some products are easy to understand on the basis of reading a single ad or data sheet. Other products require more explanation—from the detailed view provided by specifications to the high-level view provided by a backgrounder or white paper.

Background information can describe a product's design, architecture, or underlying technology. It should help the reader understand the concept or logic behind the product's functionality, or how the product fits into a larger environment, trend, or strategy. You may need to present definitions and classifications to explain a new term, new application, new process, or new technology in your background information. In this case, using an analogy or metaphor as part of your definition or classifying by type or some other common attribute can help your reader understand the concepts.

While most background information can be presented in body copy, other good methods for conveying technical concepts include decision trees, architecture diagrams, comparison charts, and flow charts.

Applications

Application information helps the reader understand what he can do with your product in his specific situation. This information can address the reader's interest in improving his work environment, operations, tasks, information availability, or in standardizing equipment, systems, and work processes. It can be organized by industry, by type of company or user, by operation type, by information need, or any other relevant factor.

Application information should describe in very specific terms how your product will meet the reader's needs and requirements. It should also address concerns the reader may have about adopting your product such as hidden costs, implementation effort required, training needs, and ongoing support and management activities. Also describe the benefits the reader can realize from the application, especially if it replaces a method of achieving the same result that does not involve the use of technology.

Upgrade Announcement

Promoting upgrades to current customers is a special form of a product announcement. These guidelines cover the special issues related to a product upgrade:

- Use reason-why copy to describe the new applications or capabilities that are possible with the upgrade. *One of the handiest new printing features is the ability to print pages in any sequence.*[101] (More information on reason-why copy is presented later in this chapter.)
- Present detailed information on the new features available in the upgrade. Customers need to understand the differences between the new version and their current version. Describe the existing product functions that will be continued in the new version. Describe any changes to training programs, service plans, or support procedures that will accompany the upgrade.
- Reconfirm the reader's initial decision to purchase your product by restating your key messages, emphasizing your com-

pany's commitment to providing improvements, or providing quotes from product reviews or other satisfied users.

- Provide complete information on how the customer can obtain the upgrade; many companies use a reply card or order form for this purpose. Include pricing and shipping details; indicate if the product is available through dealer or retail channels; describe what information (such as a registration number) the customer must supply with the upgrade order; specify any time limits, conditions, or incentives attached to the upgrade offer.

SALES INFORMATION

Some marketing documents are directed to the people who will actually sell your product, such as sales representatives, dealers, and value-added resellers (VARs). This information must tell these people what they need to know in order to sell your product. For dealers and distributors who carry multiple products, this material must also motivate them to make the effort to sell yours.

Depending on the complexity of your product and distribution channels, sales information can be packaged in a memorandum, bulletin, booklet, bound sales guide, or multidocument sales kit.

Here are some ideas on the types of information to provide for sales personnel:

- **Market information.** Describe market conditions, present relevant market research data, identify market segments by customer type, location, operating environment, industry, or other factors.
- **Target customers.** Profile typical prospects, whether they are companies or people. Describe the problems and requirements, current situation, decision-making process, and information needs of each prospect group. These groups may classify prospects by application need, job function, industry, company size, current product implementation, or other criteria.
- **Sales techniques.** Describe the typical sales cycle, present selling ideas, list typical prospect objections and effective responses, and include examples of worksheets and other tools available to support the sales process.
- **Product information.** Include copies of all sales literature, press releases, clips of press coverage, and other material that will give a salesperson a complete resource for product information.
- **Competitor information.** Describe the strengths and weaknesses of competitive products and give advice on how to sell against them.

- **Promotion plans and resources.** Provide schedules for advertising, trade shows, seminars, and other activities planned to promote the product. Describe the literature, consulting services, and other resources available from your company to assist sales representatives. As an option, include reproducible masters for product ads and brochures that a dealer can customize and reproduce.
- **Ordering procedures.** Describe the procedures and timeline a customer or salesperson must follow to order the product. Include example order forms or other ordering documents.

Pricing Information

One product may have several prices: the Manufacturer's Suggested Retail Price (MSRP), typical retail price (called "street" price), wholesale prices granted to dealers, upgrade prices for current customers, and quantity discounts. In press releases and sales literature, the MSRP (also known as the customer price) may be the only price listed, but an indication may be given that dealer and quantity-discount prices are available upon request to the manufacturer. Any published information on pricing may be subject to local commerce laws or trade regulations. These vary by country and sometimes by local market (see Chapter 8).

In a catalog or direct-mail piece that sells the product directly to the customer, clearly state the product price and the price of additional options or fees such as shipping costs.

SERVICES INFORMATION

Some high-tech companies are primarily service providers, offering consulting, integration, or other services. In the selling of high-tech services there are several considerations that are different from those for selling products. For example:

- It is difficult for prospects to evaluate the quality and applicability of services for their particular needs before they actually make a purchase. Buying services is perceived as a higher-risk activity because there often is no substantial way to perform a "test drive" or see the projected results in advance.[126]
- The service company's reputation and presentation are critical marketing elements. The prospect will make judgments based more on subjective factors—especially about the "feel" of the potential relationship with the service provider—than on an objective comparison of features or specifications that can be made with tangible products.

- Customers must rely more heavily on vendor promises; your text must ensure that those promises match what is a realistic relationship with your company. These promises are both explicit (statements of deliverables) and implicit (unstated assumptions about quality or nature of the service experience).
- You must thoroughly explain the concept behind your service to give prospects a reasonable sense of what they are buying. Describe the distinct value-added aspects of your services; what will a prospect get from your services that he couldn't produce himself or obtain from another source?
- Be clear about the differences of your service over that provided by competitors. Prospects must be able to recognize and value these differences. Describe the capabilities, facilities, expertise of staff, clients served, quality guarantees, or other factors as supporting evidence and a form of differentiation.

Even if your company is not primarily a service provider, you may need to communicate information about the service and technical support programs associated with your products. This information is often presented in brochures and data sheets and can include:

- A description of technical support programs, such as initial and extended warranties, on-site or telephone support, or differences in response-time guarantees or cost packages.
- Hours available; phone, fax, and electronic bulletin board numbers; electronic mail addresses.
- Information on consulting and customization services, training courses, and similar programs.

COMPANY INFORMATION

Documents such as corporate backgrounders and capabilities brochures focus on a company instead of a product. Company information also can appear in product materials as part of the product's positioning or to give readers confidence in "the company behind the product."

Company information often includes:

- **Market overview.** Information on markets served by the company, including size, needs, opportunities, trends, company positioning, and competitors. This information may include a profile of typical customers. It can be organized by product line, industry, market size, or location.

- **Product information.** A description of products the company develops, manufactures, and sells as well as service and support programs.
- **Capabilities statement.** For services companies, a capabilities statement typically describes the services offered and special expertise or experience of the company's employees. For product companies, this statement also can describe key technologies, development and manufacturing capabilities, and support operations.
- **Organizational history.** Information on when and how the company was founded and key events or accomplishments in the company's history; a description of relationships with parent or subsidiary companies.
- **Sales information.** A description of the company's sales methods, marketing partnerships, and distribution channels. Separate information may be presented for domestic and international sales, including a list of key distributors or customers.
- **Patents.** Information on the award of patents, licenses, or certifications by testing laboratories, standards bodies, government agencies, or other programs. This information also can describe compliance with regulations, standards, or military specifications.
- **Financial information.** For public companies, this material presents the most recently published financial results. For privately held companies, it may list annual sales or the major investors and funding sources (e.g., venture capital firms). **Note:** Financial data and investor-relations material is a type of company information that marketing writers may produce. This information has special requirements and considerations that are beyond the scope of this book, and so is not discussed in detail here.
- **Staff biographies.** Information on the education and experience of key management and technical employees and their roles in the company.
- **Facility information.** Description of sales and support offices, manufacturing plants, laboratories, and distribution centers and other facilities including location, type of work performed, specialized equipment, and other resources.

Strategy Discussion

An article or white paper may present a company's plans or strategies for a technology area or market. Sometimes called a statement of direction, this discussion is intended to give customers broad information about a company's product plans without tipping off competitors about specific designs or implementation details. A strategy discussion can encompass:

- **Phases.** When a strategy will be implemented in stages over a lengthy time period, this information describes what each phase contains and estimated dates when it will be initiated or completed.
- **Trends.** A discussion of trends that are influencing this strategy.
- **Benefits.** The value of this strategy for customers.
- **Competitive positioning.** How this strategy compares with that of competitors and how it fits into the strategies of alliance partners or other key players in the industry.

Alliance Announcement

High-tech companies often form partnerships, joint ventures, or alliances with other companies to develop new products or reach new markets. Information about these alliances can appear in press releases, newsletter articles, or company backgrounders.

Alliance information can include:

- How the alliance will benefit customers and prospects, and if appropriate, the benefits to dealers and other alliance partners.
- The products, sales territories, or market segments covered by the alliance agreement.
- The responsibilities of each partner for sales, support, or other activities.
- The reasons for creating the alliance.
- The structure of the relationship (e.g., merger, agreement to cooperate, or exclusive marketing rights).
- Dates: when the alliance was formed, when it will begin activities or introduce a product.
- A description of each company involved in the alliance: size, product line, capabilities, location, and financial information.

CUSTOMER INFORMATION

While some companies are very secretive about their customers and the nature of their business relationships, customer information is a valuable component in marketing materials. Remember to obtain approval from the customer for all information before publishing the material.

New Business Announcement

Companies often announce major contracts or other high-dollar purchases awarded by significant customers. These announcements typically appear in press releases or articles in the company's newsletter. A new-business announcement can describe:

- What the customer bought: product, training, support, and other services.
- Monetary value of the contract or sale, and time period and geographic areas covered.
- Customer description and information on the customer's environment or application.
- Customer reasons for selecting your product.
- Information on your product and company.
- Information on other parties involved in awarding the contract or implementing the project, such as in the case of a large project that involves multiple vendors.

Testimonials and Case Studies

Testimonial is the general term for any positive customer statement about a company or its products. A testimonial is a brief endorsement quote that is used in marketing materials (specific legal guidelines apply to endorsements; see Chapter 8). The key to writing an effective testimonial is to be specific in describing problems, solutions, and results. Don't use a bland quote such as "Your company makes an excellent product. We're very happy with our choice."

A *case study* is an article that fully describes a customer's use of the product. A case study describes the customer's need or prior situation, why the product was selected, how it was implemented, and the results or benefits the customer has obtained. Case studies can be used in the promotional materials for a product, or in a customer newsletter, or be submitted as an article to a trade publication (see Chapter 11).

EVENT INFORMATION

Marketing materials can be developed for events such as user group meetings, seminars, and conference presentations. These materials can include announcements and invitations, audio/visual materials for a presentation, and follow-up articles or reports. Event information can include:

- Date, time, location, and cost of the event.
- Registration procedure.
- A description of the event's purpose, target audience, and agenda.
- An outline or description of the presentations or discussions at the event.
- Benefits or incentives for attending the event.

SUPPORTING EVIDENCE

Material that supplies supporting evidence for your messages, views, or claims is essential when your objective is persuasion. When making product claims or talking about features, be sure you clearly show the "why" or "how" behind it with your supporting evidence. Types of supporting evidence include:

- **Past performance.** *Over the past 30 years, in fact, IBM Microelectronics has developed many of the industry's most significant "firsts" in semiconductors, packaging and electronics manufacturing technologies.*[53]
- **External validation.** *The product's superiority was recently endorsed by MIDRANGE Systems readers, who voted it the most reliable and innovative of its type.*[106]
- **Research.** *According to an IDC report, the number of new LAN nodes went from 39,280 in 1989 to 71,110 in 1990 to 109,160 in 1991.*[106]
- **Product tests or reviews.** *PC Magazine independently defined and ran a battery of real world performance tests to compare database server software.*[107]

Your presentation of supporting evidence from external sources must be honest and fair. Clearly state the source of the information and the relationship of that source to your company (see the guidelines for endorsements in Chapter 8).

Association is another form of supporting evidence, for example, using customer case studies in your ads when your customers are well-known and highly respected. But make sure this association represents fairly the relationship between your company and the customer.

Statistics and Numbers

Market research studies, opinion polls, survey findings, and test results can all provide supporting evidence for your message in a marcom document. But, as the writer Mark Twain once said, "There are lies, damned lies, and statistics." You need to choose your data and statistics carefully and present them accurately and fairly. Be especially careful about the language you use to describe the statistics—don't use words that will convey an inappropriate interpretation.

These techniques can improve the impact of the statistics you cite:

- Place the statistic in close proximity to the idea or message that it supports.
- If the statistic is particularly favorable, use it as the clincher for your argument, placing it at the end of the sentence or paragraph.
- If you are citing a group of statistics or evidence from multiple sources, start with the least significant and build to the most significant. Or, frame your evidence by both starting and ending with a good statistic.
- Show the equations or calculation procedures if appropriate to the document's audience.

When presenting any type of numerical information, Blundell suggests these techniques for making it easier to read and understand:[16]

- Don't place too many numbers too close together within a paragraph. Consider placing them in a table or chart instead.
- Round and shorten the number if precision isn't critical, for example, stating $2.6 million instead of $2,611,423.
- Instead of showing a complex number show a ratio, for example, 1 out of 4.

Test Results

Product tests are a common source of supporting evidence for high-tech copy. When reporting test results, if they are preliminary or need additional confirmation you can use qualifiers such as *preliminary, appear, indicate, explore.* Clearly distinguish between those results you believe are fully proven and those that require additional validation. If you are quoting test results achieved by an independent testing lab or a trade publication, be very careful that you quote the information completely and accurately. Cite the source and give a date where possible, acknowledging copyrights and permissions where appropriate (see Chapter 8).

QUOTES

There is nothing like a positive quote from a third party to en-hance the believability of what your materials say about your product or company. Quotes are valuable for:

- Adding credibility to your claims, especially if the quotes are from customers, trade publications, or industry analysts. *"If you can click a mouse, you can create stunning presentations with this program."*—PC/Computing, 11/91[49]
- Presenting the perspective of an authoritative source who can say things that you should not say yourself.[9] For example, this quote from a customer contains a negative message about the company's competitors: *"We selected Wellfleet because they were the only ones who honestly presented their protocol suite and could offer the partnership approach that we required."*[110]
- Stating your message or information more forcefully or elo-quently than you could in the narrative. *"OS/2 has been tested over and over again in real-life environments and it has consistently demonstrated an unbeatable reliability."*[53]
- Emphasizing a key point or stating it in everyday language. *"When you pull up a report, you see a figure and say 'What was that for?' Hit QuickZoom, you go right to the trans-actions and there's your answer!"*[111]
- Humanizing the information with real-world stories and exam-ples. *"I've never taken a computer programming class in my life, yet I was able to get the results I needed with NOW!"*[92]

What makes a weak quote:

- One that isn't relevant for the document, because of the source or the content of the quote.[9]
- One that states generalities instead of specifics: *"We were very pleased with [the product's] performance."* This quote would have more impact if it described a measurable result: *"The product increased our performance by at least 30 percent."*
- One that merely repeats an idea that is presented elsewhere in the body copy.[9]

Collect positive quotes made by customers, reviewers in trade magazines, test lab reports, market researchers, and industry or financial analysts. The specific quotes you use in a particular doc-ument will be based on its objectives, the nature of the quote, and the relevance of the source to your target audience. As a result, it is unlikely that you will use every quote from every one of your sources. Instead, choose only the most cogent, concise, provocative, or captivating quotes to use in your document. Think of quotes as the spice for your text, not the meat.

When you use a quote, make sure you are presenting it within the correct context. For example, if a quote about your product's performance is taken from a test report, your context should not imply that these results were achieved by an actual user. In addition, verify all references to names, places, dates, and other facts that are included in a quote. Use parenthetical text to explain acronyms or technical terms that may be unfamiliar to the reader.

Creating Quotes

For some projects you will be writing a quote for a person who will approve it as part of the review process for your draft document. When you write a quote for someone, make sure it sounds like something the person would actually say instead of something that was borrowed from the marketing text of the piece.

Editing Quotes

This section applies to quotes obtained from a customer or other person from whom you obtain approval for the quote before publishing it. See the next section for guidelines on quoting product reviews and other published material.

There is a certain amount of editing you can perform on a person's quote. Hardly anyone speaks in concise, carefully crafted, grammatically correct sentences. Your job is to take the person's direct statement—with its stumbles, excess verbiage, and incorrect grammar or word usage—and turn it into an understandable, coherent quote. While the primary purpose of this editing is to make the quote easier to read, you must be very careful about your editing. The modified quote *must* remain true to the original in meaning, emphasis, and spirit. Minor tweaking to correct grammar, remove excess and unnecessary words to make a complete sentence, or to improve the clarity of the quote are acceptable. But more extensive editing may change the meaning of what the person actually said—something you must avoid, both to be fair to your source and to avoid the potential for legal trouble (see Chapter 8).

You also may need to rearrange quotes that appear in different parts of an interview to fit into the continuity of your written piece. This situation can arise when your interview subject goes off on a tangent, then comes back to the main question, or when you collect quotes at different times or from different sources. Again, verify that this rearrangement will not change the meaning or impression given by the speaker's words.

Paraphrasing quotes is another form of editing. For example: *According to Sastri of MediaVision, OEMs should expect to see integrated graphics/video capture/compression chip sets and boards from several different companies as early as mid-1994.*[112] This technique is useful for summarizing several direct quotes that are not strong enough to appear by themselves. Again, be sure that your paraphrase correctly reflects the context, spirit, and actual words of the quote, and don't add information to the paraphrase that wasn't in the original quote.[9]

You also can use paraphrasing to break up a lengthy quote that may otherwise bore the reader or make your source appear too verbose. It also lets you put framework information around the quote, such as to explain the topic discussed in the quote itself. In this case, quote only the most powerful statement directly and paraphrase the rest.

Caution: Be aware of what happens when you use a partial quote. You may raise questions in the reader's mind about the part you left out—that you may be quoting only the complimentary part of the statement.

Quoting from Other Material

So far this section has described considerations for using quotes obtained from people in an interview situation. Most of these guidelines also apply to quotes you derive from product reviews, market research studies, or other published information. However, considerations of copyright and fair use may apply to these quotes (see Chapter 8).

Citing Sources

Always credit the source when using any direct or paraphrased quote and obtain permission for using the quote whenever possible. Because most people are sensitive about being quoted, always ask your source to approve the quote itself and its use in the piece. There are two primary ways to give credit where it's due:

- Include the person's name, title, and organization as part of the quote statement. *"Using T1 lines has been the most economical way for us to handle combined voice and data applications," said Mel Morrison, Manager of Network Systems for Alaska Airlines.*[12]

- Cite the publication, survey, article, or report where the original information appears. *"The Raidion's low price alone makes it worth considering"—Byte, August 1992[113],* or *PC Magazine states, "Oracle7 was the hands down winner on our performance tests, outperforming the others by a wide margin."*[107]

Sometimes a customer or other source will allow you to publish information as long as they remain unnamed. In this case, use language such as *one customer . . . , a customer in the banking industry . . . ,* or *a study from a leading market research firm indicates . . . .* However, these anonymous sources weaken your message, and may cause the reader to think that the information is fictional. Use a quote from an unidentified source only when you have no other way to present the information.

OTHER CONTENT TYPES

The remaining content types described in this chapter are generally applicable to almost any subject matter found in high-tech marketing documents.

Offers

An offer statement describes any incentive you are giving the prospect to respond to your material or purchase your product. Offer statements are used extensively in advertisements, brochures, and direct-mail materials.

The specifics of the offer will vary substantially based on the product and how it is marketed. However, offers generally take one of two forms: a purchase offer or an information offer.

A *purchase offer* describes conditions or options related to buying the product. A purchase offer may be included in retail materials, ads, and direct-mail pieces.

Purchase offers can be either a hard offer (pay for it when you buy it) or a soft offer (try it before paying). An example of a hard offer is: *Buy Q&A Before 10/3/92 and Get QuickBooks for Free!*[13] Demo disks or evaluation units are the most common soft offers for high-tech products: *If you're comparing word processors, order your free working model of Ami Pro 3.0 today by calling . . . .*[49]

In any purchase offer, state exactly what is included in the offer such as guarantees and terms, expiration date, an add-on product, or other merchandise or services packaged with your product. Use words that will increase the prospect's confidence about buying a product, especially if your company is not well known. These words include: no risk, guaranteed, unconditional return, or free trial period. However, make sure that these statements accurately reflect what your company will offer and deliver.

If you are selling your product in other countries, different regulations may apply to what you can offer and how a purchase offer is stated.

Information offers include literature packets, booklets, evaluation guides, and other materials that support a lengthy, complex sales cycle or promote attendance at an event. For example: . . . ***call your local distributor or Analog Devices at . . . for your free selection kit and high performance amplifier brochure.***[90] Describe the material the reader will receive and the benefits it provides.

Comparisons

Comparative information can come in several forms:

- Comparisons between your product and its competition, commonly called "comparative advertising." As these examples show, competitors may be named or unnamed:

  A spreadsheet that's easier to learn and use than 1-2-3 and Excel![102]

  No other network laser printer . . . .[103]

- Comparison of different models within a product line.
- Comparison of a product's capabilities with a nontechnology method for achieving the same result. Or, to state it differently, describe the problems the reader will have *without* your product.

One disadvantage of making comparisons with competitive products is that your readers may not have known who your competitors are until they read your material. This may cause them to postpone a purchase decision until they have explored the competitive product.

Comparisons are typically based on features or performance measurements presented in the form of a point-by-point matrix or chart. Any comparison should be specific and objective so the reader will not see it as being unfairly slanted in your favor. And, to keep you out of legal trouble, the comparison must be absolutely accurate and defensible (see Chapter 8). However, comparative advertising of any type is not allowed in some countries (see Chapter 9).

Indirect, general comparisons can help you avoid a lawsuit, but your reader may not find them believable. Don't use unexplained comparisons such as *It yields superior performance.* You should always provide the answer to the first question a reader will have about this type of statement: "Better performance than what?" Your answer to this question should be specific and based on facts.

Use comparison to:

- Show differences or similarities between products based on features, performance, application, or price.
- Show alternatives for applications, configurations, or other decisions.
- Deliver a negative message (see Chapter 3).
- Show scope or ranking of your product or company.
- State what a product is not. *X is not an operating system.*[104] This form of comparison can be an implicit way to highlight the product's key differentiating factor or a reader's problem.

While focused on ads, the guidelines below are useful for making appropriate product comparisons in any type of marketing material. They were developed by the American Association of Advertising Agencies.

- **The intent and connotation of the ad should be to inform and never to discredit or unfairly attack competitors, competing products or services.**
- **When a competitive product is named, it should be one that exists in the marketplace as significant competition.**
- **The competition should be fairly and properly identified but never in a manner or tone of voice that degrades the competitive product or service.**
- **The advertising should compare related or similar properties or ingredients of the product, dimension to dimension, feature to feature.**
- **The identification should be for honest comparison purposes and not simply to upgrade** [your product or company] **by association** [with a perceived market leader].
- **If a competitive test is conducted it should be done by an objective testing source, preferably an independent one, so that there will be no doubt as to the veracity of the test.** [Note: See the discussion of test results and product reviews in the section "Supporting Evidence" later in this chapter.]

- **In all cases the test should be supportive of all claims made in the advertising that are based on the test.** [In other words, don't misstate or distort the test results to be more favorable to your product.]
- **The advertising should never use partial results or stress insignificant differences to cause the consumer to draw an improper conclusion** [in favor of your product or against its competition].
- **The property [feature] being compared should be significant in terms of value or usefulness of the product to the consumer.**
- **Comparatives delivered through the use of testimonials should not imply that the testimonial is more than one individual's thought unless that individual represents a sample of the majority viewpoint.**

Problems and Solutions

Describing a problem and how your product or service solved it is a very common content type in case studies, articles, and brochures. Use the ideas below to describe problems and solutions effectively.

- Describe how the task or problem was addressed before the customer purchased your product. What were the dimensions of the problem? What did the customer want to do but couldn't given the situation? What issues, needs, or other circumstances prompted the customer to consider your product?
- Describe the changes that occurred as a result of implementing your product. Relate these changes back to the problems or needs identified in the "before" section of the document. For example:

Problem: A component supplier to a medical instruments firm needs access to a materials list on her HP 3000, her client's inventory system on a VAX, and word processing files on her UNIX server.

Solution: 3000 Connection—gives simultaneous access to HP 3000, VAX, and UNIX-based hosts along with LAN services.[15]

A solution can be described by the results delivered by your product, both quantitative and qualitative. These are common types of results:

- **Financial:** Increased revenues, reduced costs, or avoided expenses (quantitative).
- **Operational:** Increased efficiency, greater ease or flexibility in performing tasks, reductions in errors or unproductive work time (qualitative and quantitative).
- **Marketing:** New customers or product sales, new markets, new product offerings, increased customer satisfaction (quantitative and qualitative).
- **Organizational:** Improved employee retention or morale, improved information and decision making (qualitative).

Reasons

Often presented in a bullet or numbered list, reason-why copy typically appears in ads, direct-mail pieces, and brochures. Reason-why copy tells the reader explicitly the major benefits of your product. It is a great way to keep your writing focused on the reader's interests:

Headline: *10 Great Reasons to Upgrade to Stacker 3.0 for Windows and DOS!*

Reasons (abbreviated list):

1. *New Stackometer™ . . . you can monitor the space on all your disk drives as you work.*

2. *New Flexible Setup gives you more control and more choices.*

3. *New Stacker Tuner™ gives you unequaled flexibility in managing your system.*[105]

Issues

High-tech marketing communication isn't always focused on a product or company. White papers, backgrounders, and articles often present a company's viewpoint on controversies or issues in a market or technology area. These documents provide analysis and interpretation of what the issue means for the reader. For example, this excerpt discusses a set of issues:

Whatever their situation, organizations should consider three primary issues affecting their e-mail strategies. These issues are the rapid growth in the number of e-mail users, the proliferation of PC LANs, and the emergence of new productivity-enhancing workgroup applications.[108]

Writing about an issue can be tricky because the nature of the debate can change so quickly. In your copy, be careful about your content, your phrasing, and how you present assertions and supporting evidence.

You may want to create material that defines the parameters or nature of the discussion about an issue. This technique is called "setting the agenda" in the reader's mind. For example, with this statement the company was apparently attempting to change the debate from a comparison of specific products to a higher-level view of customer requirements:

> *The new era of internetworking is characterized not by the merits of a single device, but by the robustness of an entire internet—and the resulting gains in an organization's productivity.*[43]

Trends and Developments

Market or technology trends are another common topic for white papers, backgrounders, and articles. For example, this passage describes a trend:

> *A major trend of corporate information systems in the 1990s will be downsizing—using smaller, cheaper, yet powerful processors to support corporate application requirements.*[108]

When describing a trend, you need to cover information such as:[16]

- **Scope:** How big is it? How many users have already adopted it? What do the market forecasts predict?
- **Locale:** Where is this being developed or adopted? What is its breadth of coverage?
- **Diversity:** How does the development reveal itself? Is it affecting multiple markets, applications, or platforms?
- **Degree:** To what level are people, places, or things involved with or impacted by this trend?
- **Perspective:** What other trends or developments are contributing to or impacting this one? These factors could include economic, social, political, legal, psychological;[16] and more specifically for high-tech products: business conditions, market activity, technology evolution, and competitive factors.
- **Alternatives:** Describe the other choices available or countermoves to this trend or development.

When writing about a trend, use a variety of sources for quotes, viewpoints, and explanations; include both direct participants or affected parties and external, neutral observers. Talk to people who are close to the action, not just the executives several layers up who can describe something only in very broad, lofty terms.

Anecdotes

Anecdotes add human interest to your subject matter, helping the reader personally relate to the information. They are appropriate for case studies, articles, and brochures. When presenting an anecdote, consider using fiction techniques such as dialogue, fore-shadowing and flashbacks, or cutting between scenes. Create a sense for your reader of immediacy, of being there, of being able to feel or visualize the circumstances or actions.

> *The air smells of sweet flowers as you drive through the gardens, bypassing traffic and admiring the spring colors. Without warning, you car shakes violently for an instant, smoke rising, then comes to a complete standstill. You try in vain to restart the engine. Frustrated, you reach for the car phone and call the service station whose number you unfortunately know all too well.*[109]

Where can you find a good tale to tell? Talk to your customers or beta users about their experience with a problem, with your product, or at an event. Talk to the behind-the-scenes people—the developers, installers, and support personnel who go through heroic or creative measures to accomplish a task or meet a deadline. Look for stories, ideas, or activities that are coincidental to your primary message, but help to show the value of your product, service, or activity.

> *11.05 P.M. A lonely stretch of highway near Bellingham, Wash. Technician Tom Brosman, who just changed the nearest cell site, came upon a serious highway accident and reported it by placing one of the first calls on the new switch. Then he called the Changeout Control Center. "The new system just paid for itself," he said.*[62]

Examples

Examples can be critical for clarifying your topics, supporting your assertions, illustrating concepts, or supplying evidence that reinforces your messages. Use examples to show:

- How a product or service can be applied in a typical user environment.
- Potential benefits or results.
- A function or process.

Choose your examples carefully, making sure they indeed support the point you want to make. You also need to match the interests of the audience for the piece, and be sensitive to varying cultural interpretations of examples (see Chapter 9).

EXERCISES

1. Take several different types of existing pieces and analyze them for the content types they include. Compare how they handle the content types with the guidelines presented in this chapter. What could you improve? Do you have content types that are not described here? If yes, can you define guidelines for handling them in the future?
2. List all existing and potential sources of supporting evidence for your marcom projects. For each source, describe the type of information available and how you might use it in your projects.
3. Write a complete list of feature and benefit statements for your product. Are you making a clear distinction between features and benefits? Does every feature statement have a corresponding benefit statement?
4. Take an existing marcom document and highlight all acronyms and jargon words. Identify which words are essential to conveying the message or for audience acceptance. Then identify the terms that could be replaced by nontechnical words and make the appropriate revisions in the text.
5. List all the sources where you could obtain quotes for your product or company and list the types of quotes you want to obtain from each source. Or, look at all quotes and reviews in your file. Which quotes or comments would be the most effective for your product's positioning or messages?

CHAPTER 7

Text Techniques

Adding Power to Your Copy

High-tech copywriting can be creative and fun, but it also can be frustrating and challenging to do well. On one hand, you are free to explore a range of writing styles and forms of expression. On the other hand, you face high expectations from your audience for the appeal, readability, and relevance of your piece. In a marcom document you can use a broad vocabulary, loose sentence structure, metaphors, even humor. But you must also deliver a realistic, informative, and convincing presentation about your product, service, or company.

Good copywriting skills require continual practice. You will find yourself constantly striving to improve the clarity, power, and impact of your writing. Look at a marketing piece that does well at holding your interest and delivering its message. You are likely to find the piece is successful because it uses a variety of techniques such as:

- Language that is easy to understand yet is potent and expressive.
- Phrasing that follows the natural, varied rhythms of speech.
- Formatting devices that guide your eye through the key points.
- Verbal imagery that amplifies a message or clarifies a concept.

This chapter describes a variety of techniques that will help you transform your raw content into an interesting, polished brochure, article, or other marcom document. Some of the techniques presented here may seem contradictory or inappropriate to certain projects. Some will not be appropriate for documents that will be adapted for international markets. Indeed, if you tried to apply all of these techniques to each marcom document, you would not be successful. Instead, think of these techniques as ingredients you can selectively add to your typical writing style to create the unique recipe you will need for a particular marcom document. Just as you wouldn't combine certain flavors when cooking, you will want to blend these techniques carefully.

GETTING ATTENTION

Catching a reader's attention is the first task of any marcom document. It involves more than just a headline set in 200-point type. But how do you pack your words with the right kind of punch? This section presents a range of ideas that can be effective when you apply them creatively and appropriately in your document.

Power Words

Your words should grab the reader's attention immediately and keep it until the end of the piece (or at least until the end of the key points you want to make). Power words are lively, specific, and concrete; they are active verbs, descriptive nouns, and vivid modifiers. These guidelines will help you select power words:

- **Nouns.** Use the most specific nouns you can find for the subject of your sentence. Examples of power nouns include: *tasks, results, efforts, answers, islands [of computers].*
- **Verbs.** Use verbs that express the action specifically. Examples of power verbs include: *yield, synergize, escalate, generate, maximize.*
- **Modifiers.** Use adjectives and adverbs that deliver a specific punch or flavor to the point you want to make. Examples of power modifiers include: *keener, staggering, foremost, enduring.*

The opposite of power words are qualifiers such as *somewhat, almost,* or *possibly.* You may use qualifiers when the subject or assertion of your statement is in doubt or if you indeed want to temper or hedge your statement.

Another type of qualifier is any form of the verb *can;* the reader may ask "so does it or doesn't it?" Use forms of *can* only to indicate that options or choices are available for the action the verb describes.

Evocative Language

How do I know what I think, until I see what I say?—W.H. Auden

Words that conjure a sensory meaning for the reader can have a very strong impact. To find evocative language, think of words

that will create a vision, a sound, or a feeling in the reader's mind.
For example:

VoiceView: A Sight for Sore Ears.[34]

Did you get the picture of someone who has been talking on
the telephone for too long? This example is effective not only
because it evokes an image, but also because it talks about a problem familiar to almost anyone. This attention-getting technique
intrigues the reader into continuing further into the document.
When using this technique, be sure your phrasing paints a complete and accurate picture.

Here is another example of evocative language:

Scream Saver for Windows[35]

Did you hear a scream in your mind? This is an example of
onomatopoetic language—words that sound like what they
describe. Your goal when using words that create a distinctive
sound in the mind's ear is to achieve euphony (pleasing to the
ear), not dissonance.

Alliteration is another technique based on sound, in this case,
the repetition of the same letter or sound. For example: ***Protection.
Performance. Productivity.***[36]

Emotion

Suggesting a positive or negative emotion for your reader can add
greatly to the impact of your text. Using emotion doesn't mean
telling a sentimental story about how your product has achieved
triumph against overwhelming odds. Instead, use emotion that is
appropriate to your audience and their circumstances, and use it
in measured doses. *Frustration* is one of the most common emotions referenced for technical products. After all, everyone recognizes the experience of trying to get this blasted thing to work! . . .
*as I sit here watching my spreadsheet crawl on my PC, I'm think-
ing to myself, "This is making it easier?"*[37]

Sources of emotional appeal to your readers include:

- **Wishes and dreams, ambition or prestige.** *What if you could . . .*
  or *Now, the faster processing you've wanted is here.*
- **Comfort, ease, and convenience.** *Dallas Semiconductor's
  digital potentiometers, unlike their mechanical counterparts,
  can be set remotely. No dials. No screwdrivers.*[38]
- **Fear, skepticism, or confusion.** *Downtime could cost you a
  lot more than just access to your data.*[39]

- **Challenges.** *You've got 60 days to create a computer-based training system for 5,000 employees—and you're not a programmer.*[40]

Many marketing messages are designed to evoke FUD (Fear, Uncertainty, and Doubt) in the reader. FUD is an extremely powerful—if tricky—technique for grabbing a reader's attention and motivating a response or action (see Chapter 3). *What else are they slashing when they slash prices?*[41]

Caution: Be careful when using any of the negative emotions such as confusion, fear, or anger. When you do, always show how the reader can overcome or avoid this negative situation with your product. And, make sure your use of positive emotions doesn't imply a promise that is more than your product can deliver.

Relevance

Think about what catches your eye—the ads or brochures that describe a familiar problem or situation, right? The more tangible, the more "real-life" you can make your information, the more the reader will relate and respond. Examples of familiar problems or situations include:

- **Time pressures.** *Saves Time. Something you don't have a lot of.*[42]
- **Industry or business trends.** *One result of this trend [an increased demand for remote access] is that many Cisco customers are adding remote offices and small sites to their internetworks.*[43]
- **Preparation for disasters or for the future.** *Whether it's a crashed disk or an unretrievable file, computer failures seem to occur at the worst possible times.*[44]
- **Financial concerns.** *You need to create a local presence, but you're wondering whether you can afford to open a branch office.*[45]

Draw the reader into the document by addressing her directly with "you" and "we" words throughout the copy. Put the reader into the scene:[10] *... which meant [you had to] weave the cable up, over, around and through office obstacles . . . .*[33]

Copy that conveys relevance is effective for grabbing a reader's attention when used in a headline or opener, and for holding that interest when it appears throughout the document.

Emphasis

Two techniques can help you improve the emphasis of your text: where you place your key message or statement, and the use of formatting devices.

Put the point you want to emphasize either at the beginning or the end of your sentence. Place your emphasis at the beginning when you want to make sure the reader understands your topic or message immediately. Place it at the end when you are delivering a "punch line" or if it will be the last statement a reader will see in a paragraph, section, or document.

Formatting devices are a way to make individual messages, phrases, or words stand out from the rest of your text. These devices include use of a second color, exclamation points, commas, boldface and italic type, bullets, em dashes, ellipses, and uppercase (but don't use uppercase if your document includes acronyms). Formatting devices are especially useful for highlighting benefits, quotes, definitions, or to deliver the payoff for a teaser or anecdote. They can draw your reader's attention to key points and improve the rhythm of your writing. The example below incorporates several of these devices:

Want to get more from your Aldus software?

- More *productivity?*
  With practical techniques that reduce time and effort, while improving results.
- More *profitability?*
  By avoiding costly printing problems and preparing files so they print right the first time.
- More *self-reliance?*
  Through troubleshooting system, printing, and file-management problems—all by yourself!
- How about *all of the above?*[46]

Exclamation points add a sense of excitement or urgency to your message and are especially effective in a headline, pull quote, or call to action: *Remember that this is a risk-free offer!*[47]

One thing to keep in mind when you use formatting devices is that a reader may look only at those words that have received special typographic treatment. Stand back from your printed piece and look only at the words highlighted by a formatting device. Are these the right words for the emphasis you want to accomplish?

Inspiration

Convey a sense of satisfaction or achievement that your reader can obtain with your product or service. Give your readers positive, exciting reasons for buying your product or agreeing with your views. Think of this technique as a form of evangelizing your product—a concept that Apple Computer adopted with great success when it launched the Macintosh computer in the early 1980s. You can create inspiration by invoking:

- **Leadership.** After all, everyone likes to know they'll be in good company when they buy your product. *Voicelink is used by the world's most respected companies. [It] gives you the competitive edge you need to succeed.*[48]
- **Strategic values** . . . *this breakthrough technology will improve the decisions you make and the actions you take. While leveraging the technological resources already in place in your organization.*[49]
- **Future opportunities.** *Calling Centers are a New Business Opportunity for Utilities.*[45]

CREATING RHYTHM

> *Words march to a beat. Sentences have rhythm. Their pace can be fast or slow; their cadence, soothing or staccato. The skillful writer controls the dance of words by carefully manipulating the structure of sentences. Long sentences can flow gently, picking up momentum as they go. Short sentences can create a tense, insistent rhythm. Repetition can add accent and meter.*[8]

The cadence or rhythm of your writing is a subtle form of holding a reader's interest in your document. Text with an even rhythm—created by words with the same number of syllables and sentences of similar length—may be easy to read but may also put your reader to sleep. When evaluating the rhythm of your copy, consider the overall pace you want to establish for the document as well as for the individual elements, paragraphs, and sentences. Do you want to keep a varied rhythm throughout, or build momentum gradually to a crescendo that is delivered in your conclusion or call to action?

Check your rhythm by reading your text aloud. To the reader, your writing should seem like a satisfying, engaging conversation. If it sounds stilted or if you stumble over phrases while reading, you have a rhythm problem. To get your words back on the beat write it like you would speak it, but without slipping into grammatical sloppiness, a disrespectful tone, or inappropriate use of idiom.

Paradoxically, one of the best ways to improve the rhythm of your writing is to break it. Use short sentences. Long sentences. Varied paragraph lengths. A mix of active and passive voice. But remember to make your rhythm compatible with the style and tone of your piece. You can change your rhythm within a piece by using any mix of the techniques described in this section.

Varied Sentences

Using different sentence lengths can improve the rhythm of your text. However, avoid very long or complex words and sentences that will slow down or trip the reader. For example:

> *SKYLIGHT is a low-cost, easy-to-use, yet powerful database management system designed to give Windows application developers a refreshing alternative to the cumbersome and non-intuitive database managers currently available.[50]*

Without looking, can you remember what this sentence was talking about at its beginning? It would be better broken into two sentences:

> *SKYLIGHT is a low-cost, easy-to-use, yet powerful database management system. It gives Windows application developers a refreshing alternative to cumbersome, non-intuitive database managers.*

When they contain clear, simple language you can use a mix of long sentences, short sentences, and fragments, and declarative sentences and those with subordinate clauses. *We handle more applications than all other providers combined. Collect call billing. Suspend, restore, disconnect. Innovative solutions that lower costs, improve customer service, raise revenue—and work perfectly with other databases.*[119]

Rhyme and Wordplay

Rhymes, a clever turn on a familiar phrase, and other forms of wordplay can add rhythm to your text. Consider these headlines: *Unmiring Wiring*[51] (rhyme), or *High Performance for disk, DAT, and the other things*[52] (wordplay). Wordplay often means giving new meaning to familiar phrases, such as *Welcome to the LAN of plenty.*[53] Wordplay also can incorporate product or company names, such as this tag line for a set of sound chips called JAZZ: *It's time to JAZZ up your designs.*[54]

To develop ideas for wordplay, look at the product's features, benefits, or applications; you can also consider the behavioral characteristics of your target audience. Look for words that can have different meanings in different contexts.[10]

Rhyme and wordplay are most effective in sales pieces; they may not be appropriate for white papers or other serious editorial material. While these techniques are often used in headlines, they also can be applied with positive results to other document elements.

When creating wordplay based on sound, make sure the meanings of the words you select are truly appropriate for the message you want to convey. Also, consider whether your audience will understand your wordplay, especially if your document will be translated or read by an international audience.

Parallelism

Parallel structure creates a sense of rhythm within a sentence or paragraph, between paragraphs, or in a bullet list. Parallelism means using the same sentence structure for related topics, such as when you start each sentence in a paragraph with a verb, or each item in a bullet list with an adjective.

One form of parallelism is to use word combinations that have balanced sounds, syllable counts, placement, or meaning: *The Way It's Packed, Stacked, and Backed.*[55]

Another form of parallelism is repeating key words, messages, or phrases like a mantra:

Easy to Buy

Easy to Install

Easy to Use

Easy to Expand[56]

This example shows you can use a combination of repeated structure and repeated words to create a sense of rhythm.

Cautions: First, repeating unusual words or inappropriate jargon may trip the reader, especially if they are defined poorly or not at all in your text. The reader may skip over the unfamiliar word or phrase the first time, but become annoyed when she encounters it again and again.

Second, too much repetition of the same words or phrases in a piece can lead to staleness and lessen the impact of your message. Watch for overuse of your favorite words when you review the drafts of a piece. Use the search capability in your word processor to find these words, then replace them selectively with carefully chosen synonyms.

Document Elements

Look at how you are using the different elements in the piece. Subheads, pull quotes, sidebars, callouts, and captions can all be effective tools for improving the appeal and rhythm of your document, especially for breaking up lengthy blocks of body copy (see Chapter 5).

ASKING QUESTIONS

Questions are an especially effective technique for use in headlines and closing statements. For example, the headline *What Does it Take to Get High-Quality, Obsolescence-Proof Electronic Publishing?*[57] could be followed by the closing statement, *Can you afford cheap publishing software?*

Use questions to prompt the reader to analyze a problem or to reconsider a competitive product or viewpoint. Questions are also key to building the FUD factor (see Chapter 3). This technique is most effective when the questions are directed to the reader or when they are written from the reader's perspective. Using first or second person in your questions helps the reader's understanding and is more likely to encourage him to continue reading in order to find the answer.

You can sprinkle questions throughout your text to build your case gradually, or list the questions in a separate section or sidebar. You can create a sense of mystery or intrigue by posing a question in a headline or opener, then answering it later in the document. A question-and-answer section (Q&A) is an approach that is often used in white papers, press kits, or articles.

When writing questions, don't limit yourself to those actually asked by your customers (although these are usually the most relevant to the reader's interests). By writing the questions yourself, you can highlight product features, reinforce your marketing messages, or overcome a reader's potential objections to your arguments. *How can you do more with less? How can you bring your products to market faster? How can you get more out of your existing technology investment?*[49]

Caution: When asking questions, make sure that they do not exclude or filter out your prospects.[8] This is more likely to happen with closed-end questions (answered with a yes or no) than with open-end or "what if" questions.

CONTRASTING SEMANTICS

The semantic contrast technique creates a juxtaposition of words or phrases that make your point in a surprising, engaging way. This juxtaposition is typically based on antithesis, the contrast of two words with opposite meanings. But semantic contrast also can create a symmetry between words based on their usage or purpose in a sentence, as in this example: *We give you big-system performance. We give you small-system flexibility.* Here, the direct contrast is between *big-system* and *small-system*, while an indirect contrast is made between *performance* and *flexibility.*

This technique offers great flexibility in its application to different types of information and materials. Here are two ways to use semantic contrast for the most impact:

- Illustrate a product's features or make a selling point. *When your systems are complex, your choice is simple.*
- List choices and alternatives for implementing your product or solving the reader's problem. *[This truck] is designed to haul loads for your customers, and lighten them for your company.*[58]

USING IMAGERY

It is always easier for a reader to understand something new when you can compare it with something familiar. Taking a new or highly technical product or issue and describing it in a familiar way is one of the benefits of using any of the imagery techniques: analogy, metaphor, allusion, and personification.

Analogy suggests similarity between two things based on a substantial amount of similar or shared attributes. It is a useful technique for describing the characteristics of a product, service, or activity. *This is a Convention Like Woodstock was Just a Concert.*[59] Analogy can be a literal, concrete comparison of things that belong to the same class (convention and Woodstock are both events) or a figurative comparison of two things that are completely different: *Like the owners of starter homes that have become too small for growing families, many users feel their local-area networks are busting at the seams from new, bandwidth-hungry applications.*[60] Analogy may be used to compare things based on a relationship of one-to-one, one-to-many, many-to-one, or many-to-many.

Metaphor suggests comparison by using symbolism or describing a technical idea or feature in terms of something that is nontechnical. This technique relies on the power of showing something in a new light or describing something complex in terms that are simpler and more familiar to the reader. Metaphor must use symbolism in a way that the reader can recognize and interpret correctly, such as in this example comparing a network wiring device to an airport: *The first transportation hub that handles more connections than O'Hare.*[61] A few of the many sources of metaphor include current events, sports, entertainment, music, nature, or hobbies. Metaphor compares things in a one-to-one relationship.

Allusion is an indirect reference to something. For example, an article about an all-night installation project in the Seattle area was titled "Sleepless in Seattle," alluding to the film with the same title.[62]

Personification gives a human quality to an inanimate object. For example, in this ad the computer monitors it promotes are made to address the reader directly, as if in a conversation: *Pardon us, but would you mind if we sat right here on your desk, a mere two feet away from you, for the next few thousand hours?*[63]

These guidelines will help you make effective use of imagery:

- Be especially careful that your language and visuals work together to support the image. For example, an advertisement that shows a photo of gears can use the words *gear up, mesh,* and *whole works.*[64]
- Make a verbal connection to the subject or story in your document. For example, an advertisement that described the communication needs of the healthcare industry used this headline: *Looking for a specialist in data systems and solutions? I'll refer you to Bell Atlantic.*[65] In this example the words *specialist* and *refer* are drawn from the vocabulary of the target audience.
- Decide whether you want to carry the image throughout the piece, both visually and verbally. For example, a brochure for a product called Concert displayed the metaphor of a classical orchestra with subheads labeled *The Overture, The First Movement,* and *Finale,* as well as related words in the text such as *tuning, harmony, movement, tempo, players, unison,* and *orchestration.*[66] When metaphor is a major concept for your piece, look through your thesaurus and dictionary and create a list of all the nouns, verbs, adjectives, and adverbs related to that metaphor. Use this list when writing the text to help you convey the image thoroughly and concretely.

Cautions: The various forms of imagery can be powerful for improving the memorability of your piece. But they also can be hazardous if you aren't careful about how you use them. These are among the problems your writing can create when it incorporates imagery:

- People may not understand your allusion or metaphor, or may have different interpretations and associations with the image.
- You may be tempted to overextend the image in ways that decrease its usefulness or that are inappropriate to the subject matter.
- You may try to make an inappropriate image fit, when presenting the information in a straight, expository form would be a better approach.
- You may be using images that are clichés or rely too much on idiom or fads.
- Your image may perpetuate an unfair stereotype of people, places, or things. An image that may be perfectly acceptable to one audience may be offensive to others.
- It is easy to create mixed-up images. Choose one analogy or metaphor and stick with it. For example, one ad used an image of *a bridge* in both the visual and the headline, but then ignored it in the text, talking instead about *benchmarks, promises,* and *steps.*[68] Mixed images confuse your readers and dilute your message.
- Your image may be stated incorrectly. For example, this passage alludes to the film *The Wizard of Oz: Where Are We? Not in Kansas anymore, Toto. In the summer of 1992, the cyclone of ATM is cutting a swath through the user and service provider landscape.*[69] Well, even Toto (a dog) could have told this writer it was a *tornado* that transported him and Dorothy to Oz. Imagine the surprise of Kansas residents if a cyclone (a rain and wind storm similar to a hurricane) had indeed struck.

SHOWING PARADOX

Paradox is when something seems to be two things at once or when something seems self-contradictory. For example, *Recent studies reveal 25 MHz is now faster than 50 MHz*[70] (presumably not feasible), or *We perform field service even when there's no field*[71] (in a story that described a service trip to an offshore oil well). Use paradox as a technique to describe a feature, problem, solution, or need.

Paradox is an effective technique because it catches the reader off-guard and piques his interest in learning how this apparent impossibility can be true.

ADDING HUMOR

Humor and puns can be a great way to make a point if they are used intentionally and carefully. For example, an article about a company called XLNT Designs Inc. was titled *Totally XLNT [excellent] FDDI Management*[72]—in this case, using idiom to make a pun of the company's name. Or, this statement about a fiber-optic cable: *. . . there's light at the end of the bundle*[73] makes a pun out of a familiar proverb. (These cables transmit light through fibers that are bundled together in a cable.)

Caution: An attempt at humor can lead to bloopers that are the embarrassment of any marketing writer. Also, consider whether your audience will understand the joke. Remember that all forms of humor—including sarcasm, irony, parody, and puns—often don't translate well into other languages. And you must be certain that your humor won't offend your readers. Avoid any jokes or puns that imply racism, sexism, or cultural slur.

WATCHING THE BASICS

This book is not intended to be a review of the basic principles of good writing. However, the principles described in this section have special application to marketing writing.

Contractions

If you are using an informal style in your document, you may want to use contractions such as *it's, won't,* and *aren't.* Contractions help to maintain a conversational tone, but they can slow down the reader if used extensively, because of the time the reader needs to decode them.

Caution: Do not make a contraction of a product name or other trademarked text. Such usage can jeopardize the status of the trademark (see Chapter 8).

Conjunctions

In most marketing documents it is acceptable to start sentences with conjunctions such as *And, Or, But, Yet,* and *Because.*

Slang and Idiom

Slang and idiom, if used cautiously, can be effective in some marcom documents. You can use slang if you have a small, homogeneous audience that fully understands your meaning. But if your readers come from a variety of backgrounds, age groups, or cultures, your slang may not have any meaning, or worse, it may be offensive. Slang also presents a problem for translators, and can make your piece seem dated when the hip slang of today goes out of fashion tomorrow.

Narrator's Voice

The narrator's voice in a document can be active or passive; in first or third person. In most cases, you want the directness of active voice in your writing. But passive voice can be a good way to improve the rhythm of your text. If your document needs a formal writing style, passive voice may predominate.

These guidelines are helpful for choosing the narrator's voice:

- Use active voice to present facts, assertions, conclusions, summaries, or supporting evidence.
- Use passive voice to show indirectness, uncertainties, or complexities: *Notification of critical problems is escalated to all levels of your organization.*[114]

The use of the second person *(you)* to address the reader, combined with the first person plural *(we)*, is common in marcom documents because it creates a sense of direct communication between the company or author and the reader. However, many marcom documents are written in the third person in order to create a sense of objectivity. No matter which narrator's voice you choose, use it consistently throughout the document.

COMMON MISTAKES IN HIGH-TECH COPY

Sadly, many marketing pieces don't meet the guidelines for good writing that are described in this book. Maybe it is due to the influence of marketers who are too caught up in their promotional zeal. Maybe it is due to writers who don't fully understand what they are writing about. You can avoid these problems not only by following the guidelines in this book, but also by checking your material for the mistakes described in this section.

Mistake #1: Excessive Hype

The word *hype* is an abbreviation of *hyperbole*, which means exaggeration or overstatement. Of course the first job of marketing is to make a product, service, or company seem like the best in its category. As a result, it is tempting to use nothing but superlatives such as *best, most, perfect,* or *greatest* when writing about a product. But readers view these superlatives with skepticism unless they are followed by strong supporting evidence. Overuse of superlatives is where your copy can get into the most trouble. It can cause your statements to lose credibility in your reader's mind because she won't find them believable. Or, in the worst case, it can misrepresent a product, causing legal and ethical problems (see Chapter 8).

Of course, no self-respecting marketer will describe a product as "Ralph's Pretty Good System" (to borrow from author Garrison Keillor). Hype can have a place in some materials, such as advertisements, direct-mail pieces, and trade-show invitations, where your message must compete for the reader's attention in a very cluttered environment. And strong adjectives and adverbs *do* play an important role in conveying your message and product positioning. But not every product needs to be described as the latest, most advanced, proven, complete, sophisticated, integrated, value-added solution to any problem your customers will ever have. Instead, a more realistic presentation will enable your readers to draw this conclusion for themselves based on the strength of your information's content and presentation.

One key to controlling hype is to watch the nature and number of adjectives and adverbs you use to describe a product. Some marketing materials read like entries in a "Let's See How Many Fancy-Sounding Adjectives We Can String Together" contest. For example, one ad uses these words in close proximity: *sleek, miraculous, sublime, whopping, cinch, bevy*.[115] All of these are powerful words, but give them some breathing room!

To break your gushing words of praise into more palatable chunks, try these techniques:

- Replace multiple adjectives or adverbs with just one that is more evocative or concise.
- Limit yourself to a maximum of two adjectives or adverbs that you attach to any particular noun or verb.
- Try to find a more precise noun or verb that will eliminate the need for a modifier.
- Instead of using a modifier, rework your point into a separate feature or benefit statement.
- Use bullets to break up your points. Modifiers are easier to swallow when you dole them out in smaller portions.
- Make sure that your supporting evidence backs up any comparative or superlative language that you use.[8]

Bendinger suggests this activity: "After adding up all the adjectives . . . ask one question. Is there one adjective strong enough to build [an advertising] campaign on? It may be the only one you need."[20]

Mistake #2: Forgetting to Sell

In contrast to ads or brochures that are trying too hard to sell, some high-tech marketing materials seem to ignore selling altogether. Here are some of the factors that contribute to this mistake:

- Use of empty phrases where a selling point could be made. Many marcom documents include a phrase like this: *The following is a list of our product's benefits.* Okay, your reader will know what to expect from the information that follows. But why waste a good opportunity to make another selling point? Instead, you could write: *Here are just some of the ways our product can improve your efficiency:.*
- A bland or missing call to action. Your product brochure includes this lifeless call to action: *For more information, contact our headquarters or your local authorized dealer.* Or worse yet, the brochure doesn't include any call to action. (Specific ideas for strengthening your call to action are presented in Chapter 5.)
- You don't state your key messages and benefits clearly. Instead, you only hint at what they might be.

Always look at your material with this question in mind: "Is it taking advantage of every opportunity to sell the reader on our product, service, or company?"

Mistake #3: The "Blah, Blah, Blah" Syndrome

How often have you read a marketing piece that seemed to say the same thing as another—even though the pieces were from two different companies? The reason may be that they use the same trendy words and phrases, such as *robust, integrated, object-oriented technology, paradigm*—the list can be a long one. Called *hype, buzzwords,* or *jargon,* this language pervades all areas of high technology. While some terms have become accepted into common usage, other words may have a much shorter life.

Some marketers feel their materials won't be effective without the latest trendy words. This can lead to the "Blah, Blah, Blah" syndrome, where a document contains all the latest language, regardless of whether it has become cliché, or has any real meaning for the product or any power for delivering the key messages. As a result, the document may leave an impression that is the exact opposite of what you want—where prospects and journalists discredit or ignore your information as "just another bunch of noise."

To avoid this mistake, make a list of the words and phrases that are currently trendy in your industry or target markets.

Identify whether and how you have used this language in mar-com materials. Did it really support your objective and strengthen the document's impact? If not, write a list of synonyms or alternate phrasings you could use to make your text more specific, relevant, and interesting.

Mistake #4: Lack of Clarity

You shouldn't make your readers guess what messages you are trying to convey, why they should be interested, and what you want them to do. For example, could you guess what the headline of this ad is about? *A Klee it's not. But who needs big dots.*[67] (*Hint:* Paul Klee is an early twentieth-century painter.) The accompanying photo is the only initial clue that the ad is for a computer monitor.

A better headline for this ad might be: *A monitor equal to your masterpiece.* This alternative headline clearly states that the ad is for a monitor and presents a benefit statement with *equal to your masterpiece.*

Excessive use of passive voice, overly long sentences, striving for conciseness over clarity, and the use of complex words instead of simple ones are the most common culprits when a document is difficult to understand. Here's an example:

> *Reliability, availability, and maintainability is ensured by [the product's] built-in reliability, symmetric multiprocessor architecture with comprehensive redundancy options for no single point of failure, on-line hot swap and dynamic reconfiguration capabilities, and an easily maintainable hardware and software design.*[75]

The clarity of this text could be improved considerably by splitting it into several sentences and rephrasing the subsidiary clauses:

> *The product has a symmetrical multiprocessor architecture that is highly reliable, available, and maintainable. It offers comprehensive backup options so there is no single point where failure can occur. You can exchange components and reconfigure the unit while it is online. The product's hardware and software is designed to make it easily maintainable.*

Vagueness, whether intentional or not, is another problem that detracts from the clarity of a marcom document. This example contains so many generalities the reader can't really determine the subject:

Vertical integration helps assure reliable, cost-effective products based on the latest technology.[76]

Unless you have spelled out elsewhere the meaning of "vertical integration," "cost-effective products," and "latest technology," the reader isn't likely to have much interest in this sentence because it doesn't tell him anything specific. Here's one way this example could be improved: *Our products work together. This makes them more reliable, more cost-effective as your needs change, and able to add the latest technology without disrupting your operation.*

A way to test your material for clarity is to check it against the Gunning Fog index (see Bibliography). This index is a widely used method that measures sentence length and word complexity to determine the readability of a passage. Usually, the more readable your text, the better its clarity. However, keep in mind that a formula can tell you only whether someone is likely to stumble when reading your material—not whether your text actually makes sense.

To avoid ambiguity, check your dictionary and usage guides regularly to make sure you are making the best word choices. Here are other techniques:

- First, write your text as you would speak it. Don't worry about being grammatical, polished, or complete or your first try. Then, rewrite this text into a more formal style. Test your piece for clarity using the guidelines discussed earlier in this chapter.
- Take out words, sentences, and paragraphs until you have the minimum necessary to communicate your key messages. Then add back your deleted text, a bit at a time, but only those elements that truly strengthen your copy.

Mistake #5: Jam-Packed Jargon

Your product has many wonderful features, applications, and benefits. That doesn't mean you should tell your readers about them all in the same breath. For example, this headline from a press release is a real mouthful that fails to make its point because it is so dense with jargon:

11 milliOhm, 70 Volt MOSFET with 300 Watt Ratings; New IXYS TO-247 MOSFET Offers Lowest Rds(on) at 70 Volts.[77]

Your message will be more effective if you spread your jargon and technical details over several sentences or paragraphs. Build your case incrementally, allowing your reader time and brain space to absorb your message. Specifically:

- Avoid squishing a laundry list of product features, benefits, or specifications into a single sentence. Put them into a bullet list or use multiple sentences instead.
- Watch the number of acronyms you use, especially for non-technical audiences. Always spell-out the acronym in full when you first use it. Instead of using an acronym repeatedly, use the full name again at frequent intervals in the text. Or, create a generic way to reference the thing represented by the acronym.
- Avoid noun clusters and multiple compound adjectives. Write sentences that clearly show the individual subject-action-object relationships.
- See Chapter 6 for additional guidelines on handling jargon and acronyms.

Mistake #6: Overimportance

Condescension or pomposity is the close cousin of hype that often appears in articles, backgrounders, white papers, and proposals. When discussing issues, problems, trends, or architectures, you have a natural desire to seem as authoritative and expert as possible. But this can lead to writing that is a turn-off to your readers and cause them to devalue what you say. Want proof? Just look at the letters-to-the-editor section of your favorite trade magazine. There is nothing like condescension to get a reader angry enough to write.

Overimportance also can be expressed as an attitude or tone that implies arrogance. *Ambra. What more can we say besides "call soon"?*[74]. While your product may indeed be the best in its category or your company the leader in its market, you still have to convince every reader to adopt this belief for himself.

These guidelines will help you avoid the mistake of over-importance:

- Keep your tone and language familiar and down to earth.
- Don't preach to readers.
- Watch your formatting. For example, a product brochure that uses initial caps on all of the words in a headline: *Take Advantage Of The Widest Variety Of Interface Options Available Anywhere.*[78] In this case, the words alone are strong enough to carry the message.

Mistake #7: Negativism

Most marketing material presents information with positive, upbeat language. Yet some materials, especially those that present negative messages or comparative information about a product, can suffer from an excess of negativism. This problem can be caused by placing too much emphasis on negative words or messages, or by using too many words that could have a negative association for the reader.[7]

Negative words are *de*motivators, as Kaplan pointed out: "Readers are more interested in what is than what is not. The key word is not. It is a signal that tells the readers what follows isn't important—don't give it a second thought."[4] For example, this headline: *Go Ahead . . . Add Network Users. See If We Care!*[154] Given the phrase "see if we care!" you might be tempted to turn the page without reading the rest of the ad.

Negative statements are more difficult for readers to interpret correctly than positive ones. Even when you want to present a negative message as part of your competitive positioning, you will want to balance it with stronger positive statements about your product (see Chapter 3).

Mistake #8: Forgetting the Audience

Given the complexity of most technical products and the fast pace of most marcom environments, it's easy to lose sight of your reader when writing the copy for a particular piece. This mistake typically manifests itself in either of two forms:

- **Featureitis:** An excessive focus on the product's capabilities without relating what these features mean to your reader. Balance your feature statements with benefit statements that answer these questions in the reader's mind: "Why should I be interested in this? What will this feature do for me?"
- **One Piece Fits All:** Don't try to make one piece be all things to all people, unless you are clearly segmenting and identifying the content for each audience. Segmenting techniques include using subheads to identify the audience or isolating information for a specific audience into a sidebar.

A good marcom plan, creative platform, and document plan can also help you remember your audience (see Chapter 1).

Mistake #9: Irrelevancies

Information that is irrelevant to the message, objective, and purpose of your document will distract your readers. Or, even worse, these irrelevancies will raise unnecessary questions in the reader's mind; "Oh yes, what about that?"

This mistake can creep into your writing when you feel you need one more bit of evidence to support your message, when you feel you have white space to fill or a quote that is too vague. You want to give your readers just enough information to make a decision or take an action—and no more.

Mistake #10: Errors

After multiple drafts and even more reviews, it is easy for errors of fact or omission to find their way into a marketing document. Not only can these errors be an embarrassment, they may cause legal problems (see Chapter 8). Using checklists of facts and giving the document to an expert reviewer who is seeing it for the first time are two methods you can use to avoid errors in the information.

Another form of error arises from lack of careful proofreading. Misspelled words, improper grammar or word usage, incorrect punctuation, reversed images, and missing text can damage your credibility in the reader's mind. After all, the reader might think, if you can't put together a simple data sheet correctly, can he trust you to deliver a quality product?

EXERCISES

Getting Attention

1. Take an existing marcom document and use different colors to highlight power words and those you think are weak or qualifiers. Based on this exercise, create two lists. The first is power words that are appropriate for the product and that you can use in future projects. The second list is qualifier words you want to avoid.
2. Develop a list of evocative words or phrases that could be appropriate for the product.
3. List the emotions, both positive and negative, that could be relevant to the prospects for the product. Can any of these emotions be used to convey the marketing messages? Write several phrases or copy ideas that express these emotions.
4. List the problems, trends, circumstances, or other factors that would be relevant to the target audience for a marcom document. Take a few of these factors and write a sentence or paragraph that conveys their relevance to the reader.
5. Take a few sentences or paragraphs from a document and identify how you can apply formatting and punctuation to improve the emphasis, interest, or clarity of the text.

6. List the aspects of the product that could be used to create a sense of inspiration in your text. Write a headline or sentence that presents these aspects with a strong sense of excitement and motivation.

Creating Rhythm

1. Take an existing piece and analyze the average sentence length and typical sentence structure. Identify the changes you could make to vary the sentences for improved rhythm.
2. Write a headline that uses rhyme or wordplay.
3. Look at existing marcom material and identify where parallelism appears or where it could be applied to improve the clarity and impact of the text.

Asking Questions

1. Develop a headline that poses a question about the product.
2. Develop a list of questions that incorporates all of the key messages for the product.

Semantic Constrast

Write a sentence or headline about the product that uses semantic contrast.

Using Imagery

Identify an analogy, metaphor, or other form of imagery that can be used for the product. Describe how you would incorporate that image into the different elements of a brochure or other marcom document.

Showing Paradox

Write a feature statement for the product that uses paradox.

Adding Humor

Identify at least one characteristic of the product that could be the source of humor in your material.

Avoiding Mistakes

1. *Excessive Hype:* Choose the single best adjective or adverb for the product, then write a list of synonyms you can use for variety. Do the same for the next best or next most important adjective, and continue until you have identified the most essential modifiers you want to use for describing the product.
2. *Forgetting to Sell:* Take an existing marcom document and identify the bland words and phrases. Revise them to improve their selling ability.

3. *Lack of Clarity:* Take an existing marketing document and mark out every word, phrase, sentence, or paragraph that isn't essential. Then start restoring your deletions, one at a time, but try to make the restored text more specific and potent.

4. *Lack of Clarity:* Look at each paragraph, sentence, and long word in the text of a marcom document. How can you rewrite it to make it simpler and more specific? Analyze what the text loses in this rewrite and what it gains.

5. *Lack of Clarity:* Read an existing document aloud. If you have trouble following the meaning as you go along, other readers will too. Mark the segments that are causing trouble and rewrite them to improve their clarity.

6. *Excessive Jargon:* Find all the questionable technical jargon in the text of an existing document. Identify how you can restate this information in plain language or reformat it to make it easier to understand.

7. *Forgetting the Audience:* To determine if a document has lost its audience focus, use different colors to mark each place where you use the words "you" and "we" (and their variations). How does the usage of "we" words compare with the usage of "you" words? Your message will be more powerful if you can balance most of your "we" statements with "you" statements.

8. *Forgetting the Audience:* Repeat the exercise above, but this time mark feature and benefit statements and analyze the balance between them.

9. *Irrelevancies:* Take an existing marcom document and look for information that is irrelevant to the document's message, objective, or purpose. Evaluate how the tone, content, or impact of the document will change if you remove that information.

CHAPTER 8

Legal and Ethical Issues

Avoiding Problems in Your Materials

The information in this chapter is intended to give you an overview of the legal considerations involved in writing marcom materials. It is not intended to give legal advice. In addition, the discussion of legal issues in this chapter covers practices that are common in the United States, but may not be applicable in other countries. In addition to national and local laws, your marketing communication projects may be subject to government regulations or guidelines from a standards organization.

Copywriters must not only be concerned about what's *legal*, but also about what's *right*. While ethical dilemmas vary widely with each situation, some are common to nearly every type of marketing communication project. This chapter also presents an overview of ethical problems and suggests a set of considerations that apply specifically to high-tech copywriting.

WORKING WITH AN ATTORNEY

When it comes to legal issues, the single best thing you can do is consult with a qualified attorney who can address the specific factors that apply to each of your marketing projects. Most companies require that an attorney review all significant marcom materials, including brochures, data sheets, and press releases.

Some copywriters feel that attorneys veto the most creative elements in marketing materials. However, there are solid reasons why your legal counsel takes a very cautious approach to the words and images in any marketing document. The potential for liability or other legal claims is simply too great to ignore an attorney's suggested changes to your text or images.

This does not necessarily mean you must incorporate every one of your attorney's edits verbatim. There are often many alternative ways to express the same concept or information that will be acceptable to both your attorney's sense of caution and your sense of marketing impact. Whether it involves a single word, a sentence, or an entire section of your document, you can probably reach a compromise with your attorney.

Here are additional ideas for working effectively with an attorney during the review process:

- Remember that your attorney may not have the technical knowledge required to judge whether a document contains false information or improper claims. A detailed or highly technical document also should receive an appropriate technical review.
- Attach an explanation of the document's objective, purpose, planned use, audience, and relationship to other materials (you may want to adapt this from your document plan). This will help the attorney understand the context behind the document's content.
- Indicate the type of input you want from the attorney, whether it's a review for potential legal concerns or assistance in rewriting the document.
- Develop a list of words, phrases, and boilerplate text acceptable to both you and your attorney that can be used in any document for your product or company. This can expedite both the writing and review processes.

TRADE LAWS

Business activity in general, and advertising in particular, is governed by a variety of federal and state fair-trade laws in the United States. Federal trade laws are based primarily on the Lanham Act, with supporting regulations from the Federal Trade Commission (FTC). State laws and regulations may be administered by a variety of departments, agencies, and commissions. In addition, the marketing of biotechnology products is regulated by the U.S. Food and Drug Administration.

Whether on a national or local level, fair-trade laws cover a variety of practices in advertising and marcom. These include the statements you make about a product's functionality or performance, safety warnings, use of testimonials, information about pricing and special offers—in short, anything you say about the product and how it is sold.

Product Claims

Federal law prohibits claims about a product that are unsubstantiated, exaggerated, or ambiguous with a deceptive intent. Product claims cover any statement about features, performance, quality, options, costs, warranties, and other characteristics that may influence a purchaser's decision. State consumer-protection laws also cover advertising practices, often with severe penalties for ads that contain false or deceptive claims.

The capabilities and features you describe must be available at the time you run an ad or distribute a brochure. If the capability will be available in the future, you must indicate this fact clearly: *This feature will be available in 4th Quarter 1994.* In a addition, you must be absolutely truthful about statements that a product is:

- The first available in its field.
- New. The product must be commercially available for six months or less to be advertised as "new."
- Approved by a government agency, has received a patent or approval from a regulatory agency, or was developed by a recognized research laboratory.

A statement made in an advertisement or other marketing document doesn't need to be an outright lie to be problematic. These types of statements are also considered an unfair practice:[133]

- Statements that are false or misleading because they don't disclose complete information.
- Statements that are partially true or true only in certain circumstances.
- Statements that may be deceptive by themselves but are clarified by other text that appears in the "small print."
- Statements that are factually accurate but convey a false impression. "Each sentence in an advertisement, considered separately, may be literally true and yet the entire advertisement as a whole may be misleading."[14]

As an additional incentive to ensure the accuracy of your marketing materials, the Lanham Act allows a competitor to file suit if you make a false representation about your product in your advertising—even if you don't mention the competition.

This does not mean you need to use only noncommittal language in your materials. The FTC recognizes that a company can be expected to praise the features, capabilities, performance, and benefits of its products (called "puffing"). The key is to make sure that all of your claims are based on a truthful representation of what your product and company will deliver.

Offers and Pricing

FTC regulations contain strict rules about the language that describes offers and product pricing. This language includes:[14]

- The words "free," "sale," "clearance," and other language that implies special pricing.
- The words "proof," "evidence," and other language that implies scientific verification.
- Any language that describes environmental claims.

FTC regulations also apply to offers of premiums and contests and sweepstakes that are conducted through advertising or other materials. The references listed in the Bibliography contain more information on each of these issues.

Quotes and Endorsements

Your materials may not include a quotation from, or reference to, fraudulent or nonexistent testimonials, surveys, or endorsements. For example, an "endorsement" by a fictitious person is considered to be an unfair trade practice. In addition, you cannot use testimonials or endorsements if the person no longer uses the product or if the product has changed so substantially since the endorsement was made that it could no longer be considered a fair statement.[14] You should obtain a signed consent from the person or company involved before publishing the endorsement quote in any promotional material.

If you quote a survey or study, especially when comparing competitive products, the survey must be designed properly and the conclusions fair and truthful.[132] You also must be careful not to present the quote in an inappropriate context—one that would distort the meaning or implication of the quote. Cite the source as a part of the quotation or in a footnote.

Warranties and Guarantees

Most companies offer some form of a product guarantee or warranty. A warranty is a statement that your product is of a specific quality or offers a specified performance level. A guarantee is a statement of what your company will do to repair, replace, or refund a product that is unsatisfactory or defective. Both types of statements can be made with a time limitation on their enforcement.

The concept of a warranty or guarantee may seem simple at first: a statement of what your company will do if the customer experiences a problem or is not satisfied with your product. However, beyond offering good customer relations, warranties and guarantees also create legally binding conditions that you should carefully consider when writing any type of marketing material. You also must remember there are two types of warranty statements from a legal perspective: an explicit warranty and an express warranty.

An explicit statement is what usually comes to mind when you think of a warranty or guarantee. For example, *No Risk Guarantee! Remember, if you're not satisfied with QuickBooks for any reason, you can return it within 60 days for a full refund.*[111] An explicit warranty tells the customer exactly what your company will do and what he must do to receive a repair, replacement, or refund under the warranty. It also must describe any other conditions, limitations, or terms that apply to the warranty or guarantee.

In the United States, the Magnuson-Moss Act spells out detailed requirements for explicit warranty statements made for consumer products; this Act may be applicable to your product. Consumer products also may be covered by an implied warranty about their quality and use; consult a qualified attorney for guidance.

The other type of warranty is called an *express warranty*. You may be inadvertently creating this type of warranty if your material is promising more than what your company intends to deliver. Meyerowitz explains: "Express warranties can be created in virtually any advertising, marketing, or packaging materials and can be created without the use of the words 'warranty' or 'guarantee.'"[132]

An express warranty can be created by any written description, specifications, or visuals depicting the product, because a prospect would reasonably expect that the product will conform to the description or depiction. This covers text that appears in ads, catalogs, brochures, documentation, order and quotation forms, as well as the product's packaging. An express warranty also can be created by product samples—in the case of high-tech products, this includes demo disks, working models, and evaluation units.

In addition to printed materials, an express warranty can be created by a salesperson in an oral presentation. Also, trade customs within the industry or geographic market may create warranties.[132]

There are two essential ways to check that your copy does not create warranty problems. First, develop standard text for your explicit warranty statements and use that text consistently in all marketing materials. Compare the other text in the document with the explicit warranty statement; are they in conflict? Second, check whether the text in the document implies a greater promise than is covered by the warranty. Are all statements in the text and all visuals accurate in the way they describe and depict the product?

Disclaimers

As a defensive measure against rapidly changing product features and market circumstances, many companies develop a standard disclaimer statement that appears on all marketing materials. For example, *ADC Kentrox reserves the right to change specifications without prior notice.*[149]

Product Safety Warnings

Some high-tech products can be used safely only in certain conditions or by following specific procedures. If your product could potentially cause any health or safety problems for a user, your marketing materials may need to include safety warnings. Consult an attorney with expertise in product liability laws for guidance.

POSTAL REGULATIONS

The postal authority in every country regulates any commercial activity that is conducted through the mail. Of particular concern to copywriters are regulations that cover direct-mail materials and practices. For example, some postal authorities allow promotional copy to be printed on an envelope, while others do not. These regulations can vary widely for each country; obtain this information as part of your marcom planning activity.

FINANCIAL REGULATIONS

A number of regulations from the U.S. Securities and Exchange Commission cover the disclosure of any information that might impact trading in the stock of a public company. This includes claims about products and capabilities made in your sales materials—if it can be shown that those claims influenced an investor's decision to buy or sell your company's stock. If your stock is traded on exchanges in other countries, additional or different regulations may apply.

In addition, do not use a company's confidential information for personal gain or disclose it to others who might improperly gain. Notify your employer or client of any existing or potential conflict of interest as it applies to the company's stock or other financial transaction.

Many companies have internal policies about the use and disclosure of sensitive information. In addition, the Bibliography lists several references for learning more about financial disclosure and other investor communications.

COPYRIGHTS

U.S. laws give the author of a work complete copyright protection once it has been expressed in a fixed form such as a printed document or software. While you do not need to place a copyright notice on each copy of the work, doing so creates stronger protection under international copyright agreements. The strongest form for a copyright notice is:

Copyright © 1994, (owner's name). All Rights Reserved.

For example:

Copyright © 1994, Janice M. King. All Rights Reserved. or
Copyright © 1994, MarkeTech. All Rights Reserved.

For revised works, the copyright notice needs to include only the latest year in which the work was published; it does not need to include every year in which the work was written, issued, or revised.

For a substantial work that may have commercial value in itself or a long life, you may want to consider registering the copyright with the U.S. Library of Congress. In addition, you may want to register the copyright with the appropriate government agencies in each country where you will distribute the material.

Material from Other Sources

Some marketing documents incorporate material—text or images—from other sources that is protected by a copyright. You must obtain permission from the copyright owner for any excerpt you use—no matter how small the block of text or how seemingly inconsequential the image. Copyright protection for text includes the original language and any translation.

In the case of most text excerpts, it is a simple process to obtain permission for use. It involves contacting the copyright owner (usually the company or individual who wrote or published the document), and sending a letter that describes the exact text that will be reproduced, provides a sample of how it will appear in your document, and describes the publication circumstances. This letter may include a space for the copyright owner's signature, indicating agreement with the proposed use and terms. In most cases, permission to use brief excerpts on a limited basis are given without payment of a fee. However, the copyright owner may demand a fee for more extensive excerpts or more significant uses of the source material.

Copyright and usage permissions also are a significant concern for the use of photos and illustrations in any marcom document, and for still images, video clips, and music in multimedia documents. Use of these elements often involves payment of a fee and a very specific agreement on the particular use, time limitations, quantity of publication, and distribution of the document. When negotiating these usage rights, make sure that your agreement covers all planned uses for the element.

Work for Hire

If you are an employee, the copyright for any creative work you produce as part of your job belongs to your employer.

If you are a freelancer or consultant, or if you contract for the services of outside creative resources (e.g., writers or designers), you should be aware of the process for transferring copyrights. Unless the terms of the contract or work agreement explicitly transfer the ownership rights to the text, design, image, or other work product, the creative resource retains copyright ownership. This means that the creative resource must grant permission for the company to use the text or image for purposes or in applications beyond those initially covered in the contract. It also means the creative resource can use the text or image in other projects and grant permission to other companies to use or adapt it.

In most cases, companies that produce high-tech marketing materials either develop agreements with external creative resources that acquire all rights to the work (including the copyright) or contract (and pay for) usage rights on a project-by-project basis. (This latter practice is much more common for images than it is for text.)

TRADEMARKS

A trademark is a word, name, symbol—or a combination of these—that a company uses to distinguish a product from others that are similar in design, operation, or function. A service mark is the same as a trademark, except that it applies to nontangible services performed by a company. Trademarks are important because they help to create a particular brand name and image for your product and service, and by extension, for your company. The remaining discussion in this section references only trademarks, however the principles apply to service marks as well.

Trademarks can be created for a company's logo or for the company name, but only as it identifies a concrete product or service. For example, Microsoft by itself identifies the company and cannot be protected as a trademark. However, Microsoft® Windows™ identifies a specific product and can be protected as a trademark, as can the Microsoft logo.

Trademarks involve two considerations for copywriters: properly using the trademarks owned by your company, and acknowledging the trademarks owned by others.

Trademark Notation

All trademarks, whether owned by your company or others, should appear with the correct notation in your materials. Use the following symbols:

- ™ for an unregistered trademark
- ℠ for an unregistered servicemark
- ® for a trademark or service mark that is registered with the U.S. Patent and Trademark Office. Trademarks that are registered in other countries may be covered by different rules for notation.

Use the symbol on the first or most visible appearance of the trademark in your material; you do not need to include the symbol on subsequent appearances. For example, if you included the trademark symbol in the product name in a headline, you would not need to include it where the product name appears in the body copy. For newsletters, catalogs, or other documents that have distinct articles or entries, use the trademark notation again with each new article or section. Include a statement on each marketing document that indicates your ownership of each trademark: *Microsoft is a registered trademark and Windows is a trademark of Microsoft Corporation.*[150]

Trademark Usage

Present the trademark in the correct word form: always as an adjective, never as a noun or verb. The correct word form is a necessity to prevent your trademark from becoming a generic word that can lose its protected status. For example, Xerox Corporation has made extensive efforts to protect its trademark of the word Xerox™ to describe a photocopying process. These efforts have been necessary because the word *xerox* has been widely adopted by consumers as both a noun and verb synonymous with photocopying.

These guidelines will help you avoid turning your trademark into a generic term:

- Always treat your trademark as a proper adjective (starting with a capital letter), and always use it with a generic noun that describes your product or service. For example: *the Windows NT operating system.*[150]
- A trademark can be used in shortened form after first reference within a document. For example, if you use Microsoft Windows at the first reference, you can use Windows in any later reference in the same document.
- Don't use your trademark as a noun, a verb, a possessive, or a plural (if not already a plural).
- Don't change the spelling or hyphenation, or use the trademark in an abbreviation or acronym. However, you can create an acronym from a multiword trademark, such as *Transaction Monitoring Facility™ (TMF™).*[151]
- Use a different typeface where possible to distinguish your trademark from the surrounding text.
- Your company name may be a trademark only when it appears with a product or service name (which itself may also be a trademark). For example, *The Microsoft® Windows™ operating system* is a correct usage of the company trademark, while *Microsoft Corporation today announced* . . . describes the company and thus cannot use the trademark symbol.

Fueroghne suggests this test to determine if you are using a trademark correctly in a sentence: If you remove the trademark, does the remaining sentence make sense?[153] If the sentence still makes sense when you remove the trademark, you are using it correctly.

Develop a guide to proper usage of your company's trademarks or include this information in your marketing style guide. Distribute this guide to employees, outside marcom, advertising, and design firms, resellers, strategic partners, or other people who might have occasion to produce materials about your company and products.

Using Another Company's Trademarks

If another company's trademark appears in your document, you must acknowledge its ownership. Use the appropriate symbol when the trademark appears in your document and include an acknowledgment statement such as: *Windows and Windows NT are trademarks of Microsoft Corporation.* And, because it sometimes can be difficult to determine if all the product names you mention are trademarks, or who owns those trademarks, include a general statement such as: *All other trademarks are property of their respective owners.*

In some cases, your company may license the trademarked name or logo of another company's products. Refer to the owning company's guidelines for proper usage of that trademark or logo. Also, be aware that images can be reflective of a trademark. For example, one company used images from the Star Trek films in its advertising, and included a reference to the trademark's owner, Paramount Pictures, even though the words Star Trek were not used in the ad's copy.[120]

PATENTS

Check with your attorney before you publicly release information about a product or process that your company may want to patent. Releasing information too soon could jeopardize your company's ability to obtain a patent in one or more countries. Different countries have different laws that cover whether an idea can be patented after information has been disclosed publicly.

TRADE SECRETS AND CONFIDENTIAL INFORMATION

Because high-tech markets are so competitive, most companies are understandably reluctant to release information that may be considered proprietary or a trade secret. This usually includes information such as detailed designs, processes, methods, or components in a product; description of manufacturing processes or sources; sales methods, marketing expenditures, and contract details; customer lists or information on customer relationships; and details on alliances.

To ensure that you are not inadvertently including proprietary information, all marcom documents should be reviewed by a company executive and your company attorney before release or distribution. Your company may have written policies regarding the release of information or may be subject to government regulations that cover release or nondisclosure.

In some situations, confidential information may be released to a person or company under a nondisclosure agreement. This typically occurs when two companies are exploring an alliance or other business relationship, or when a company conducts a press tour in advance of a new product announcement. In this situation, the person receiving the information agrees to treat it as confidential, and not disclose it to any other party without permission from your company. This limitation usually has an expiration point—a specific date or upon termination of the agreement or business relationship. In the case of a press tour, giving a journalist information under a nondisclosure agreement allows you to create advance awareness for your product without concerns that the journalist will publish a story before you make a public announcement.

Your company may have an existing nondisclosure agreement that you can use for marketing communication purposes, or contact your company attorney for guidance.

PRIVACY RIGHTS

Most high-tech marketing communication is so product-oriented that privacy rights are not a major consideration. However, if your materials use the image, name, or information for an identifiable person or company, you must take the steps to protect the subject's right to privacy.

Individual Privacy

When publishing information, there are two primary considerations for protecting a person's privacy: using the person's name or likeness and disclosing information about the person's beliefs, statements, or actions.

Permission for use applies to any material (including press materials) that contain information about or images of a person. You must obtain a signed consent form for use of the information or images from that person before you publish the material. If a photograph shows a group of people, obtain a signed consent form from every person in the group. Even for employees of your company, you must obtain a signed consent form before using their photos, names, or other information in any promotional material. The release should specify the form, media, and duration of usage rights the person is granting for the image.

Some projects involve the use of a fictitious person or company name. Yet especially for a person, it can be difficult to create a name that will not belong to someone somewhere in the world—causing a problem of privacy rights. A safer alternative is to use an employee's name instead, after obtaining a signed consent form for this use.

Another concern of individual privacy is disclosure of a person's information. As a matter of common business sense, most copywriters are unlikely to publish information about a person that is embarrassing or confidential, or to portray a person's image, statements, or actions in a false context. To avoid problems, always obtain written permission from the person on the specific text to be published and its planned use. In some cases, this permission may apply only to certain media or uses, and apply only to a specified time period.

A variation of privacy rights applies to celebrities—called publicity rights. You cannot use the image, name, or other identifying characteristics without permission from the celebrity or her estate. These restrictions apply to celebrities both living and dead and apply also to "lookalikes" or "soundalikes."

Company Privacy

Privacy concerns extend to information you may want to publish about other companies, whether they be customers, alliance partners, or competitors. Do not publish another company's information, such as in a case study, without obtaining written permission from an authorized representative of that company.

When publishing material about other companies, disclosure of confidential or proprietary information is a primary concern, as is presentation of their information in a false context. Also, do not use a fictitious company name without labeling it as such in a footnote or parenthetical note in the text. For example, *Companies, names, and data used in scenario and sample output are fictitious.*[88]

COMPARATIVE ADVERTISING

You must use extreme caution when writing material that compares your product with its competition. Your statements must be factual, complete, and based on verifiable evidence. Otherwise, a competitor may file a lawsuit alleging unfair trade practices under the U.S. Lanham Act, which states that you cannot make materially false representations about another company's goods, services, or commercial activities. These provisions can apply even if you do not name the competitor, if there are really only two leading products in that market.[132]

Comparative advertising of any type is illegal in some countries outside of the United States. Work with an attorney in each country where your advertising or marketing materials will appear to ensure they will comply with local laws.

PROPOSALS

Information presented in a proposal can become legally binding if the proposal is incorporated into the purchase contract. In this case, you must ensure that the proposal contains accurate information on items such as the functionality and performance of products, level and types of services to be provided, schedules, task responsibilities, and costs.

ETHICS

Ethical considerations always present difficult challenges: Who's right? What's right? What should be said or done? For a high-tech copywriter, these considerations involve the responsibility of the writer to her readers, to her employer or client, and to third parties such as customers or journalists.

The situations where ethical questions arise in high-tech marcom can vary widely, and each requires individual evaluation. The discussion here addresses some of the common ethical dilemmas in marketing communication and suggests a series of questions to evaluate the ethics of any marcom project. You should be aware of these situations, and plan in advance your response or course of action.

Overstatement

Filled with zeal for promoting a product, a marketer or copywriter may be tempted to make unjustifiable exaggerations about the product's features and performance. This overstatement can appear in many forms, including:

- Misrepresenting a product's design, functionality, or other characteristics in descriptive text, specifications, or images.
- Implying that features, options, or other product capabilities are currently available when in fact they will not be available until a future date.

- Promising certain results that may require additional products, conditions, resources, or activities that are beyond the company's control.

Inappropriate Interpretation

Another problem of information accuracy is making an inappropriate interpretation of fact, comment, or description. This can occur in a number of forms, such as:

- Making an inappropriate attribution of your company's involvement in an activity, or the value of the solution or results delivered by your company.
- Making inappropriately selective use of facts or comments, for example, including only the information that reflects favorably on your product or company while ignoring information that may negate or alter the implications of that information.
- Implying a falsely positive interpretation by making neutral or negative comments seem more positive than they are.
- Paraphrasing a quote or other text to convey a false impression.
- Using formatting devices to add emphasis to text that was not there in the original form; this may not be a problem if you include the words "emphasis added" immediately following the altered text.

Alteration of Images

Today designers can use computers to scan and alter photographs, illustrations, diagrams, and other images. While not strictly an ethical issue for copywriters, you should keep in mind the implications of this ability to alter or enhance "reality," especially as they apply to product images and data charts.

Certain minor modifications to images are acceptable, such as those made to correct flaws or improve clarity. However, extensive changes that substantially alter the proportions or appearance of the product may cause problems of misrepresentation or express warranty (see discussion earlier in this chapter). In addition, magazines and newspapers may not accept the image for publication, or may require that it be labeled to indicate the alteration. These concerns may not apply in cases where the image has been altered so dramatically that it makes only a symbolic representation of the product it depicts.

Charts that present statistics can be manipulated to distort the meaning or relationship of the data. This becomes especially problematic because many readers give charts only a cursory look, seeking only a sense of the information presented. For an excellent discussion on accurate presentation of statistics, see Edward Tufte's book *The Visual Display of Quantitative Information* (see Bibliography).

Plagiarism

Plagiarism involves copying or borrowing text, images, or ideas from another source without authorization or acknowledgment. All sources should be cited, and the material used only after securing the necessary copyright or usage permissions (see the discussion on Copyrights earlier in this chapter).

Interviews

Obtaining and using information from interviews can present several ethical considerations:

- How you represent yourself, your company, and your planned uses for the information in order to get an interview from a customer or other source.
- The questions asked during the interview. These must be worded carefully to avoid prompting the source to make statements that are inaccurate, incomplete, or misleading.
- The context of the interview. Any information or quotes taken from the interview must be presented in an accurate context when published.
- Recording interviews on audio or video tape—whether in person or over the telephone. Many countries require that you obtain permission from your source before recording an interview. In addition, local laws may restrict your ability to record telephone conversations; check with your telephone company or the appropriate regulatory organization about what is permitted. And because many people are simply uncomfortable with the recording process, respect any request from the source that you not record the interview.

Ethical Considerations for High-Tech Copywriters

A number of professional organizations have developed codes for ethics or standards of practice that are relevant to high-tech copywriters. In addition, your company may have a set of policies that cover ethics or it may be required to comply with government regulations about ethical practices. Cultural considerations also may play a part in your development of a set of ethical guidelines.

The considerations suggested here are drawn in part from the ethics codes established by several professional organizations, including the International Association of Business Communicators, Business Marketing Association, Public Relations Society of America, Direct Marketing Association, the American Association of Advertising Agencies, and the Associated Press Managing Editors. However, these considerations have not been reviewed or approved by any professional organization or other governing body.

These ethical considerations may help you produce fair, honest, and ethical materials. Yet, no set of standards can predict every potential ethical problem you may encounter. Remember that you will need to apply common sense, good judgment, and a sensitivity to the people and implications involved to determine the best response to each situation.

Ethical considerations for marketing communication address these questions:

- Does the material present all information accurately and honestly, and with a fair representation of its context? Can all information about product features and performance claims be readily substantiated? Do all images make an accurate depiction of the product or service? Are all pricing and offer statements complete and not misleading? Are errors of fact, omission, or improper interpretation acknowledged and corrected promptly? Is information that is based on a composite or hypothetical person, company, or situation clearly identified as fictional?
- Does the text include appropriate citations for information drawn from other sources? Is the information summarized, interpreted, or paraphrased in a manner that does not distort its original meaning or context, and does not make inappropriately selective use of facts or comments?
- Have you respected the rights of individuals and companies for privacy and protection of confidential information? Does the information comply with all restrictions of nondisclosure agreements or other confidentiality requirements?
- Have all necessary approvals and releases been granted before publication or distribution? Does the material comply with all copyright and other restrictions on use of text, information, or images?

- Is the material sensitive to variations in standards, tastes, and communication protocols among different audiences, communities, and cultures? Does the material avoid words or images that stereotype or objectify people or groups, or that imply discrimination or disparagement?
- Does the material comply with all legal and regulatory requirements, organizational policies, and industry or professional standards?
- Were interviews, testimonials, or other information from a customer or other source obtained after accurate representation of the interviewer, company, and purpose?
- Does the material avoid promising or implying the delivery of results that involve activities, events, or resources that are beyond the company's control?

EXERCISES

1. Identify or develop a company policy for legal review of your materials. Identify all legal, regulatory, financial, and confidentiality factors that must be considered before a document is approved for publication.
2. Develop a guide to trademark usage for your company.
3. Develop a set of legal boilerplate text.
4. Identify any company or government ethics policies that apply to your projects.
5. Identify the ethical issues you have resolved in the past. Would the considerations presented in this chapter be relevant to those issues? If not, what additional or alternative considerations would apply?

CHAPTER 9

International High-Tech Marketing Communication

Adapting Your Materials to the Global Market

While the United States remains a major source of and market for high-tech products, no company can ignore the significant sales opportunities available in other countries. Nearly all forms of technology are disseminated globally, and the pace of that dissemination is quickening. Localized products that previously were delivered several months after the U.S. launch are now part of a simultaneous, multi-country introduction.

These factors are behind a growing volume of international marketing communication. Advertising, collateral, press materials, and direct mail are among the materials being adapted or specially developed for each geographic market.

This chapter describes the general issues around international marcom, presents an overview of localization practices, and offers writing guidelines for materials that will be localized. While the information presented here is applicable primarily for materials that will be adapted from American English, it also may be useful to writers working in other languages. Because international communication is a topic too large to cover completely in this book, the Bibliography includes many references for additional exploration.

GENERAL ISSUES

Farinelli describes the most significant issue for marcom targeted to international audiences: "Our international marketing errors are usually errors of omission—not errors of commission. It is not that we misinterpret the culture of a country—typically, we do not do any interpretation at all. We simply assume that international markets are 'pretty much like here, except that people might speak a different language.'"[139]

As these remarks indicate, one of the most important things you can do for an international marcom project is to give it the same high level of attention and quality as any other communication effort. From the reader's perspective, you don't want to make your international marcom seem like an afterthought to your domestic efforts.

Beyond this general concern for quality, which factors are critical to developing successful international marcom? First, avoid the arrogant assumption that if international customers want your product strongly enough they will accommodate themselves to the same messages and text that are targeted to your domestic audience. This arrogance implies a serious lack of respect for your customer.

Second, you must learn about—and respect—the linguistic, cultural, and business differences that exist in each country or market. For example, technologies that are widely available in your home country may not be available at all in certain international markets. Also, don't treat parts of the world—such as Europe or Asia—as a single market and don't think of Europe as just Western Europe; the Eastern European countries are becoming important markets, each with its own characteristics. Market segmentation, audience concerns, buying factors, and sales cycles will likely be different in *each* country, and these differences should be reflected in your materials.

Here are a few of the representative differences between international and U.S. marcom:

- **Company image.** A strong, consistent company image is important when you are marketing outside of your own country, where your company may not be known at all or may be confused with another company in the same industry or with a similar name. Long-term company relationships are important in most markets outside of the United States.
- **Product awareness.** More time is required in many markets to build awareness of your company and products.
- **Direct mail.** Prospects outside of the United States and Canada receive a significantly smaller number of direct-mail pieces than prospects in those two countries. As a result, your direct-mail campaigns may have higher response rates. However, local postal regulations may not permit self-mailers or teasers on the envelope of a direct-mail package. Your copy and design also must accommo-

date the longer line lengths and greater number of lines in most international addresses.

- **Legal guidelines.** Advertising and direct-mail laws can vary significantly among countries, especially in regard to purchase offers and comparative advertising. Copyright and trademark registrations and notations are often different. As a precautionary measure, your marketing and press materials should be reviewed by an attorney who is thoroughly familiar with the laws and regulations in the target country.
- **Text organization.** Material may need to be organized in different ways to accommodate differences in learning styles and reading orientation. Or your materials may need a much greater level of detail for some countries where this is expected. In contrast, some cultures place a high reliance on the context of information exchange.[138]
- **Visuals.** Appropriate images, symbols, and colors vary widely among cultures.

COORDINATING MARCOM IN MULTIPLE MARKETS

With all of these differences, it may seem impossible to create any level of commonality among your marketing materials for multiple countries. And while localization factors must be considered separately for each marketing campaign, some high-tech companies have successfully created coordinated, global materials. Here are a few guidelines:

- Develop a single concept that can be adapted successfully for the different countries you want to reach. This may be in the form of a common text and visual theme that is supported by detailed information adapted for each market.
- Coordinate the effort among the different translators and in-country marketing and public relations agencies involved to ensure consistency of terminology and messages.
- If you want to adapt an existing English-language document, verify with the in-country reviewers that its messages will be understood and its content will meet the needs of the local audience.
- Consider the spillover of information from the American press. Many U.S. publications are read by prospects in other countries, or their articles are reprinted by the local press.
- Be clear about what you are offering and when for each country, especially when describing localized versions of your product.

- Incorporate market information specific to that country: previous successes, implications, local business or regulatory trends, and local applications. Use quotes and case studies from in-country sources.

As an example, consider one company's message development strategy, which has two parts: corporatewide and country-specific. The corporate messages address company directions, overall product features and benefits, product positioning, and technology advantages. The messages are then customized to each country to address market segmentation, strategies, applications, and customer profiles relevant to that country.[140]

A more specific example is provided by the advertisements from Intel Corporation shown in Figure 9.1. The same visual concept and layout was used in all three ads, which appeared in computer magazines published in the United States, Germany, and France. Common to all of the ads are the messages about 70 percent improvement in performance, simplicity of installation, and single-chip upgrade. Also, the offer of a demo disk is the same in all three ads. But there are differences in the content as well. For example, the French ad does not address the concept of power-hungry software, which appears in both the American and German ads. However, the German ad does not include the use of the word "boom" (a reference to the cannon) that appears in both the French and American ads. As these examples show, the same concept can be used in different markets—but with adjustments in messages to make them locally appropriate.

While the Intel examples show how a single concept can work across multiple markets, it may not be successful in all cases. You need to evaluate each project individually in light of the product and market characteristics.

ADAPTATION AND LOCALIZATION

Translation is often used synonymously with localization. However, translation is only one step in the process of developing materials that are suitable for international markets. Instead of translation, you need to think about a process that adapts and localizes your messages and information to meet the needs, interests, and practices of each local market. In most cases, this effort requires more than simply translating the text developed for an English-speaking, American audience. For example, the formality of tone, the choice of words and visuals, even the length of your

Bis zu 70 Prozent mehr Leistung für Ihre leistungshungrige Software.

Jusqu'à 70% de perfor mances en plus. Et boum!

Figure 9.1   These ads show how a common concept was adapted to meet different language and market considerations.

Source: Intel Corporation. Reproduced by permission.

piece can vary substantially when accommodating linguistic and cultural differences among international readers.

As Grüber explains, "Copy adaptation works on the premise that today's consumers are highly attuned to advertising copy. If it doesn't ring absolutely true, it loses credibility. Copy adaptation helps to create a strong international image within different national contexts, getting the advertising message across with all the freshness and impact it had in the original campaign."[141]

Which Materials? Which Languages?

Most high-tech companies choose to produce localized materials for those countries where:

- A significant market opportunity exists for the product.
- English (or your native language) is not widely understood.
- Local laws require translation of product advertising and other materials.
- Competitors use localized materials.

Localization can be considered for all of your materials, including brochures, reply cards, demo disks, and press materials. The specific materials you adapt may vary by country, based on market needs or whether your company sells directly or through in-country dealers. You also may need to consider different viewpoints on the type of information that should be presented in a document. For example, prospects in each country may have different ideas on the content and type of information included in a direct-mail package.

You may need to consider regional dialects when localizing materials. For example, the English spoken in the United States is slightly different from that spoken in the United Kingdom; the French language as spoken in Canada is different from that spoken in France; the Spanish language spoken in Spain is different from what is spoken in Latin America. And the language may have additional local dialects within each country. Adapting your text for only one market can make your material stand out in a way that will be perceived by the reader as subtly negative. Decide whether your translators should create a separate version of the material for each specific market or find a version of the language that will be understood by readers in all markets.

You will need to decide whether to produce separate documents for each target language, or a single, multilingual document. If producing a multilingual document, you must choose a format such as one of the following:

- The text appears completely in one language, followed by the complete text in each additional language.
- The text appears in parallel columns, one column for each language.
- The text appears in alternating paragraphs for each language.
- English or native language is used in the base document, with a localized appendix or wraparound document.

Working with Translators

The translation process involves these general activities: finding a qualified translator, supporting the translation process, and working with local reviewers to verify the accuracy and appropriateness of the translation.

Grüber notes, "Adaptation relies on the skills of professional copywriters, living in their own country, writing in their own language and in touch with local trends. It is also a question of teamwork: between copywriters and technical specialists in the case of technical copy; between the copywriters of the different countries for very creative multi-lingual campaigns; and, whenever possible, between the adapters and the local managers to ensure company terminology is respected."[141]

Because localization means more than just matching words, it will likely involve some amount of rewriting—making a good writer in the target language critical for the success of your piece. As Victor notes, "At best, a translation provides an *equivalence*, not an exact reproduction of meaning. This holds true for all words, even the most concrete of expressions."[24]

For marketing materials, you will want to find a translator who is also a copywriter. This skill will enable the translator to successfully adapt the message and positioning, tone and style, and product personality—as well as the words themselves. Most localization experts recommend that the translator be someone who is a native speaker of the language and who either resides in the target country or visits regularly.

You can make a translator's job easier in several ways. First, provide support materials in both your native language and the target language that will help the translator understand the technology, the market, and applications for your product. This material also will help the translator assess how others have handled information similar to what is presented in your materials.

Second, coordinate the efforts of multiple translators and your other international communication resources. This guideline applies whether you are working with the same or multiple languages. An effective way to coordinate the efforts of everyone involved is to appoint a single lead translator or translation company.

Remember the cascading impact of changes made to the text after it is delivered; translation compounds this problem. Finally, write your English copy with translation in mind (see the next section for details).

Working with In-Country Reviewers

Once an initial translation is completed, it should be reviewed and proofread by your marketing staff or distributor in the target country. These reviewers should check the accuracy of the translation for technical information, marketing messages, and appropriate cultural considerations. They should verify the translation of both words and meaning, and the accuracy of hyphenation, punctuation, and accent marks. However, remind the reviewers that the intent of this process is to verify the translation, not to rewrite or add to the document.

In addition to the review by in-country staff, some companies perform a reverse translation on critical documents. In this process, the translated text is retranslated—by another translator—back into the original language. A reverse translation helps both you and the translators verify the accuracy of the first translation.

Developing a Translation Glossary and Style Guide

An essential resource for you, your translators, and your reviewers is a common glossary and style guide. These documents become especially critical when you are working with multiple translators, agencies, and reviewers who are located in many countries. Freivalds notes, "Without specific guidelines from the client, the individual overseas agencies would interpret English after their own fashion, or worse, cling to the belief that only a literal translation of what needs to be said will do."[142]

Your translation company may own a glossary of the common terms in your industry that it can apply to your projects. In this case, supplement the glossary with terms, acronyms, and abbreviations that are unique to your products or markets. In projects that involve multiple languages, work with your translators to ensure consistency of terminology and usage across languages and across all materials, including marcom, public relations, packaging, and documentation. Ask your in-country reviewers to check the accuracy and completeness of your glossaries before translation begins.

When creating definitions in the glossary, define both what a thing does and what it doesn't do. Your glossary entries should be as concrete and detailed as possible—even include an illustration if that will help the translator select the correct word. Also, list the terms that should not be translated such as product and company names, trademarks, publication titles, and technical terms that are widely used and understood in English or other original language.

An international style guide is one means for creating a consistent corporate identity when using multiple translators in multiple markets. For some high-tech products, especially computer software, localized style guides developed by the industry leaders (such as Apple, Microsoft, and Sun Microsystems) may be a helpful resource. For example, if your company markets products for the Macintosh computer, using the same terms that Apple Computers uses in its materials may be appropriate.

WRITING GUIDELINES FOR INTERNATIONAL MARCOM

This section lists many techniques that will help you consider the international implications when you are writing English-language documents. Add your own techniques to the list based on the specific circumstances for your products and markets. In addition, the translation resources you use may follow different practices.

General

- **Translation spread.** When preparing an English-language document for translation, you must consider the differences in physical space required by other languages. This is called the translation-spread factor. For example, Latin languages such as Spanish and French increase the copy length by 20 to 25 percent while German and Scandinavian languages increase copy length by 25 to 30 percent. In the other direction, Japanese and Chinese characters *decrease* the text size. While translation spread may seem to be only a formatting problem, it can be difficult to overcome for document elements such as sidebars, headlines, captions, and callouts, which may have limited space on the printed piece. If you are working with a rigid or tight format, identify portions of the copy that could be deleted from the translated version to make a fit.
- **Document format.** Consider the reading orientation of languages such as Japanese and Arabic, where the text is read from right to left and bottom to top. Can a different reading

orientation be accommodated by the layout and document elements in your piece?

- **Market-specific information.** Are all of the products and services described in your materials actually available in each of the target countries? Your materials should indicate whether the product is available only in a single language (e.g., English) or list the localized versions that are available. Sales information, contacts, offers, and other information may need to be customized for each international market.

Writing Style

- **Variances in copy styles.** In general, marcom outside of the United States adheres to a formal writing style and may have less "hard-sell" language. American informality is very difficult, and sometimes impossible to translate into other languages and cultural contexts.[137] Identify and adhere to the preferred style for each country or market segment.
- **Repeat key messages.** This repetition can reinforce the content and overall impression of the piece.
- **Keep ideas distinct.** Presenting one topic at a time simplifies the translation process and reduces the possibility of error. Use active voice to avoid confusion about the subject-action-object relationship that can arise when a statement is written in passive voice.
- **Avoid negative statements.** Negatives can be confusing enough in the reader's native language and translation compounds this problem.
- **Verbal courtesy.** Adhere to local guidelines for courtesy in written communication. For example, salutations in direct-mail letters are usually very formal.
- **Local laws.** Advertising laws in some countries do not allow the use of superlatives or claims such as your product being dominant in its category.

Word Usage

- **Use all words consistently.** Reduce your use of synonyms and choose words that have a single primary meaning to avoid mistranslation.
- **Use technical terms appropriately.** Remember that some languages create new words for a technical term and may have multiple words to indicate variations in that term or to handle different parts of speech. Other languages use the English word or a phonetic equivalent. Avoid introducing

new words that will be difficult to translate, even if you provide a definition.

- **Acronyms.** Always include the component words of the acronym on first usage in the text, and consider using the full words instead of the acronym throughout the document. Be especially careful about acronyms that may have multiple meanings. In addition, a single technology may be referenced by different acronyms in different languages. However, it may be acceptable to use acronyms if they are widely known in the industry, regardless of their originating language.
- Watch for compound adjectives and noun clusters, for example: *remote access router series.* To facilitate a correct translation, rewrite this noun cluster as: *a series of routers for access from remote locations.* When using a modifier + noun + noun combination (common in English), identify which noun is associated with the modifier, because in some languages the modifier follows the noun.[127]
- Watch for sentences that contain long strings of prepositional phrases. Long sentences in general can make translation more difficult. Vögele suggests these guidelines: Each sentence should contain a maximum of 15 words and 30 syllables, with an average of 10 to 12 words. Only a few subordinate clauses should appear in the entire text.[31]
- Watch for ambiguity or vagueness in the original text; this will be compounded by the translation process.
- Write full sentences; include articles (e.g., the, an) and eliminate contractions.
- Watch for words that are the same whether they are used as nouns, verbs, or adjectives. For example, *display* can be used in these ways: *display a screen* (verb), *on the video display* (noun), and *install a display adapter* (adjective). Use these words in only one part of speech.
- Avoid idiom and local slang in both the original text and the target language and for both technical and nontechnical terms. Also, remember that when using general terms such as "government," specify which country is involved.

Content Types

- **Subject matter.** Are you describing a technology that is considered controversial or unethical in other countries? Are you discussing issues that affect customers in only one part of the world, or that have different implications in other areas?

- **Formats.** Items such as units of measure, currency, dates, times (24-hour clock), large numbers, and telephone numbers vary in their appearance among countries and may vary even within a country. Specify which measurements and units you are using in the original text. For example, when you state an amount as $5 million, specify whether this is in United States, Canadian, or Australian dollars.
- **Quotes.** Handling a quote involves a decision about translating it or presenting it in the original language. If you present the original, include all special characters and punctuation. Follow the quote with an accurate translation that is placed in brackets or highlighted with another type of formatting device. Also, include in the translation a definition of any specialized terms that appear in the original quote.
- **Imagery.** Check whether your examples, metaphors and analogies, emotion, humor, wordplay, and other text techniques will translate correctly. In many cases, these items are very specific to a culture. Winters notes, "Has that metaphor been *completely* researched; that is, will it intellectually work, make sense, and have the desired cognitive connection?"[6] In addition, avoid gender-specific language and examples because they may not accurately represent gender roles in other cultures.
- **Local laws.** Check local laws for the types of information that cannot be included in marcom materials. For example, some countries do not allow advertising that compares your product with its competition. Offers are another content type that is subject to different local regulations.
- **Call to action.** The call to action should include detailed instructions on how to respond for each country, such as returning a reply card or calling an in-country contact for more information.
- **Trademark notation.** In some cases, a product may be sold under a different name in different countries to avoid a negative meaning. Product names that remain in the native language and are trademarks should not be translated.

Document Elements

- **Visuals.** All photographs and illustrations must be culturally appropriate. For example, different cultures attach different meanings to colors and symbols; what may have a positive meaning in one country may have a negative meaning in another. The use of cartoon-style drawings may be acceptable in some countries but perceived as inappropriate for business communication in others. For screen shots and diagrams, place callouts in a separate legend and use only key letters on the image itself to avoid space problems when translating. Photographs of software screen displays should show the localized version whenever possible.

- **Boilerplate.** To avoid the cost and problems caused by repeat translations of similar text, develop approved boilerplate and other blocks of text that can be used in multiple documents for each market.

EXERCISES

1. Look at the international editions of trade publications or marketing materials that have been localized. Analyze them (to the extent of your language abilities) for the types of messages they present, and use of document elements, content types, text techniques, and visuals.
2. Develop a translation glossary and style guide for your product.
3. Take a document written in your native language and identify the changes that would be necessary to prepare the text for translation.

PART THREE

High-Tech Marcom Projects

The chapters in this part describe common marketing materials for high-tech products and services. In addition, Chapter 13 presents a discussion of the emerging importance of electronic media in marcom. The information for each type of material has a similar structure, presenting a description of the characteristics, uses, and content ideas. An example document is also presented for the most common material types.

Not every company uses all of these materials and your company may use others that are not described here. In addition, as a marketing writer you may focus on a limited range of project types, such as sales materials only or press materials only. Use these chapters, together with Chapters 5 through 7, to spark your ideas and guide your efforts on each of your marcom projects.

CHAPTER 10

Sales Materials

Reaching Prospects and Customers

The majority of projects for high-tech copywriters involve product materials such as brochures, catalogs, and direct-mail pieces. Often called sales collateral, these materials provide information and support the sales cycle for a product or service. While prospects are the primary audience for sales materials, these documents also may have a variety of secondary audiences including customers, dealers, alliance partners, journalists, analysts, and investors.

The most common types of sales materials are described in this chapter. The specific mix of materials will vary for each product, depending on its characteristics, markets, and sales cycle. In addition, you may develop different sets of materials for different markets and develop localized materials for international sales.

ADVERTISEMENT

An advertisement is a paid message from a company that appears in a print or broadcast medium. This section focuses on print ads, because few high-tech companies advertise on radio or television. Print ads can range from two-line listings in the classified section to a multipage, four-color spread. Most advertisements for high-tech products appear in trade, business, or consumer magazines; local or national newspapers; distributor catalogs; and card decks (see separate section on card decks later in this chapter).

Many high-tech companies use minimal advertising compared with companies that produce consumer or other business products. The reason is that most high-tech products are too complex and expensive for a prospect to feel comfortable buying just on the basis of an ad. Instead, high-tech companies often use advertising to generate inquiries about the product (called product or brand advertising) or to build awareness of the company in the market (called image advertising). In the case of products that have a low price or involve a low-risk decision, a company may use advertising to generate an immediate order from the prospect (called direct-response advertising). (See Figures 10.1 through 10.3.)

Ads can be the most challenging of marcom projects. The copy must deliver a high-impact message that is also clear and engaging—and do so with a minimal amount of text. Within the ad, the headlines, body copy, and visuals should all work together to reinforce the key message or offer. And while ads often allow for a great deal of creativity, it can be a daunting task to develop an ad that will stand out from others and produce the desired results.

Content Ideas:

An ad can use any of the document elements described in Chapter 5. Many of the text techniques described in Chapter 7 are especially effective in ads. In terms of content, an ad should present a single message or offer. The copy should emphasize benefits over features, state the key message or offer clearly, and finish with a strong call to action.

Effective ads incorporate these principles:

- The headline is powerful, attracts the reader's attention, and draws the reader into the body copy.
- All copy is easy to read and understandable upon first reading.
- The visuals and copy work together to support the overall message of the ad.
- The call to action is strong and complete.
- The key message or offer is clear and easy to recognize.
- The ad attracts the target audience.
- Text techniques and document elements are used appropriately.

In addition, ads for high tech products often include:

- System requirements or platform support if this information is necessary for the reader to determine interest in your product.
- Feature information when this is critical for differentiating your product and for the purchase decision.
- Pricing information.
- Testimonials or quotes from product reviews; symbols for product awards or certifications.

Voice Mail, Visibly Enhanced.

Desktop Voice Processing so cutting edge nobody can match it. Yet so easy, anybody can use it.

Repartee® Voice Processing offers an amazing enhancement of voice mail on your local area network: TeLANophy™ (tel·*LAN*·o·fē). TeLANophy integrates voice mail, E-mail and fax mail messages through Microsoft® Windows.™ And pops up on your screen to announce incoming calls.

TE L A N O P H Y

With the ability to sort and see, you gain unheard-of control over messages. Mouse-directed call handling is a dramatic advance that opens up new territory in personal flexibility and time management. Plus TeLANophy's graphical user interface makes Repartee even easier to use.

TeLANophy and Repartee were created by Active Voice, a leader in voice mail with more than 15,000 installations worldwide. We make a whole line of voice processing systems suitable for every size company.

TeLANophy is certain to change your view of voice processing. Call us for details.

TeLANophy. Voice Mail with a Vision.™

Circle reader service card number 35

ACTIVE VOICE

©1993 Active Voice Corporation   Seattle 206.443.9440 x 700   London 089.251.8741 x 386   Melbourne 03894.1699 x 301

Figure 10.1   This product ad is intended to present an overview of the product and encourage inquiries for more information.

Source: © 1993, Active Voice Corporation. Reproduced by permission.

The world's leading banks, hotels, retailers and publishing firms. They rely on Hughes for satellite, wireless and enterprise network solutions to make their businesses work better.

WE'VE INSTALLED MORE INTERACTIVE VSATs THAN ALL OTHER COMPANIES IN THE WORLD COMBINED. BUT WHO'S COUNTING?

At Hughes Network Systems, our success is measured by the success of our customers who keep a step ahead of the competition with the help of our networking products and services.

To learn more, call Jack Shaw, Chairman and CEO, at (301) 601-7401 or fax (301) 428-1868. **The Best Value in Global Networking.**

HUGHES
NETWORK SYSTEMS
A unit of GM Hughes Electronics

Figure 10.2   This image ad has the objective of positioning the company as a leader in its industry.

Source: © 1994, Hughes Network Systems, Inc. Reproduced by permission.

Figure 10.3 This direct-response ad contains detailed information on features and benefits, as well as a guarantee to motivate the reader's decision.

Source: © 1994, Knowledge Point. Reproduced by permission. Copywriter Ian Alexander.

ADVERTORIAL

An advertorial is an *advert*isement written and designed to resemble the edi*torial* material in a magazine or newspaper. Often written in the form of an article, an advertorial is paid for by the sponsoring company and may be written by the company's staff, a freelance writer, or one of the publication's editors or reporters (policies on who writes advertorials vary with each publication).

Advertorials may be placed on one or more pages in the publication or bound in as an insert (Figure 10.4). An advertorial must be labeled as advertising, and most publications require that it use a different type style, layout, or page size to distinguish it from the editorial content. While advertorials can cover almost any topic, they usually have content similar to that in articles and white papers (see Chapter 11 for articles; white papers are discussed later in this chapter).

Advertorials can be used to:

- Present more information than can fit into a typical ad.
- Support the desired positioning for a product or company.
- Present the company's viewpoint on an issue or trend.

In addition, reprints of the advertorial can be used as a sales document for the product or company.

Content Ideas:

An advertorial can incorporate any of the document elements described in Chapter 5 and address many of the content types described in Chapter 6. While advertorials are usually written with a journalistic style, some of the text techniques in Chapter 7 may be appropriate in moderation.

BROCHURE

A brochure typically is a multipage booklet that describes a product, service, or company. Data sheets (discussed later in this chapter) also can serve as brochures, and many companies produce disk-based or multimedia brochures (see Chapter 13). Still the most common are print brochures, which can have a wide variety of formats and levels of production quality. They can be formulaic, as in a set of data sheets that follow a standard format, or highly creative, as in a product or corporate showcase brochure (Figures 10.5 and 10.6).

Customers can order QVC's most popular items without waiting, by using Perception Technology's interactive voice processing system.

Others With Perception

QVC is joined by other organizations in the pursuit of enhanced customer service and call center efficiency. Twenty-four hours a day, seven days a week, Perception Technology systems enhance service, reduce costs, and improve productivity for:

- 80% of the Bell Regional Holding Companies
- 5 of the top 15 banks
- 10 of the top 20 Universities
- Many government agencies, including the largest IVR customer, the IRS.

Direct Order, Direct Results

West Chester, PA -- QVC customers are shopping faster and easier than ever before. And QVC is increasing its sales volume. The Secret: a state-of-the-art interactive system from Perception Technology.

A leader in the use of interactive communications, QVC credits its improved service capabilities to an expanded VRU (Voice Response Unit) from Perception Technology. Using the easy-to-use, self-serve system, customers can bypass conventional customer service representatives and place orders using the buttons on their touch-tone phones.

See us at Voice Spring '94!

"The Perception Technology system has put us in a win-win situation," says QVC Vice President John Link. "During call crunch times when all of our representatives are helping customers, callers have the option of ordering electronically - with no waiting. For QVC, it means increased sales and fewer customer complaints. Our trained customer reps are free to assist callers with more complicated orders or questions. Best of all, the VRU is flexible for users and operators. If, at any time, customers would like special help, they can switch to a customer representative."

With the success of QVC's new interactive system, only one question remains: What's next?

Call Response Needs Analysis

If you want some help on a cost justification analysis call 1-800-284-DEMO (3366). We can assist you in putting together a plan tailored for your telephone system, computer architecture, and need for service.

For a research report on the voice processing industry and how it impacts you, call **1-800-284-DEMO (3366).**

PERCEPTION ©
TECHNOLOGY
A Division of
Brite Voice Systems, Inc.
40 Shawmut Road
Canton, MA 02021
Offices Worldwide
617-821-0320

Figure 10.4 An advertorial presents information about a product in a form that blends the promotional techniques of advertising with the journalistic techniques of an article.

Source: **Perception Technology, a division of Brite Voice System, Inc. Reproduced by permission.**

A brochure is a critical communication medium because it may be a prospect's only source of information about your product or company. Brochures serve as the cornerstone of most sales efforts, with distribution through direct-mail campaigns, at trade shows, in presentations by a salesperson, or as a fulfillment piece for inquiries generated by advertising or publicity programs.

Many high-tech products cannot be described adequately in a single brochure. In addition, companies often have "families" of related products that are targeted to different markets, applications, or platforms. In these cases, companies often produce multipart brochures or a brochure set, with individual brochures for each product, market segment, platform, or application type.

The following are the most common types of brochures for high-tech products:

- **Product overview.** An overview brochure typically presents a complete description of a product or product line. The information may be at a high level to accommodate different audiences and different uses. Keeping an overview brochure at a high level can also make it usable for a longer period of time, an important consideration if it involves expensive production.
- **Capabilities overview.** A document that describes a company's expertise, services, and resources. A capabilities overview is used to market a service company or a service program provided by a product manufacturer. This document also can show "the company behind the product" for high-cost, high-commitment products.
- **Market-specific brochure.** Some high-tech companies produce different brochures for each market segment. This type of brochure presents the features, benefits, examples, and case studies that are most relevant to that market. In addition, these brochures may be localized for each country where the product is sold internationally.
- **Direct mail.** Brochures are an essential component of direct-mail campaigns, either as a self-mailer or part of a package. The term "self-mailer" indicates the brochure has a built-in address area that allows it to be mailed without an envelope. The content, format, and length of a direct-mail brochure will depend on whether its goal is to generate prospect names

Project Management

Designed to work the way you do.

Tools you use to manage projects.

On time and within budget.

Bayshore Travel is a thriving business like yours. The company is planning to open a new branch office, which will require careful coordination of schedules, resources, and costs. The general manager uses Microsoft® Project and Microsoft Excel, powerful software tools for the Macintosh® that will help the company manage the expansion effectively. Let's follow along as the general manager prepares time and cost estimates for the president and chief financial officer (CFO).

First we use Microsoft Project to plan tasks, priorities, and responsibilities. Several different phases will be required: finding a new·location, performing necessary renovation, and planning details of the move itself. The general manager can view Microsoft Project information in a Gantt Chart to display the project graphically on a timeline.

Microsoft Project makes it easy to create Gantt Charts, for a snapshot of project tasks. Custom bars give you flexibility to detail special conditions.

Resources can be accurately scheduled across projects. Special conditions, like the date when a new lease must be signed, can be highlighted for effective decision making. Tasks are arranged easily and logically, both from the top down and bottom up.

Figure 10.5   This brochure fits into a standard letter-size envelope, making it suitable for inclusion in a direct-mail package or for a retail display.

Source: © 1991, Microsoft Corporation. Reproduced by permission.

(sales leads) or to actually sell a product. (See the section on direct-mail packages later in this chapter.)

- **Video, demo disk, or multimedia brochure.** Although very expensive to develop and produce, electronic-media brochures are growing in popularity. They can be especially effective for explaining new technologies and for marketing high-priced, sophisticated products (see Chapter 13).

Microsoft Project and Microsoft Excel

Business tools that make business sense—to help you stay on top of every aspect of project management. Gantt Charts and PERT Charts for visual tracking of schedules and task relationships. And the spreadsheet functions you need for powerful financial and data analysis.

When it comes to understanding business, Microsoft leads the way in Macintosh applications. With products that work together—to enhance each other—for everyday business solutions. Easy-to-use commands with a click of the mouse.

Microsoft Project. The truly versatile business project planning system. With the flexibility and power to manage schedules, resources, and costs. Customize project information to suit your individual needs. And create boardroom-quality presentations.

An unprecedented number of ways to look at projects:

- Easy-to-understand Gantt Charts to view project schedules on graphical time scales
- PERT Charts to show task relationships
- Spreadsheet-like view for a quick check on resource allocation
- Outlining to easily group and arrange project tables in a hierarchical order
- Split views to see any two screens at once
- Resource histogram that displays resource workloads and over-allocations across multiple projects

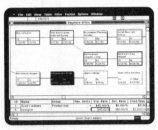

With Microsoft Project's PERT Charts, you can view and define relationships. Making changes is as easy as clicking the mouse and selecting the specific data files you wish to display or edit.

- Automatic resource leveling to identify both resource availability and costs quickly, across multiple projects
- Icon bar that gives easy access to commonly used functions
- Filters for viewing information exactly the way you want
- Extensive style options, so you can choose from different colors, symbols, patterns, shadings, text fonts, and border styles
- Custom reports you can easily adapt to your needs

Microsoft Project gives you visual tools to manage time, money, and people across multiple projects.

Figure 10.5 *continued*

Content Ideas:

A brochure can accommodate any of the content types, document elements, and text techniques described in Chapters 5 through 7. The ideas given below cover the types of information typically included in a brochure for a technology product. The order here reflects the most common sequence for presentation of these items in a product brochure.

- **Overview.** A summary description of the product, its target customers, and key benefits.
- **Product features and benefits.** A description of the product's features and benefits, as well as options for product configuration or

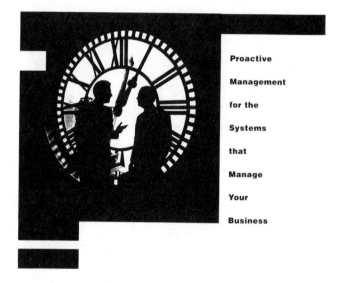

O M E G A C E N T E R

Proactive

Management

for the

Systems

that

Manage

Your

Business

!Candle·

Figure 10.6   This product showcase brochure was produced in full color with high production values. It is accompanied by detailed product data sheets.
Source: © 1994, Candle Corporation. Reproduced by permission.

operation. This section also may include a description of accessory products and services offered by your company or other vendors.
· **Product operation.** A description of how the product works including test results, architecture or design information, and screen shots or sample output.

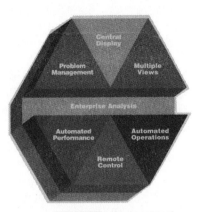

OMEGACENTER systems management:
an integrated approach

Advanced systems management with OMEGACENTER

OMEGACENTER controls and protects your systems using three integrated dimensions:

▲ Status management

▲ Comprehensive analysis

▲ Automation

Enterprise-wide status management

To provide a single point of control for managing the entire enterprise, Candle introduced "status management" to the industry in 1988. It includes:

▲ A central display – At a glance, OMEGA-CENTER's graphic display depicts the health and status of critical systems and applications across the enterprise.

▲ Multiple views – Easily tailored to the needs of every data center area – senior management, operations, help desk, etc. – to highlight information of specific interest.

▲ Problem management – For coordinated problem resolution and improved communication across data center groups and sites.

Comprehensive system analysis

Working with status management, OMEGA-CENTER's analysis probes your enterprise, collecting and analyzing information key to managing your systems. It helps you proactively solve problems via:

▲ A solution-oriented approach – Including hundreds of recommendations based on 15 years of experience to speed identification and resolution of problems.

▲ Ease-of-use – With a CUA interface, featuring extensive help facilities, pop-up windows, and action bars for rapid product navigation.

▲ Detailed analysis – Taking the guesswork out of solving problems, OMEGACENTER provides powerful, leading-edge performance analysis.

Automation for self-managed systems

Automation allows you to react to problems at the same speed they occur – machine speed. OMEGACENTER automation brings you:

▲ Automated performance – Working with your site policies, priorities, and OMEGACENTER analysis, problems are detected and resolved automatically.

▲ Automated operations – That extend beyond the console to disparate data center management tools, and even interface with NetView.

▲ Remote control – From an outboard platform, you can manage remote data centers and non-IBM platforms, notify personnel, and report on environmental conditions.

All working together for total systems synergy

Every OMEGACENTER component works together and integrates to leverage systems management and increase your control. From a single data center to a global enterprise, OMEGACENTER manages and improves your systems' performance, throughput, availability, and reliability.

Figure 10.6 *continued*

- **Product applications.** A discussion of how the product can be implemented to support certain capabilities or solve certain customer problems.

- **Customer information.** One or more brief case studies or a list of major or representative customers.
- **Awards, endorsements, and reviews.** Brief, positive quotes from current customers, excerpts from product reviews in trade magazines, and citations of awards or certifications.
- **Comparison charts.** Word charts that compare products within the same product line, or a product with its competitors.
- **Product specifications.** The technical details about the product's physical and functional characteristics.
- **Service and support programs.** A description of repair, service, and technical support programs; training programs; consulting services. This section may also include warranty and guarantee information.
- **Company information.** A discussion of the company's expertise, history, and operations; sometimes presented in the form of a letter from a company executive. This section also may include information on relationships with alliance partners.
- **Ordering and pricing information.** Detailed instructions on ordering or buying the product. A list of dealer and sales offices, and information on demonstration lines, demonstration disks, or evaluation units.
- **Images.** Photographs, illustrations, or diagrams of the product, its concept, architecture, usage, application, or positioning.

CARD DECK

A card deck is a package of reply cards, usually produced by a trade magazine publisher, that serve as mini-advertisements for products. Deck recipients return the individual cards directly to the manufacturer to request more information or to order the product. Companies also use card decks to promote catalogs, application guides, videos, and other marketing documents (Figure 10.7).

Because of the limited size, make only one offer or sell only one product per card. Make this offer recognizable at a glance as the prospect is flipping through the cards. The headline for the card is the easiest way to capture the reader's attention in a card deck.

Although space is limited, the amount of copy on a card will vary depending on your objective. Use less copy if you want to generate inquiries; more copy if you want prospects to buy the product from the card.

Content Ideas:

Promotional cards typically use only headlines, body copy, and bullet lists as document elements. They can accommodate any of

Figure 10.7   Cards in deck can sell products directly (top) or generate inquiries (bottom).

Sources: Ontrack Computer Systems (top). Ontrack is a registered trademark of Ontrack Computer Systems, Inc. American Power Conversion (bottom). © 1993, American Power Conversion (bottom). Both reproduced by permission.

the ideas listed in the "Product Information" and "Offers" sections in Chapter 6. In addition, cards can benefit from many of the text techniques listed in Chapter 7.

- Use the headline to present a clear, brief statement of the offer or key product benefit.
- Present a call to action such as *Call Today!* or *Return This Card Today.*
- Include only the key features or benefits; don't overload the card with copy.
- List your toll-free, direct-dial, and fax telephone numbers to encourage faster response.
- Instruct prospects to tape a business card to the card as an alternative to completing the response information. Place the response form in the return address area of the card to maximize the copy space on the reverse side of the card.
- If the objective is to generate inquiries, consider including a small number of profile questions in the response section to prequalify the prospects.
- State the pricing and ordering terms if prospects will purchase the product from the card.
- Assign a code to each card deck to help you track responses.

CATALOG

A catalog is a booklet that presents a collection of products sold by a company, distributor, or dealer. Most commonly used for mail-order sales, a catalog also can serve as a reference book to support sales by dealers or direct-sales staff. Some companies produce their own catalogs, while others participate in catalogs published by distributors or resellers (Figure 10.8).

A consistent format for the product descriptions in a catalog will help readers find information quickly. For example, a format could open with a statement of the product's key benefit, follow with a description of additional features and benefits, present a summary of technical specifications, and end with the part number and price.

Content Ideas:

Catalogs can incorporate many of the product and company information types described in Chapter 6, as well as any of the document elements described in Chapter 5 and the text techniques in Chapter 7. Most catalogs also include these elements:

- A table of contents or product index.
- A welcome letter from a company executive.
- Ordering instructions for phone, fax, and mail orders. Telephone number and hours of operation for order center. Printed order form with information on ordering procedures, payment policies, shipping options, and expiration date on prices.
- Charts to show options available for each product.
- Cross-references to related and accessory products.
- Instructions on how to obtain additional product information.
- Guarantee or warranty statements.
- A list of sales office or dealer locations.

DATA SHEET

A data sheet is usually a two-page or four-page document that presents detailed information about a specific product. The focus of the writing is primarily on the product, with information on features, functionality, and applications. Benefits statements play a secondary, supporting role. Many companies create a standard format for data sheets to ensure consistency of style, content, and presentation (Figure 10.9).

Data sheets often supplement a product overview brochure, presenting detailed information on product features and specifications. They also serve as reference material for sales staff and dealers, as an inexpensive handout for trade shows or retail sales, and as a fulfillment piece for an advertising or direct-mail campaign.

Content Ideas:

A data sheet can contain many of the same content types and document elements as a brochure. If a data sheet is the only document where you present the technical specifications for the product, see the guidelines for this information in Chapter 6. See the section on brochures earlier in this chapter for other content ideas.

DIRECT-MAIL PACKAGE

"Junk mail" is the derogatory term often applied to direct mail, which in actuality is one of the most important pieces in the

Figure 10.8   This catalog is used to sell products directly to customers.
Source: Photo courtesy of IBM Corporation. Reproduced by permission.

Buy any ThinkPad and receive LapLink V, file transfer software (serial cable included), and SonicPro alarm card for only $99 (2299432).

Softnet FaxWorks®

FaxWorks takes traditional fax software to the next plateau with the latest in fax viewing speed and clarity. FaxWorks Pro includes OCR, advanced annotation tools, FaxTracker® technology and direct scanner support.

FaxWorks V3.0 for Windows
(MM23231) $29
FaxWorks Pro V3.0 (MM11365) $89

Hit the road with AutoMap!

Before you hit the road on business or vacation, check your AutoMap. Just tell it where you need to go, and it maps out the shortest (or the most scenic) route—and you never have to fold it back up.

AutoMap for DOS (MM14189) $55
AutoMap for Windows
(MM39914) $55

Bring Your Office with You!

Scherrer Resources software

These powerful programs are a dream come true for sales professionals. Besides keeping all your information and contacts in one quick-access database, they can also do analysis and forecasting. The built-in word processor (with support for laser

fonts) lets you turn out professional-quality reports, letters and mail merges from your portable computer.

Sales Ally ....**Call!**
Broker's Ally ....**Call!**
Realty Ally ....**Call!**

The wireless portable LAN!

This affordable, error-correcting, wireless LAN adapter keeps you and your ThinkPad connected to your office's network while you move about.
Proxim RangeLAN™ ....**Call!**

Xircom® Pocket Token-Ring and Ethernet Network Adapters

With these adapters, it's easy to connect your notebook or laptop to a 4 or 16bps Token-Ring Network or Ethernet LAN. Exclusive SmartRing™ software available on the Token-Ring Adapter reduces memory requirements by more than 50%.

Xircom Pocket Token-Ring Adapter II
(MM90341) $615
Xircom Pocket Ethernet Adapter III
(MM54375) $384
See page 32 for additional communications options

Xircom Adapters

Make it just right.

IBM PC Direct has plenty of options for your new ThinkPad. We also have accessories for IBM N45SL, N51SLC, N51SX, L40SX, and CL57SX portable computers, so give us a call if you don't see what you want.

Other products available

Options	Part #	Price
Grid PenRight*	MM00768	$105
Data I/O CardPro PCMCIA Drive	—	Call!
Trakker Tape 250 Back-up	MM07849	$449
Megahertz PCMCIA pocket modem	MM06627	Call!
Apex Data/Fax Modem	MM34384	Call!

Certified for use with a ThinkPad 710T.

Call **1 800 IBM-2YOU** 1 800 426-2968
8am-midnight M-F, EDT; 8am-7pm Sat., EDT.
Purchase order is available for qualifying customers.

Figure 10.8 *continued*

Master Series Token Ring Adapters

Master Your Token Ring LAN Support Problems

The *Master Series of Token Ring Adapters* is comprised of the **ISA IIA** and the **MCA II**, Andrew Corporation's user-friendly, easy-to-use token ring adapter cards. As the newest addition to the Master Series product line, the 16/4 Mbps ISA IIA has been optimized for use in larger networks where reliability, quick installation, high performance, low maintenance and rapid problem resolution are critical.

Completely software configurable. Full software configurability is provided through the ATRACT (Andrew Token Ring Adapter Card Test) utility for the ISA IIA and is inherently embedded in the MCA II. This feature allows large accounts to do rapid configuration of adapters as well as reconfiguration of existing adapters to accommodate new PC peripherals. The ISA IIA specifically allows configuration of ring speed, IRQ, DMA and all other options through the ATRACT utility. The ATRACT program reviews the existing PC configuration and notifies the installer of those devices that could potentially conflict.

Diagnostics provide quick fault isolation. Following adapter installation, the diagnostic functions of ATRACT may be run in order to test all operation characteristics (e.g., complete hardware diagnostics, data transfer tests, ring insertion tests while remaining off the ring, and ring insertion tests while on the ring).

LEDS for easy troubleshooting. Diagnostic LEDs on the end bracket provide the user with preliminary evaluation of node operation. The user can determine if the card is operating at 16 or 4 Mbps and whether the card is inserted into the ring. LEDs on the MCA II indicate if the card is inserted into the ring and if it's passing data.

Half-length card for flexibility. The ISA IIA has been designed as a half-length card to provide additional flexibility for PCs with limited space. This feature is valuable for a variety of PC clones that do not adhere strictly to length tolerance, perhaps bending longer cards.

Upgradeable RAM allows for future growth. Both the ISA IIA and MCA II come standard with 128K RAM. RAM upgrades of 512K and 2MB are provided for server or high-performance workstation environments that are expected to operate at a high rate of utilization (e.g., large file transfers) Additional RAM, coupled with wide data path, allows for high-performance communications. The ISA IIA utilizes an 8 or 16 bit path while the MCA II offers a 16-bit path and 16, 24 or 32-bit addressing. Both adapters utilize bus master technology.

Additional features:

• On-board media filter for UTP cabling with automatic detection.

• 16 or 4 Mb selectable operation.

• 128K RAM on board with upgrades available to 512K and 2MB.

• Drivers for NetWare 286, NetWare 386, NetWare DOS ODI, NetWare OS/2 ODI, DOS NDIS, OS/2 NDIS, AHI/LLC, DOS and Banyan Vines workstation.

Figure 10.9   This is a typical data sheet, providing detailed product information in a standard, reference-oriented format.

Source: **Andrew Corporation. Reproduced by permission.**

Master Series
Token Ring Adapters

General

LAN Data Rates: 16 and 4 Mbps

Connectors: DB-9 for connection to shielded twisted pair network cable; RJ45 for connection to unshielded twisted pair

Cable Types Supported: Types 1 and 2 STP, Type 3 UTP. On-board media filter for Type 3 connection.

Standards Supported: IEEE 802.5 Token Ring Access Method; 802.2 LLC

Memory: 128K standard. Upgrades to 512K and 2MB optional

Warranty: Andrew five-year limited

Technical Support: Technical support is available from 6:00 a.m. to 5:00 p.m., PST (USA). European technical support is available 9:00 a.m. to 5:00 p.m. GMT or BST.

Models

ISA IIA: Supports AT-class machines (286, 386, 486) connecting to either a 16 or 4 MB token ring over UTP or STP cabling

MCA II: Supports IBM PS/2 machines based on the Micro Channel architecture (models 56, 57, 70, 80 90 and 95) connecting to either 16 or 4 Mb token ring over UTP or STP cabling

Specifications

Interrupts:
- ISA IIA: 2, 3, 5, 6, 7, 10, 11, 12
- MCA II: 2, 3, 4, 10, 11, 12, 14, 15

I/O Addresses:
- ISA II: 1A20h, 2A20h, 3A20h, 3A40h, 3A60h, 3A80h, 3AA0h, 4AE0h
- MCA II: 1A20h, 2A20h, 3A20h, 4A20h, 5A20h, 6A20h, 7A20h, 8A20h

DMA Channels:
- ISA IIA: 1, 5, 6, 7
- MCA II: Not applicable

Arbitration Channels:
- ISA IIA: Not applicable
- MCA II: 0, 1, 2, 3, 4, 5, 6, 7, 8, 9 10, 11, 12, 13, 14

Support for the following features is supplied::
- Novell Boot ROM
- Novell RPL
- IBM Boot ROM
- IBM RPL

Network Operating System support is provided for the following
- Novell 3.x
- Novell 2.x
- Microsoft LAN Manager
- All NDIS compliant operating systems
- Banyan Vines (workstation)

Hardware:
Power:
- ISA IIA: 1.0@+5V
- MCA II: 2.0@+5V

Opeating Temperature:
- ISA IIA: 0C to 40C
- MCA II: 0C to 40C

Data Width:
- ISA IIA: 16 bit
- MCA II: 16 bit

Storage Temperature:
- ISA IIA: -45C to 80C
- MCA II: -45C to 80C

Operating Humidity:
- ISA IIA: 10% - 90% non-condensing
- MCA II: 10% - 90% non-condensing

Storage Humidyt:
- ISA II: 10% - 90% non-condensing
- MCA II: 5%-95% non-condensing

Media Type 1:
- Shielded IBM Type 1, 2, 6, 9

Media Type 3:
- Unshielded IBM Type 3

Application

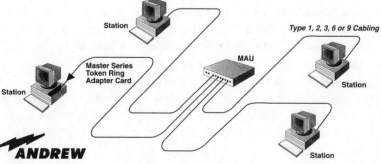

Station

Type 1, 2, 3, 6 or 9 Cabling

MAU

**Master Series
Token Ring
Adapter Card**

Station

Station

Station

Station

ANDREW

Torrance Office:	**Orland Park Office:**	**Australian Office:**	**United Kingdom Office:**
23610 Telo Avenue, Torrance, CA 90505	10500 W. 153rd Street	153 Barry Road	Ilex Building, Mulberry Business Park, Fishponds Road
(310) 784-8000	Orland Park, IL 60462	Campbellfield Victoria 3061 Australia	Wokingham Berkshire RG11 2GY England
(800) 328-2696 Fax (310) 784-8096	(800) 328-2696 Fax (708) 349-5673	(61) 3 357-9111 Fax (61) 3 357-9110	+44 734-894689 Fax +44 734 791829

Figure 10.9 *continued*

marcom mix for many high-tech products. Direct mail can generate inquiries or directly sell a product (Figures 10.10 and 10.11).

Direct-mail packages can be used in a product launch campaign or as an ongoing marketing method. Direct mail may be used as the entire sales process, where the reply card enables the prospect to order the product. More often, the direct-mail piece is the first step in the selling process, encouraging the recipient to request more information on the product or service it promotes. In addition, direct mail can be used to:

- Announce the availability of a product and motivate visits to a dealer or retail store.
- Encourage attendance at seminars or other events and visits to a trade-show booth.
- Announce new programs or sales incentives to dealers.
- Announce and generate orders for product upgrades or accessory products and services.
- Support advertising, telemarketing, and other sales activities by making multiple contacts with a prospect.

A direct-mail package usually includes a cover letter, a brochure, a "lift note" document with additional information to motivate a response, a reply card or order form, and an envelope. A variation on this package is the self-mailer, a brochure with a built-in address area that allows it to be mailed without an envelope. Catalogs also are often distributed as direct-mail pieces.

When writing direct-mail copy, repeat the offer statement and key benefits multiple times throughout the package and at least once on each piece. "No matter how interested people are in your *product*, they won't respond if they're not interested in your *offer*. Merchandize your offer in all elements of the package."[148; emphasis added] Use an integrated theme for both copy and visuals in all pieces in the package to reinforce the offer or message.

The copy must comply with national and local laws regarding the statement of offer terms and guarantees (see Chapter 8). And, the complete package must comply with legal and postal regulations on mailing content and copy that appears on the outside of the envelope.

Content Ideas:

Direct-mail pieces can use many of the document elements described in Chapter 5 and the text techniques covered in Chapter 7. Many of the content types in the "Product Information" and

Figure 10.10   This direct-mail package is intended to sell the product directly. It includes each of the pieces described in the section for direct-mail packages.

Source: © 1994, Saber Software Corporation. All trademarks acknowledged. Reproduced by permission.

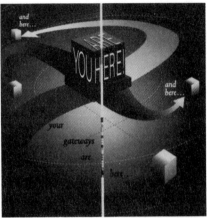

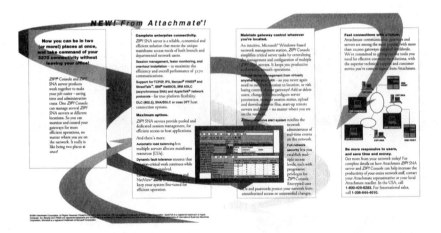

Figure 10.11   This direct-mail package is intended to promote a product upgrade, in a self-mailer format.

Source: © 1994, Attachmate Corporation. Reproduced by permission.

"Offers" sections in Chapter 6 are also appropriate for direct-mail pieces. In addition, the information below covers specific guidelines for each piece in a direct-mail package.

Envelope

- Use the outside of the envelope (both front and back if postal regulations permit) to present or continue a teaser, show the offer, or present a statement to encourage immediate action: *Limited-Time Offer* or *Act Now!*
- If you use a teaser statement on the front of the envelope it should encourage the reader to open the package. A teaser can identify the audience: *Attention Network Manager;* state the offer: *Free Demo Disk!;* present a benefit: *Locate any document in 3 seconds or less!*[134]; or announce the product: *Introducing New Quick Books 2.0!*[152]

Letter

- Consider producing different letters for different prospect groups, customizing the content to the interests and buying factors for each group.
- Most direct marketing experts indicate that long letters (3 or 4 pages) generate a higher response rate than short letters (1 or 2 pages). A long letter is usually necessary to generate purchases, while a short letter can be suitable for generating inquiries.
- A postscript (P.S.) is essential; use it to reinforce the call to action, restate your key message or benefit, or emphasize the value of your offer.
- Place a headline or Johnson Box at the top of the letter to state your offer or key benefit. (A Johnson Box is a block of text placed within a box to catch the reader's attention.) This technique can catch the prospect's attention and encourage further reading. However, using a headline if the letter is personally addressed to the prospect can destroy the sense of personal communication.
- Restate the offer or key benefit in both the opening and closing paragraphs.
- Use the middle paragraphs of the letter to describe features and additional benefits, and to present supporting evidence about your product claims or company. Also, cover all details about the offer in the body copy, including any guarantee or warranty statements.
- The letter should have a "skimmable" format, using short sentences and paragraphs. Use subheads to state key aspects of the

offer, key benefits, or messages and formatting devices to high-light the words or phrases that emphasize your offer or benefits.
- Personalize the salutation or use a salutation that describes the person's job function or interest: *Dear MIS Manager.*
- Include a signature block to support the letter's sense of personal correspondence.

Brochure

- State the offer or key benefit in the headline.
- For selling a product, the brochure in the direct-mail package can include all of the information that would be presented in a standalone brochure or data sheet. This includes detailed information on product features, benefits, and specifications (if necessary to make the sale).
- For an information offer, the brochure can present a brief overview of the product.
- See the section on brochures earlier in this chapter for additional ideas.

Lift Note

A lift note is a brief letter, often printed on a smaller piece of paper, that gives the reader additional motivation for responding to the offer. A lift note can present a variety of information, but the following types are common:

- Provide responses to the typical objections a prospect may have to your product or offer.
- Restate the value of your offer or the key benefit of your product.
- Present testimonials: *Here's what others have said about our product.*

Order or Reply Form

- Include instructions for placing the order by mail, phone, or fax. Include your company's address, toll-free and direct-dial phone and fax numbers; hours of operation for the order center; payment methods and terms; delivery options and costs; other ordering terms; information required from the prospect to process the order such as product number, customer number, or system version. Restate your guarantee or warranty.
- Summarize the terms of the offer and your key messages about the product; some recipients will keep only the order form, so it should be able to sell on its own.[2]

- For an information offer, qualify prospects by asking them to answer questions on the reply form.
- Use a response code to track the source of each inquiry or order. Create a separate response code for each mailing list and mailing date.
- Consider a fax form if the objective is to generate inquiries or if you can accept product orders by fax.

Self-Mailers

A self-mailer is something like a brochure with a reply card attached (see the guidelines for brochures earlier in this section). Self-mailers are best suited for information offers or to encourage attendance at an event. Because of postal regulations, this format may not be usable in some countries.

NEWSLETTER

A newsletter is a news-oriented yet promotional publication that is sent to customers, employees, dealers, and other people with an interest in your products and company (Figure 10.12). A primary benefit of newsletters is that they encourage customer loyalty by providing ongoing contact and useful information on new products, services, applications, and upgrades. If your products are sold internationally, you may want to create localized editions of your newsletter for each international market.

Newsletters also can be sent to prospects, analysts, and journalists to enhance their awareness of your company. In addition, some companies produce a separate newsletter for sales people, dealers, and alliance partners.

Content Ideas:

A newsletter can incorporate many of the document elements, content types, and text techniques described in Chapters 5 through 7. Most newsletters include a mix of the following items:

- **Product and company news.** New product announcements, openings of sales offices and support centers, or other company activities.
- **Other article types.** Interviews with company staff, analysts, or industry experts on current issues or strategies; customer case studies; an editor's message or a message from the company president or other executive.
- **Brief articles or fillers.** Application tips and quotes from product reviews or market studies.

Volume 3
Issue 4

Jul/Aug
1 9 9 4

THE ADVANCED PROGRAM-TO-PROGRAM COMMUNICATION NEWSLETTER

NETWORLD+INTEROP 94

Networld+Interop is probably the single most important computer networking conference for 1994, so we sent some of our reporters to join the 75,000 plus computer professionals in Las Vegas, May 2-6. Interop has traditionally focused on TCP/IP, while NetWorld was aimed at the Novell world, but they've merged into an enormous show that spans the world of computer networking. As you'll see in the article that follows, APPC and APPN technologies were prominent offerings among the hundreds of vendors represented.

APPN in the Subarea

We headed for the IBM booth first because it had a huge crowd outside it, which turned out to be people playing the IBM "slot

Interview with Bill Carico,
President ACTS Corporation   page 4

Client-Server Case Study:
Lincoln National Life Insurance Company   page 5

APPC/APPN Technical
Conference in
Amsterdam
page 12

APPC on the
Internet
page 16

MARKET PLACE

SEE PAGE 11

machines." You plugged your token into the slot and pulled the handle — we didn't win the IBM ThinkPad but we did get a luggage tag and a t-shirt. After the slot machines, we toured the latest heavyweight hardware for SNA. The new 3746 model 900 was previewing its APPN network node capability. The 3745 Network Processor, right next door, allowed you to build composite network nodes with VTAM. And the 3172 controller is becoming an ever-better router — soon it will provide APPN support using a Pentium engine and still-broader adapter support.

APPN on the Desktop

APPN continues to grow stronger on the desktop. The AIX SNA Server/6000 (see story, page 9) offers blazing performance with its APPN end node and network node support, as well as the CPI-C programming interface. Across the booth, OS/2 Communications Manager/2 was demoing its latest dependent LU requester software, allowing LU 2 connections to VTAM over APPN.

As the range of APPN products has increased, the APPN Showcase that was started in 1993 at these shows has obviously been outgrown. APPN was everywhere. In addition to the 6611, numerous vendors were touting APPN in their routers and
Continued on page 2

GETTING STARTED WITH CPI-C

CPI-C, the Common Programming Interface for Communications, gives programmers an interface that's portable across different platforms and programming languages. This article is the first in a series that explores simple CPI-C programs in the C programming language.

The programs begin with a task familiar to most C programmers. First-time C programmers often learn to write a program that displays the phrase "Hello, world" on the screen. These CPI-C programs will do the same thing, except across a network. One program sends the phrase "Hello, world" to its partner program on another computer, which then displays it on the screen.

Getting Started

Every CPI-C application consists of at least two programs, one program for each computer where
Continued on page 13

Figure 10.12   This newsletter includes many of the content ideas described in this chapter. The masthead is especially complete.

Source: Reprinted from the July/August 1994 edition of the APPC Connection, © 1994, IBM Corporation. Reproduced by permission.

FROM THE EDITOR

We've got a busy issue this month with lots of info on new products using APPC and APPN. The parade starts on page 1 with our from-the-showfloor report at Interop and continues on through the rest of the pages with four New Product pieces.

We've also got a new slant on the "MAINFRAME IS DEAD" headline that seems to appear on every third page of the trade press these days. Bill Carico, President of ACTS Corporation, isn't sure the mainframe is dead, and gives some reasons why the dinosaur isn't in the grave yet. He argues that the mainframe in a distributed environment can provide exactly what the user wants. Read his interview, then take a look at the Case Study on page 5. Moving to APPC on page 10 discusses the same problem from a different perspective by showing how you can use FEPI to get your application data from the host down to your workstation, without touching legacy code. Serena International (X:Change article, page 12) is headed in a similiar direction — they've got a slick new product that uses APPC to let programmers do mainframe development work on workstations.

Finally, we heard your requests for more technical information — Tips and Techniques (page 6) gives a detailed explanation of data compression for networking and how it works, then Configure Out APPC (page 8) shows how you configure it on OS/2. And if that's not enough, we've got C code samples with our front-page "Getting Started with CPI-C" story.

If you like these articles, or if you don't, drop us a note (appcnews@vnet.ibm.com) or join us on CompuServe. We're looking forward to hearing from you.

Mel Jones

Jul/Aug 1994

Networld, continued from page 1

gateways. Netlink showed their latest support, while OpenConnect Systems was at the show with their APPC to TCP/IP gateway. The Cisco 7000 router was there in demo form, as was the new router from Harris Adacom. Wellfleet and Proteon both stressed APPN support using data-link switching. 3-Com is shipping APPN support today.

APPC Does Windows

For years, many were convinced that merging APPC with Windows would take some magic, but no more. APPC platforms for Windows become ever more mature and widespread, and there were lots of them on display at this year's conference. IBM's Person-to-Person application for Windows lets you hold electronic conferences via your workstation — it uses CPI-C 1.2 calls to the latest version of IBM's Networking Services/DOS to link up the different participants. (And, as we go to press, it's just won "Best United Kingdom Product" in the 1994 Ziff-Davis Europe Software Excellence Awards.)

In fact, we saw lots of CPI-C implementations. Wall Data demoed its CPICEasy platform for writing AppWare applications on its Rumba product, which has support for CPI-C version 1.2. We saw Windows support in Attachmate's Extra! for Windows Version 4, with APPC and CPI-C. DCA's APPC was present in two products, its IRMA Workstation for Windows and for OS/2. NetSoft, a long-time APPC vendor for the PC market, now offers a range of Windows platforms geared specifically for connecting to AS/400 systems, Elite/400, and NS/Midrange Client Services. Finally, while Microsoft has yet to offer a 32-bit OS/2 application (a mild disappointment), they were here in force with APPC support, showing a new release of their

Windows NT SNA Server.

Networking Tools

We also got to see some interesting tools during our hours walking the showfloor. Objective Systems Integrators demonstrated NetImpact. It uses OS/2 and APPC in connection with VTAM to show session outages and allow tracking of open problems and who's working on them. Legent has a new APPC tool named NetSpy for watching what's going on in your network. Finally, back at the IBM booth (where there were still lines for the IBM slot machines), we were very happy to see the APPC Application Suite demo with a new set of common APPC applications. The idea is to provide portable "building block" applications on all APPC

Continued on page 3

THE APPC CONNECTION is published six times a year by IBM APPC Market Enablement. Letters to the editor are welcome. Please address correspondence to:
THE APPC CONNECTION
IBM APPC Market Enablement
Department E42/502, P.O. Box 12195
Research Triangle Park, NC USA 27709
Phone: 1-919-254-4957. Fax: 1-919-254-6050
Internet: appcnews@vnet.ibm.com
IBM Mail: USIB23NQ at IBMMAIL
CompuServe: 76711,370

Managing Editor: Mel Jones
Contributors: Dawn Comfort, Zeke Crater, Marilyn Gallagher, Tim Huntley, Amy Matas, Mike Richards, Kathleen Riordan, Anne Schick, Peter Schwaller, Susan Venderbush, John Q. Walker II

2

Figure 10.12 *continued*

- **Editorial information.** Authors' biographies, an "In This Issue" contents box, "What's Ahead" column, article index, and section for letters to the editor.
- **Other information.** Examples include a calendar of conferences, user-group meetings, seminars, trade-show participation, training courses, and other events. Also, a directory of sales and support offices.

Special Document Elements

- **Nameplate.** The nameplate appears on the first page and can include the newsletter name, company or publisher name, date of publication, volume and issue. It also can include a tagline: *The Newsletter for Users of Reflection.*[147]
- **Masthead.** The masthead presents publication data for the newsletter. It can include the names and affiliations of the publisher, editor, writers, designers, illustrators, photographers, and other contributors; publication date, volume and issue numbers, copyright date, and country where printed; trademark acknowledgments and information disclaimers (see Chapter 8); contact information including postal address, telephone and fax numbers, and e-mail address; recycled paper information or logo.
- **Order form or reply card.** Give readers a way to request newsletter subscriptions, back issues, or other product literature.

PACKAGING

The product box or packaging is an important form of marcom for products that are sold in a retail environment. The copy on your product box becomes especially important if you have a low-priced product that could be considered an impulse purchase (Figure 10.13). In addition, the packaging copy can reinforce the customer's decision to buy the product when the sale is made through mail order or other indirect method. Use a consistent design and images for your brochures and packaging to help a prospect recognize your product on a crowded retail shelf.

The copy on your packaging should be strong enough to sell the product then and there. The information presented on the package must be complete, clear, and include strong statements of features and benefits. Emphasize benefits, but include all feature information that is essential to differentiate your product or to encourage a purchase decision.

Use all surfaces of the package for copy, including the top, sides, and bottom. Place the product name and your key message on each of these surfaces. Test your use of document elements on a prototype that's placed in an actual selling environment to ensure the desired messages will attract the wandering eye of a prospect.

Content Ideas:

Packaging can include many of the document elements and text techniques described in Chapters 5 and 7. The content types described in the "Product Information" section in Chapter 6 are also appropriate. In addition, packaging may include the following items:

- Quotes from product reviews or testimonials from users.
- Callouts or a text box to highlight promotional offers, premiums that are included in the package, or other sales incentives.
- Summary statement of what the product does and the target user on the package front.
- Service and support program information.
- List or description of package contents. Platform information or description of compatibility with other products. Identification of localized versions.

PROPOSAL

A proposal is a document that details a company's bid for a project or product sale. Typically a proposal includes comprehensive information on the proposed project or product, its applicability to the customer's requirements, and the capabilities of the proposing company. It also may include copies of the sales materials described in this chapter.

A proposal may be created in response to a Request for Proposal (RFP) or in a competitive bid situation. It is often developed near the end of the sales cycle, when the customer will make a specific selection from the proposals submitted by several vendors.

Because proposals can vary so widely in content and format, they are described only briefly and no example is presented here. The Bibliography lists useful references that focus on proposals.

REPLY CARD

Also called a BRC (Business Reply Card), a reply card is included in a direct-mail package, brochure, or advertisement. It provides a convenient way for a reader to request more information about a product or to register for an event (Figure 10.14). Some companies also use reply cards to obtain feedback on the quality and timeliness of the information provided.

Figure 10.13 This box for a software product provides all the information a prospect needs to make an immediate purchase decision.

Source: Intuit, Inc. Reproduced by permission.

Figure 10.13 *continued*

Join The Winning Team!

Complete this card and bring it to the ADC Kentrox Booth #4759 at NetWorld + Interop and you'll receive a **limited-edition baseball cap** absolutely free! You'll also be entered in a drawing for a state-of-the-art **SEGA Game Gear System** — complete with the **SEGA Sports World Series Baseball Game**. Create your own Dream Team... All-Star Games... the real World Series. Imagine: all 28 teams, all 700 players and — for once! — batteries are included.

Name _____

Title _____

Company _____

Address _____

City/State/Zip _____

Phone _____

Fax _____

ATTACH BUSINESS CARD HERE

List Your Vital Statistics Here

1. Which categories best describes you or your company (check only one)?
   - ❏ End User/Network Administrator
   - ❏ RBOC ❏ Alternate Carrier
   - ❏ Cellular Carrier ❏ Distributor
   - ❏ Systems Integrator
   - ❏ Value Added Reseller
   - ❏ Consultant (Indep.) ❏ Student ❏ Other

2. Which category best describes your industry group?
   - ❏ Financial ❏ Health/medical
   - ❏ State Government Agency ❏ University
   - ❏ Utilities ❏ Other

3. What is your area of responsibility?
   - ❏ Engineer ❏ Recommend
   - ❏ Sales/Marketing ❏ Approve purchase
   - ❏ None

4. I am interested in network access products for the following services:
   - ❏ T1 voice [D3] ❏ T1/FT1 (voice/data) [D2]
   - ❏ Frame Relay [M20] ❏ SMDS [M14]
   - ❏ ATM [A5] ❏ T3 [D8] ❏ E1/E3 [M21]
   - ❏ Wireless [M15]

5. What is your purchasing time frame?
   - ❏ 1-6 months ❏ 7-12 months ❏ longer

6. Are you a current ADC Kentrox customer?
   - ❏ yes ❏ no

7. Company Size (employees)
   - ❏ more than 10,000 ❏ 5,000-9,999
   - ❏ 2,500-4,999 ❏ 1,000-2,499
   - ❏ 500-999 ❏ 499 or fewer

8. Number of remote locations:_____

Figure 10.14   **This reply card gives readers a way to request additional product information. Note the use of a response incentive (the game system drawing) and the qualifying questions.**

Source: © 1994, ADC Kentrox. All rights reserved. Reproduced by permission.

The reply card may include survey questions that are designed to qualify the inquirer by asking about purchasing authority, current systems, and product needs. However, you must be careful that you don't ask too many questions or request information the prospect may feel is confidential or inappropriate to disclose early in the sales cycle.

Content Ideas:

- A statement or headline that restates what the prospect will receive and reinforces the benefit of returning the reply card.
- Instructions for returning the card by mail or fax.
- Prospect information, including name and title; company and department; postal address, mailstop, country, and postal code (allow for international variations); telephone and fax numbers; e-mail address.
- Qualifying questions. Examples include industry or business category; purchasing plans (timeframe); purchasing authority; organization size (revenues or number of employees); job function; application needs; budget size; description of current systems or configurations.

SALES LETTER

A sales letter accompanies a brochure or other marketing material. It outlines the key benefits or marketing messages for the product or service, states a call to action to encourage the reader to take the next step, and provides complete contact information (Figure 10.15).

The length of the letter will vary depending on its objective and what it accompanies. As a cover letter for materials it typically is a single page (see the section on direct mail earlier in this chapter for additional ideas on sales letters).

Content Ideas:

- Many readers will believe that only the brochure or other pieces in the mailing provide substantial information, so they will give the letter only a cursory look. The opener must be strong to compel the reader to continue through the letter. Use the opener to make an offer, provide news, ask a question, or state your call to action.
- Use a Postscript message (P.S.) or box to emphasize your key message or call to action.
- Don't repeat the person's name more than once in the letter. Otherwise, your sincerity will seem fake to the reader.

digital™

> Looking for the best platform for running Windows NT? Now, you have an opportunity to purchase the world's most powerful PC for only $4,999, a 22% savings!

JANICE KING
MANIETECH
1075 BELLEVUE WAYNE STE 486
BELLEVUE WA 98004

Dear JANICE KING,

Imagine running Microsoft's Windows NT™ operating system on a PC that's nearly three times as fast as a Pentium™ system. And up to twelve times as fast as a 486 processor.

Imagine running Windows NT on a PC that's fueled by the Alpha AXP™ chip, the world's fastest microprocessor. One that can tackle multimedia, CAD/CAM, even virtual reality and voice recognition programs.

> Now imagine the world's most powerful Windows NT platform, the DECpc AXP 150, at its lowest price ever. As low as $4,999--or just $175 per month to lease.

Take advantage of Windows NT applications that are available for the DECpc AXP 150 PC from major developers like Powersoft™, Parametric Technology ™, Intergraph™, Uniface™, Microsoft™ and many others. Hundreds of Windows NT applications are shipping now or are on the way, plus the DECpc AXP 150 PC runs your existing 16-bit DOS and Windows applications. To receive--via FAX--a current listing of Windows NT applications for the DECpc AXP 150 PC, please call **1 800 388 3228** and request document #1055.

Of course, when it comes to Windows NT support, Digital is unsurpassed. Digital provides you with more choices of Windows NT training and business consulting from Digital than any other company--including Microsoft. And with a 3-year warranty and 35,000 Digital service people to back it up, Windows NT on the DECpc AXP 150 comes with the industry's best support.

Check the enclosed brochure for more detailed specifications and easy-to-order packages. For a custom quote, or to place your order, please call **1 800 215 8763** and mention **priority code GWV**, 8:30 a.m. to 8:00 p.m. (ET), Monday through Friday.

Sincerely,

Mary Suiter

Mary Suiter
Alpha AXP PC Marketing Manager

P.S. Looking for a specific application? Call today **1 800 388 3228** and request **document #1055.**

The following are trademarks of Digital Equipment Corporation: AXP, Alpha AXP, and the DIGITAL logo. All other products mentioned are trademarks of their respective owners.

Figure 10.15   This sales letter highlights the offer in a Johnson Box, uses an engaging opener, and has a strong call to action.

Source: Digital Equipment Corporation. Reproduced py permission.

- Don't create a "one letter fits all" that promotes too many products or that contains information for both prospects and dealers. You should have a way to segment inquiries and provide targeted information for each prospect group.
- Always provide complete contact information for a sales representative or dealer. Don't make the reader call your office or go to a phone book to obtain this information.

WHITE PAPER

A white paper is an essay-style document that presents an analysis or in-depth explanation of a technology, market trend, or issue (Figure 10.16). A white paper provides useful background information to help the reader gain a better understanding of a new technical development or a company's strategy. A white paper also can be an advocacy piece that presents a company's viewpoint on industry issues and directions. Depending on your subject matter, you may want to develop multiple, audience-specific versions of a white paper.

White papers are most often produced for highly complex, expensive products that have a significant impact on a customer's operations or business. They are useful in the intermediate stages of a sales cycle, when a prospect needs a comprehensive understanding of technologies, applications, and strategies in order to narrow a list of candidate products for further consideration.

The content of the white paper should emphasize the topic under discussion—not promotional information for your product. However, you can include information about how your product and company address the issues or problems you describe in the primary paper discussion. This information typically appears at the end of the white paper and has a soft-sell approach compared with other forms of marketing materials. Taking a hard-sell approach to this information may detract from the more detached impression you are trying to achieve with the rest of the paper.

White Paper Types

- **Technology Briefing.** Explains a new or underlying technology that is incorporated into your products.
- **Industry Trend Overview.** Analyzes current market, operational, or technological trends.
- **Application Digest.** Describes potential applications for a product or technology.
- **Planning Guide.** Presents guidelines for implementing a new technology or preparing for future industry changes.

Topical White Paper

Migration
Solutions

*An overview of migration
issues for electronic
messaging systems*

Figure 10.16   Produced in booklet form, this white paper addresses one of the important issues for adopting a new technology.
Source: © 1992, Microsoft Corporation. Reproduced by permission.

- **Strategy Discussion.** Describes strategies planned by your company or that are recommended to customers.
- **Management Discussion.** Describes how technology considerations relate to financial, operational, or other business issues.

Overview

Electronic mail is growing up. No longer can it be viewed simply as an interoffice memo without the paper. Rapidly changing technology is making electronic mail and workgroup applications vital components of organizations. In the coming years, users will work together across a building or across the world, sharing not only text messages, but data of all types—from graphics to spreadsheets to sound—via electronic mail.

As a result, many organizations today face a challenging journey as they consider a change in their electronic mail (e-mail) systems. Typically, an e-mail migration means moving to an integrated LAN–based e-mail system from either a mainframe-based system such as IBM. PROFS. or from multiple, often incompatible, systems (mainframe-, minicomputer-, or LAN–based).

Why migrate to a LAN–based e-mail system? The reasons vary for each organization, but many of our customers cite benefits such as these:

- Significant cost savings
- Freed host resources
- Enhanced user productivity
- Simplified system administration
- Powerful workgroup applications

These benefits are strong incentives for migration. However, many strategic issues impact such a decision, issues that will affect your organization in the coming decade. We developed Microsoft. Mail to provide powerful solutions for each of these critical concerns:

- A reliable long-term messaging infrastructure
- Open systems
Advanced Graphical - Workgroup applications
Messaging Features. - Vendor support

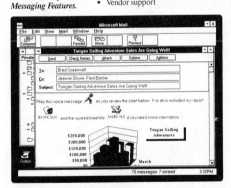

In this paper we'll explain how Microsoft Mail responds to each of these crucial issues as well as discuss the benefits to migration mentioned earlier. In addition, we'll present Microsoft's three-phase plan for a successful migration to the future of electronic messaging.

The migration to an integrated LAN–based electronic-messaging system offers exciting possibilities. Choosing the right migration strategy and tools will provide you the opportunity for unprecedented levels of productivity.

Figure 10.16 *continued*

- **Issues Analysis.** Describes the nature of an industry issue or controversy, and offers the company's viewpoint or recommendations on how customers might respond.

Content Ideas:

A white paper can include many of the content types and document elements described in Chapters 5 and 6. In addition, white papers can incorporate these items:

- A table of contents. Executive summary or overview; section summaries. Glossary, standards information, and bibliography.
- Decision criteria list or worksheet.
- Example applications or case studies.

EXERCISES

1. Analyze a marketing document for a technical product. Answer these questions as a way of evaluating the document's effectiveness, using the information presented in this chapter as a guide.
   a. What type of document is it? Is it designed as a standalone piece or as part of a collateral set?
   b. Can you identify the document's target audience(s)? How well does the document address each audience?
   c. What are the key messages presented in the document? How are they stated? How are they reinforced?
   d. Identify the document's objective and purpose. How well does the document meet each?
   e. What elements are used to organize the document's copy? Are these elements used effectively? Could you improve the flow, impact, or readability of the copy by using other elements?
   f. Which content types are used? Which writing techniques?
   g. What visuals are used? Do they reinforce the messages in the piece? Do the captions or callouts make selling points?
   h. What is the style and tone of the document? Are they appropriate for the document's audience and intended use?
   i. What is your overall reaction to the document? Do you find it interesting and informative? Or, confusing and empty? Do you need additional information that is not provided by the document? If you were shopping for this type of product, would the document motivate you to learn more about it or actually make a purchase?
2. Identify all the different sales materials you have developed (or that you could develop) for your product. How would you use any of the other document types described in this chapter?

CHAPTER 11

Press Materials

Reaching Journalists and Analysts

Press materials are directed to journalists and industry analysts with the primary objective of encouraging them to write about a product or company. Some of these materials, especially press releases, are developed for a specific marketing activity or event such as a new product introduction. Other materials, especially backgrounders, are developed to be enduring documents that a journalist can save for future reference.

Press materials are often grouped together in a press kit—typically a presentation folder that contains the press releases, backgrounders, and fact sheets related to a product, event, or company. The press kit is distributed to journalists and analysts during press tours, at a press conference or trade show, or in a mailing.

This chapter describes all of these press materials. Articles contributed to a variety of publications are also an important promotional resource for many companies. Articles are described in this chapter because they typically involve working with the same editors who are recipients of press materials.

ARTICLE

An article is an essay, analysis, case study, or other material that you contribute to a magazine, newspaper, or professional journal. (The general business press rarely accepts articles written by outside resources.) While articles can be planned as part of new marketing activities, such as a product launch, they are also an effective form of ongoing publicity for a product or company. This is because articles typically cover high-level topics that are not dependent upon short-term changes in a product or market conditions.

Articles can be developed to generate publicity, provide education, or promote the desired positioning for a product or a company. Articles also are an effective medium for building awareness and support for a technical strategy or issue. After publication, article reprints can be used as part of the sales collateral for a product.

Articles are usually not written as a speculative project. Instead, they are commissioned by the publication, based on the topic ideas you suggest in a press kit (see section later in this chapter) or on a "pitch" letter that proposes the article to an editor.

Some articles have a very specialized content, suitable only for a particular publication. Other articles may be of interest to multiple, noncompeting publications. To address the different audiences of multiple publications efficiently, develop a base article or outline that can be tailored to each publication. For example, if you are writing a "How to Select a . . ." article, it could be easily tailored by incorporating relevant examples, quotes, or decision factors for different vertical market publications. However, verify each publication's policy on multiple submissions before you place the article.

Article Types

This discussion focuses on feature articles that are submitted by a company to a trade publication or professional journal (Figure 11.1). News articles are not described here because they are typically written by the publication's reporters and editors.

For an article, choose a type based on the planned topic, your objective for writing an article instead of another document, and the publication's standards.

- **Product-selection guide.** Covers "How to select a . . . "(fill in the blank with your product type). This article gives information to help prospects in evaluating potential solutions to a problem, in particular, your product against its competition. This article type also can set the purchasing agenda in a prospect's mind.
- **Technology primer.** Explains the concepts, architecture, or applications of a product's underlying technology. A primer is a good educational resource for describing new types of technology, or to introduce a technology to new markets.
- **Research findings or analysis.** Reports the methodology and results of a technology research project, an attitudes or per-

ceptions survey, or a market research effort. This article type usually includes a large amount of statistics, data, and other supporting evidence for the results or conclusions.

- **Case study.** Describes a customer's problem or need and how your product provided a solution. This article type serves as an important reference for your product or company. (See the section on case studies later in this chapter.)
- **Trend analysis.** Discusses current or future trends in your industry, market, or technology. This article type is especially effective for positioning your company as knowledgeable about its industry or market.
- **Editorial or opinion piece.** States your company's position on a current issue or controversy. This article type is often used to correct a misperception or advocate a certain viewpoint.
- **Profile or interview.** A profile presents a biography or an overview of a company or person. An interview reports the information gathered in a question-and-answer session with a company official, industry expert, customer, user panel, or other people.

Planning the Article

Develop an article plan after you determine the article type, topic, and target publication. In addition to the guidelines given in Chapter 1, planning an article involves:

- **Matching the publication's style.** Most trade magazines and journals publish an information sheet about writing style, content expectations, and audience interests. In addition, look at several issues of the publication to understand the content, organization, and tone of its articles.
- **Meeting submission requirements.** Confirm the editor's due dates for an outline and the full article. In addition, confirm the editor's expectations for number of words in the article and the use of sidebars, callouts, and other document elements. Verify the procedure for submitting the article to the editor, such as disk type and file format.
- **Handling product mentions.** Ask the editor about the number of times your company or product can be named in the article. Most trade publications are very strict about this limit and editors are savvy to subtle forms of self-promotion that you may place in the article.

Network Communications

Janice King

A Guide to Planning a Wide-Area Network

What are the three key ingredients in creating a wide-area network? You guessed it: planning, planning, and more planning. Even the most LAN-savvy technicians and administrators may find connections beyond their local areas somewhat daunting. If connecting to the public telephone network seems like one of life's great mysteries, relax. Learning how to design a solid, serviceable WAN isn't that difficult. There are many options available for creating WANs, as well as the equipment, software, and services needed on both sides of the internetwork boundary.

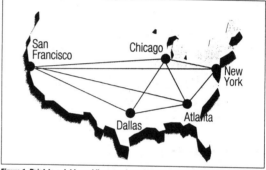

Figure 1. Point-to-point leased lines require a dedicated line to each site.

Choosing a WAN

The first thing you need to decide is which type of WAN is best suited for your existing and anticipated communication demands. This in turn will determine the best data routing schemes and required internetworking equipment. A few factors to consider when choosing a WAN include the following:

■ Number and location of LANs. Will the WAN link only a few LANs in fixed locations or will it facilitate communication among a continually changing "community" of LANs? Are the LANs located in a campus setting, in buildings across town, or in offices that are strewn across the globe? Is communication with customer, dealer, or supplier LANs also required?

■ Transmission demands of applications. Is data sent in a continuous stream (such as on-line transaction processing) or short, intense bursts (such as batch file updates)? Will the WAN accommodate data-filled graphics and imaging applications?

■ Potential bandwidth use. Will the LANs require a continuous, dedicated link for communication, or could they share a high-capacity line with other equipment?

WANs today can be divided into two categories: point-to-point leased lines that directly link multiple sites to each other, and network "clouds" that indirectly link sites through packet service technologies, which include frame relay, switched

multimegabit data service (SMDS), and eventually asynchronous transfer mode (ATM). WANs are also classified according to their implementation: as an internal, private network that uses customer-premise equipment (CPE), or by access to a public service provided by a local-exchange or interexchange carrier (LEC or IXC, respectively). With CPE, the customer owns the hubs, routers, and switching equipment and connects directly to the carrier from its site. With an LEC or IXC, the equipment is owned and maintained by the service company.

Point-to-Point Options

Leased Lines. A private network based on dedicated leased lines is

---

Figure 11.1   Example of a how-to article. It is designed to present useful reference information for readers. Reprints of such articles can be used as part of your sales collateral.
Source: NetWare Technical Journal. Reproduced by permission.

suitable for connecting a small number of LANs in fixed locations that have heavy, continuous traffic demands. Although costs are fixed, they can be expensive because each pair of node connections requires a separate line and network access equipment (see Figure 1). In most cases, leased-line networks are built upon digital T1 circuits that are provided by LECs (for networks located in a campus setting or in the same city) or IXCs (for networks that are connected across the state, country, or world).

A fractional T1 (FT1) circuit may be the answer for data volume that is too low to justify the expense of full T1 bandwidth (1.544 Mbps). This type of circuit uses a subset of the channels on a leased T1 line. The carrier company installs a full T1 line but only charges for the circuits used, providing reasonable service for low-demand applications while also offering room to grow. Another alternative is to carry voice, video, or fax traffic over the same T1 line that interconnects the LANs, allocating certain channels to each application. This spreads the cost of the bandwidth over more users or applications and requires a multiplexer or

DSU/CSU (data service unit/channel service unit) that can combine voice, video, and data traffic on a single T1 line.

Subrate Services. Subrate services are dedicated lines that have less capacity than T1 lines. Carrier-provided switched 56/64-Kbps service or a leased-line dedicated digital service (DDS) may be appropriate for low-traffic, infrequent LAN connections—such as e-mail exchange—but not sufficient for frequent, heavy LAN-to-LAN communication. Although subrate services offer an affordable entrée to LAN internetworking, traffic may quickly outgrow capacity, and subsequent upgrade to a T1 or FT1 line requires that the multiplexer or DSU/CSU be replaced.

Network Clouds

The telephone companies (US West, GTE, MCI, Sprint, AT&T, to name a few) either now provide or will soon introduce frame-relay, SMDS, and ATM packet service technologies. Packet services basically divide data of all types into packets that are routed through a network cloud to other destinations. Connections between sites are virtual, removing the need for fixed, point-to-point connections (see Figure 2).

Frame Relay. Frame-relay technology can be implemented as either a private network or a public carrier

service. By establishing a network cloud, frame relay can interconnect LANs in any location. Each LAN requires only a single T1 line into the cloud to connect to any other site on the frame-relay network. This design eliminates the multiple overlapping lines required to connect all of the sites in a point-to-point network. Within the network cloud, frame relay is connection-oriented, establishing a direct link between sender and recipient for the length of the

---

Even the most LAN-savvy technicians may find connections beyond their local areas daunting.

---

transmission. This makes it a good choice for creating an intra-enterprise network, such as for connecting regional distribution centers or sales offices.

SMDS. Local-exchange carriers currently offer SMDS to provide switched data communication among sites within a metropolitan area (SMDS offerings that extend beyond local carrier service areas are planned). Public carriers in Europe currently provide an equivalent service called Connectionless Broadband Data Service (CBDS). SMDS also uses a network cloud, with a single T1 line providing the connection from each site. SMDS employs a connectionless method, where links between LANs are established when needed, in much the same way as dialing a phone number on the public voice network.

Able to accommodate a changing mix of connected locations, SMDS is well-suited for interenterprise communication. As a scalable service offered by public carriers, SMDS can be cost-effective for small organizations that have

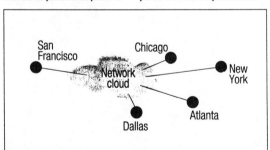

Figure 2. Network clouds create virtual connections to each site.

Figure 11.1 *continued*

Seeing Your Work in Print

When you submit an article, realize that the publication may not print it in full or without modification. Editors may make changes to the article based on their perceptions of readers' knowledge and interests, or to make your text conform to the publication's writing style.

In addition to the article text you may also want to submit other materials to make the editor's job easier. Include a list of supplemental materials, photos, customer and internal contacts, or other resources you can provide to the editor. Always include or suggest visuals that can be used with the article. Photos, illustrations, diagrams, code examples, and flowcharts are possible images that can accompany your text. In some cases the publication will use these visuals directly; in other cases, they will adapt them to their own style or use their own images.

Attach a complete caption to all photos, diagrams, and illustrations that you submit. This helps to ensure the accuracy of model numbers or other product information, and the correct spelling of names. A caption also can support the messages presented in the article text.

Content Ideas:

The text techniques described in Chapter 7 may help you transform your raw material into an interesting, polished article. An article can accommodate many of the content types described in Chapter 5 and the document elements covered in Chapter 6. An additional document element for most articles is a sentence or paragraph of author information including names, titles, and company affiliations.

BACKGROUNDER

A backgrounder is a document that provides in-depth information on a company, technology, or product. Most high-tech companies produce two types of backgrounders—one for each product or product line and one for the company. A backgrounder gives detailed, context information to a journalist, supplementing a press release that may present only the basic facts about the product. Depending on their content, white papers also may be used as product backgrounders (see Chapter 10).

While backgrounders are used primarily as press materials, they may also be appropriate to include in the sales collateral for a product or company. However, backgrounders usually have an information purpose that should be reflected in the writing style, organization, and content.

Content Ideas—Product Backgrounder:

A product backgrounder describes the design and function of a product or its underlying technology (Figure 11.2). It can accommodate any of the content types described in the "Product Information" section in Chapter 6. Most product backgrounders include a mix of the following information:

- A discussion of the product's architecture or design.
- Information on product configurations or applications.
- Diagrams to show product functionality, architecture, data flow, operational processes, configuration, or other concepts.
- A description of the product's physical characteristics.
- A description of the relationship to other products in the product line or to products and technologies from other companies.
- A description of product components, options, or accessory products.
- An overview of the product's development history.
- A discussion of future plans or strategies for product development or marketing.
- A comparison with competitive or alternative products, technologies, or methods.
- Purchasing information, including pricing, distribution channels, and availability dates.
- Information on contacts for editors (usually a public relations person) and for readers who want more information about the product (usually your primary sales information contact).

Content Ideas—Corporate Backgrounder:

A corporate backgrounder presents an overview of the company's capabilities, structure, and operation (Figure 11.3). It can accommodate any of the content types described in the "Company Information" section in Chapter 6. Most corporate backgrounders include a mix of the following information:

- A company description, including history, strategies, domestic and international operations and information on parent, subsidiary, and affiliated companies.

A Subsidiary of ADC Telecommunications, Inc.

14375 NW Science Park Dr.
Portland, Oregon 97229
(503) 643-1681
FAX (503) 641-3341

Backgrounder

Technology Backgrounder

ADC Kentrox CityCell™ 824

A New Standard in Cellular Network Access and Management

Editorial Contact:
Lynn Epstein
(503) 643-1681
March, 1993

 Printed on recycled paper

Figure 11.2   A technical or product backgrounder provides detailed information about a product's design, functionality, or underlying technology.

and overlap to provide total coverage of an area (see Figure 1). When a user is moving from one cell to another, the signal from the serving antenna is "handed-off" to the next cell. This hand-off is designed to provide the user with uninterrupted operation.

Figure 1. The cellular concept.

However, in the real world, things don't always work as planned especially as subscriber demand and network complexity increases. Sometimes, the coverage between cells doesn't overlap and dropped calls occur during the hand-off. Another problem is caused by the inability of the cellular signal to provide coverage inside structures such as office buildings, shopping centers, airports, or tunnels. Or dead spots can be caused by hills and large buildings. Added to this can be problems caused by overloading or distortion from noise or weak signals due to interference or distance from the antenna.

As cellular carriers look for solutions to these and other problems, they need to keep the following in mind when selecting a network expansion alternative:

- **Coverage** — How can they provide the required coverage when and where needed in order to eliminate dropped calls or to stimulate demand in new areas, indoors and underground, and achieve true ubiquity of service?
- **Capacity** — How many additional channels are needed to meet subscriber demand?
- **Clarity** — Is the current signal strong enough without noise and distortion?
- **Connectivity** — What is the optimum solution for the transport of information among cell sites and switching centers?
- **Cost** — Which solution provides the best coverage, capacity, and clarity at the most economical cost — both present and future?

Figure 11.2 *continued*

⁂ HARRIS

Harris Corporation
Digital Telephone Systems Division
At-A-Glance

COMPANY OVERVIEW

Harris Corporation, Digital Telephone Systems (Harris DTS), a major manufacturer of high-reliability digital switching systems, is a worldwide provider of specialized telecommunications products and solutions for integrated voice and data switching communications — both hardware and software.

Harris DTS actively participates in international standards committees, and adheres to the prescribed codes of national and international standards to ensure future compatibility in the rapidly advancing digital telecommunications network technology.

Rigorous engineering standards and extensive quality assurance have helped make Harris DTS a global leader in communications technology and equipment reliability. An example of recognition for Harris DTS' innovation and reliability is the success of our Voice Switching and Control System (VSCS). Our commercial switching technology is the foundation of the Federal Aviation Administration's air traffic control upgrade which requires 99.99999 per cent availability.

BUSINESS MARKETS

Harris DTS develops integrated voice and data switching platforms and solutions for:
• Computer-telephony integrated enhanced services
• Operator service providers
• Advanced call centers
• Public and private telecommunications networks
• Correctional institutions
• Government and defense
• Hospitality industry
• Health, legal, and financial establishments
• Businesses of all sizes

PRODUCT OVERVIEW

At the core of our telecommunications solutions is the Integrated Network Platform (INP). Designed to serve today's and tomorrow's complex and demanding public and private telecommunications networks, the INP's powerful capabilities, versatility, exceptional reliability, and easy upgradeability make it the ideal foundation for telecommunications systems around the world.

A fourth-generation voice, data and video digital switching platform, the INP provides exceptional call throughput exceeding 25,000 calls per hour, ensuring that internal traffic, customer service calls, and emergency demands are easily met. Both on-site and remote administration of databases, alarm diagnostics, and traffic statistics are possible.

The INP offers universal port architecture, full common equipment redundancy with hot standby mode and 100 percent nonblocking operation. Future growth is also included in the design. The INP's modular hardware and software allow the platform to be expanded or altered easily and economically. The INP optionally offers an ISDN Primary Rate Interface (23 B+D and 30 B+D) for readily interfacing with a sophisticated public networks offering ISDN, as well as private and leased T1/E1 networks.

Figure 11.3   This corporate backgrounder presents the essential information in a highlight format.

Source: © 1994, Harris Corporation. Reproduced by permission.

• Information on the company's key markets and position in each. May include a list of major customers and information on distribution channels and alliances.

The design flexibility of the INP accommodates the traditional business products including:

- Private Branch Exchanges
- Automatic Call Distribution Systems
- Correctional Facility Systems
- Hotel/Motel Systems

All of these functions can be integrated in a single system platform.

The INP is a multi-functional digital switching platform that offers greater flexibility in designing a telecommunications system. Some of the more sophisticated, wide range of technologically advanced hardware and software product applications the INP offers include the following:

- Protocall 2000 Enhanced Services System, automated and live operator services, pre-and post-paid (debit and travel) card calling, and inmate call management
- VoiceFrame enhanced services platform
- Integrated advanced automatic call distribution (ACD) and ACD management systems (AMS)
- Enhanced Digital Telephone Exchange switches
- Secure network switches

PARENT AFFILIATION

Harris DTS is a division of Harris Corporation, a $3 billion worldwide, Fortune 200 company that uses advanced technologies to provide innovative and cost-effective solutions to the challenges faced by commercial and government customers throughout the world. Harris Corporation's four major business focuses are:

- Communications
- Semiconductors
- Electronic systems
- Lanier Worldwide Office Equipment

Harris Corporation's technology expertise and worldwide leadership in these areas provides the Harris DTS division with the financial and R&D resources it needs to maintain technology and market leadership.

SALES/DISTRIBUTION

In the U.S., Harris DTS markets its products through a nationwide distributor network, value-added resellers, its own direct sales force, and other Harris divisions. Each member of the direct sales team specializes in select vertical markets and then serves as a consulting advisor to other salespeople and distributors in regions outside their own sales territory. Harris DTS offers business partnerships worldwide to third parties, system integrators, and value-added resellers with specific market focuses to jointly provide custom, industry-specific solutions.

For over 25 years, Harris DTS has sold its products internationally. Harris DTS' international sales comprise more than 50 percent of the division's revenue. Products are marketed through authorized, independent distributors and technology transfers in more than 130 countries worldwide, including the following regions:

- North America
- Central America
- South America
- Eastern and Western Europe
- Middle East
- Pacific Rim and Asia
- People's Republic of China
- Russia
- India
- Africa

HARRIS CORPORATION   DIGITAL TELEPHONE SYSTEMS DIVISION
300 BEL MARIN KEYS BLVD.   P.O. BOX 1188, NOVATO, CA 94948-1188   (415) 382-5000   FAX (415) 883-1626

Figure 11.3 *continued*

- An overview of products developed and marketed by the company.
- Biographies of company executives and a list of directors or investors.

- A description of quality processes and customer support programs.
- An analysis of competitors by product line or by market.
- Information on contacts for editors (usually a public relations person) and for readers who want more information about the company (usually your primary sales information contact).

CASE STUDY

A case study is typically an article that describes how a particular customer uses a product, the problem it solved, and the benefits obtained. Many trade publications make extensive use of case studies, either as full-length feature articles or as brief fillers. A case study also can be written in a brochure or data sheet format and used as part of the sales collateral for a product (Figures 11.4 and 11.5).

Case studies are a powerful marketing tool. They build credibility for a product by providing references and helping prospects understand how the product relates to their problems and circumstances.

Developing an effective case study involves showing the "hows and whys" of a customer's situation or decision. It should emphasize the results achieved by the customer, both quantitative (such as financial data or productivity statistics) and qualitative (such as operational improvements). To get this information, ask probing, open-ended questions when you interview the customer. You may want to start the interview with a list of standard questions, but explore other ideas that add to the interest of the case study when they arise in the conversation.

Before you publish the case study, obtain written approval on the text from all relevant authorities in the customer's organization. When a case study will appear as an article in a trade magazine, you may want to give your customer the byline.

Content Ideas:

A case study can include many of the content types described in the "Applications" and "Customer Information" sections in Chapter 6. In addition, a case study can include any mix of the following information:

- A "before-and-after" description of the customer's problem, environment, or operation.

- A description of the evaluation or decision process the customer used when your product was selected.
- Information on results achieved.
- A discussion of product implementation.
- Background information on the customer's industry or trends reflected by the customer's actions.
- Diagrams or photos of the customer's environment or use of the product.
- Names of contacts at the customer's organization and your company.

FACT SHEET

A fact sheet is a single page of key information about a product, event, or company. Fact sheets help reporters quickly find the most commonly requested information (Figure 11.6). They are a standard component of press kits and may accompany individual press releases.

Content Ideas—Company Fact Sheet:

A company fact sheet can include any of the content types described in the "Company Information" section in Chapter 6. Most include the following items:

- A brief company description including date founded and names of founders or company executives.
- A statement of revenue and other key financial data for the most recent fiscal year or year-to-date.
- A brief overview of products and services offered by the company.
- A list of markets or customers and a brief statement about distribution channels and international operations.
- A description of sales, manufacturing, laboratory, or other significant facilities or resources.
- Number of employees.

Content Ideas—Product Fact Sheet:

A product fact sheet can include any of the content types described in the "Product Information" section in Chapter 6. Most describe the following items:

Connecting urban doctors and rural patients

Frontier country: That's how many people describe the rugged and isolated plains of eastern Montana. Imagine driving 300 miles to visit a specialist physician in the cold, bitter grip of a Montana winter.

The Eastern Montana Telemedicine Project, sponsored by Deaconess Medical Center in Billings, is testing one potential solution. Currently in a trial period, the Project uses videoconferencing over T1 to connect five small rural hospitals and clinics with medical and mental health specialists at Deaconess.

"We have three major applications we want to develop during this trial," says Jim Reid, project director and a certified physician assistant. "First is the delivery of medical and mental health consultations between rural and urban providers. Second is continuing medical and higher education over the system. The third is what we call community development applications—use by the rural community at large."

Using a compressed interactive video link, specialists in Billings provide diagnostic and consultation services for patients and physicians at the rural sites. On-line interpretation of X-rays, EKGs, pathology slides and other medical images can be performed over the network.

Take the example of a 14-year-old boy who sustained a serious pelvic fracture during a football game. The local physician was able to transmit X-rays to an orthopedist at Deaconess, who then advised the boy's doctor on how to treat him locally.

"The boy and his mother were able to participate in the conference with both doctors," says Bert Lepel, a physician assistant at Roosevelt Hospital in Culbertson, Mont. "Without this system we would have had to send him to Billings."

Telemedicine improves communication between the patient's local physician and the specialist at Deaconess. Both doctors can simultaneously view medical images, test results or data in the patient's record. The local doctor can make the most appropriate referral and the local facility can perform more pre-admission tests and procedures. The relationship between the patient and the primary physician is preserved, resulting in greater continuity of care and less duplication of services.

The telemedicine concept can be applied with similar efficacy to mental health services. While physicians are in short supply in rural communities, there is an even greater shortage of skilled mental health providers. As a result, rural residents must travel even longer distances for psychiatric care. The Project has already proved the benefits for mental health services with a conference session established between a female inpatient in Deaconess' psychiatric unit and her children at the hometown clinic.

"This conference really encouraged her to pursue her treatment plan and return home as quickly as possible," Reid notes.

Project structure

Deaconess is a 272-bed center offering a variety of medical specialty programs in a service area that covers more than 121,000 square miles of eastern Montana, northern Wyoming and the western Dakotas. The hospital also operates a 60-bed inpatient psychiatric facility that provides a wide range of mental health services.

Deaconess has long recognized the challenges of delivering advanced medical care to rural areas. Solutions included an airplane ambulance, scheduled clinic visits by specialist physicians and a traveling physician service.

The Project currently connects five rural health-care facilities in eastern Montana with Deaconess. The network is used for medical and mental health consultations, administrative meetings and delivery of continuing medical education courses.

Practice of video-based telemedicine

Continued on page 29

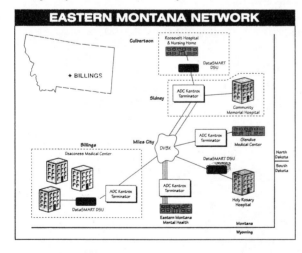

EASTERN MONTANA NETWORK

Figure 11.4   This case study was developed as a feature story for publication in a trade magazine. The diagram was submitted by the company along with the article.

Source: Reproduced by permission from *Communication News*, February 1994 issue.

AUDIO/VIDEOCONFERENCING

URBAN/RURAL continued from page 26...

has been endorsed by the American Medical Association (AMA) and the American Psychiatric Association (APA).

Financing for the Project has come from a combination of grants, in-kind contributions and hospital funds. An advisory group meets monthly via videoconferencing to address planning and policy issues.

A site coordinator at each local facility schedules the conference room and equipment. In addition, a project coordinator at Deaconess maintains a master schedule to facilitate connection of the local sites to each other and to prevent conflicts in network usage. The local coordinators also handle equipment set-up and operation, as well as registrations for the medical education courses delivered over the network.

The network

The Project network is comprised of leased T1 facilities from US West, digital service units and network access concentrators from ADC Kentrox and PC-based videoconferencing equipment from VTel.

T1s between the six sites are daisy chained to minimize costs and support multipoint conferencing. Each location can access a 384 kb/s channel for video and a 384 kb/s channel for data. Three sites also access voice circuits on the Deaconess phone switch via the T1 lines.

Equipment at the rural sites includes a video codec, two monitors, two video cameras, an audio system, control devices, graphics tablets and a fax interface. At Deaconess, this equipment package is supplemented by control consoles that can link multiple remote sites.

Diagnostic gear such as ultrasound machines, video microscopes or otoscopes with an attached video camera can be connected as camera sources. All of this equipment generates a standard video signal; interfaces also can be developed for other medical equipment such as EKG machines.

One part of Reid's job at Deaconess is to research new ways to provide medical services to the hospital's rural areas. When he first learned about the telemedicine concept more than three years ago, his first response was, "We need to pursue this."

Like all new networks, the Project encountered some stumbling blocks along the way. Excessive noise on the T1 lines was an initial problem, but Project staffers were able to work with the carrier to reduce this problem by installing a DACS at the access point in Billings and using the diagnostics capabilities of the network access equipment.

Based on his experience, Reid rec-

ommends that other health-care facilities proceed methodically with implementation of a telemedicine project.

"You need to make sure that the initial few sites work well before bringing additional sites on-line," he says. "This minimizes the number of variables you need to troubleshoot."

Project staff are promoting the Telemedicine Project facilities to local businesses and community organizations for use as a videoconferencing service at no charge during the trial period. By improving communication between businesses and their customers or suppliers, this service is expected to make a positive contribution to local economic development efforts. As an additional benefit, this revenue-generating service will help each community cover its portion of the ongoing operational costs for the network after the trial period.

Project staff will use the results of the trial as a basis for deciding where and how to expand the network in the future. Additional health-care facilities and two correctional centers within the Deaconess service area may be added to the network. A recent grant award from the Rural Electrification Administration (REA) enabled the Project to purchase the videoconferencing and network access equipment for use beyond the trial period.

CN

Figure 11.4 *continued*

- Hardware components in the product.
- Software incorporated into or supported by the product.
- Key features and benefits.
- System requirements and platforms supported; localized versions available.
- Suggested retail price, distribution channels, and availability dates.

PRESS KIT

A press kit is a collection of press releases, fact sheets, backgrounders, photos, diagrams, and other material that gives a reporter or analyst complete information about a product, service, event, or company. It is not a media kit, which is a package that publications use to market their advertising space.

Companies have used Lotus Notes to create useful applications for their sales and marketing needs including:

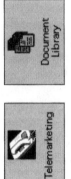

SALES AND
MARKETING

Client
Correspondence

Client Correspondence
Stores client names and
addresses Includes an easy-
to-use way to draft customer
letters mail merge documents
and faxes.

Sales
Discussion

Sales Discussion
Lets the sales team share
information and conduct
discussions without having
to be in the same room at
the same time.

Customer
Tracking

Customer Tracking
Tracks all activity related to
the customer—action items,
call reports and meeting
reports

Status
Report

Status Report
Tracks the progress of people
on any type of project. Keeps
sales team members up to
date on all activities.

Telemarketing

Telemarketing
Lets users read from a tele-
marketing script and record
the customer's information—
all within the same document.

Document
Library

Document Library
Servers as a centralized
repository for presentations
technical data and other
materials that aid the sales
process

HOW LOTUS NOTES WORKS FOR SALES AND MARKETING

These days, a single follow-up call can mean the difference between making a big sale and losing a big customer. Lotus Notes gives your team that crucial edge. Customized Sales and Marketing applications can allow the entire sales force simultaneous access to the same up-to-date information – from client correspondence to status reports to research and technical documents.

And remote-access capabilities let your people work just as easily from the road as from the office Sales representatives can communicate more directly, share ideas track trends route purchase orders – whatever they need to do from wherever they happen to be. So your sales force acts faster and moves more efficiently

By opening the lines of communication in the office and on the road Lotus Notes creates an environment where productivity and sales can be increased almost effortlessly.

Figure 11.5   An application profile is a variation of a case study that shows a product's potential use for a particular function or industry.

APRIL 1993

COMPANY OVERVIEW

Sequent Computer Systems, Inc., headquartered in Beaverton, Ore., is a leading architect of open systems solutions for commercial OLTP and decision support applications. The company develops and markets scalable computing systems that support enterprise-wide applications and information services. Sequent is the market share leader in the large ($700,000 plus) UNIX systems market.*

PRODUCTS

Sequent designs, manufacturers and markets the Symmetry® 2000 series of tightly coupled, symmetrical multiprocessing (SMP) systems which dynamically balance the processing load among a pool of 1 to 30 Intel® 486™ microprocessors. The systems range in price from $9,995 to more than $2.5 million. DYNIX/ptx® is Sequent's multiprocessor enhanced, POSIX™ and X/Open®-compliant version of UNIX® System V operating system for the Symmetry 2000 series. In 1990, Sequent was selected by UNIX System Laboratories (USL) as the primary development partner for UNIX Systems V.4 ES/MP, an enhanced security and multiprocessing version of UNIX V.4. In 1991, Sequent was selected by the Open Software Foundation (OSF) as the multiprocessor development and reference platform for OSF/1 Release 1.2. Sequent is currently developing a new family of Microsoft® Windows NT™-based database and application servers for workgroup, department-level and enterprise-wide computing.

MANAGEMENT

Casey Powell, chairman, chief executive officer and president
Michael Simon, senior vice president of corporate development; corporate secretary
Bob Gregg, vice president and chief financial officer
Dennis Peck , senior vice president of marketing
Roger Cooper, senior vice president of geographic operations

FINANCIALS

Sequent (NASDAQ: SQNT) reported net income of $3.4 million on revenues of $77.6 million for the first quarter of fiscal 1993, the strongest first quarter results in the company's history. Net income for the quarter, ended April 3, was more than triple first quarter 1992 net income of $1.0 million. Revenues for 1992 were $307.3 million.

INSTALLATIONS

Since the launch of its symmetric multiprocessing family in 1984, Sequent has directly installed more than 4,500 systems worldwide.

EMPLOYEES

Sequent employs more than 1,600 people worldwide.

*InfoCorp Unix and Applications Study, January 1993.

Figure 11.6   A fact sheet provides the essential information about a product or company in a brief, quick-reference format.
Source: Sequent Computer Systems, Inc. Reproduced by permission.

Because it includes multiple loose documents, a press kit is usually packaged in a presentation folder (Figure 11.7). You do not need to include all of the pieces described here in every press kit you distribute. Instead, choose the documents that are the most relevant to each editor, and include a list of other documents that are available.

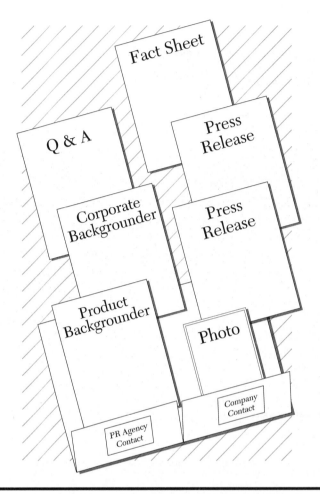

Figure 11.7   A press kit provides a variety of information about a product or company, in a package convenient for journalists.

Some companies provide their press kits on disk, as a way to both reduce costs and make information access simpler for journalists. According to Middleberg, the advantages of putting press materials onto disk include: easier handling than bulky printed press kits, easy access to information, the ability to transfer text and images from your disk to a story, and faster updates.[122] Verify the disk and file format used by each of your target publications to ensure the editors can actually use the disk when they receive it.

Content Ideas:

In addition to press releases, backgrounders, and other standard press materials, consider including the following documents in a press kit:

- Reprints of articles already published about your product or company. Always show the name of the publication and the date or issue number in which the article appeared.
- Biographies of company executives.
- Annual reports, product brochures, and the company newsletter.
- Customer case studies.
- Copy of a speech or presentation made by a company executive or technical expert.
- Demo disk or demo line information.
- List of topic ideas for feature articles or interviews related to your product, industry, or company. The goal of this document is to encourage an editor to write or commission an article based on one of your suggested topics.
- Indication of whether additional materials, photos, screen shots, evaluation units, customer and industry analyst contacts, or interviews can be provided to editors.
- Each page of every document labeled with your company name, the title or headline, date, a contact phone number, and "Page x of y."
- Complete captions for all photos, diagrams, and illustrations.

PRESS RELEASE

A press release is a document that attempts to generate publicity by announcing current news about a company, product, service, or event (Figure 11.8). A press release is usually developed as a printed piece, but also may be produced as a video news release that is distributed for broadcast on television news programs.

A special form of a press release is the *media alert*. This public relations document does just what its name implies: It alerts journalists to an upcoming event they are invited to attend. For high-tech companies, media alerts are often used to announce press conferences or special demonstrations at trade shows. A media alert is typically a single-page document that provides only the essential information about the event.

The subject of a press release must be genuinely newsworthy in order to catch an editor's attention. Many events and activities can justify a press release, including:

- **Product information.** Announcement of new products, options, add-ons, or upgrades; new applications or platforms

For more information contact:

Sequent Computer Systems, Inc.   **Hold For Release**
Mike Green or Tami Sturdevant   **Until May 3, 1993**
(503) 626-5700

Waggener Edstrom
Wendy Hughson or Arlene Watkins
(503) 245-0905

Sequent and Microsoft Expand Joint Efforts to Provide Scalable, Preconfigured SMP Servers
Programs Include Cooperative Engineering, Service and Marketing for Windows NT Servers

BEAVERTON, Ore. — May 3, 1993 — Sequent Computer Systems, Inc. today announced an expansion of its joint development with Microsoft Corporation to make high-performance servers extremely scalable and easy for customers to deploy and operate. The joint working agreement outlines the companies' commitment to cooperative engineering, service, training and marketing programs intended to provide customers with turnkey symmetric multiprocessing (SMP) application and database servers. As an initial step toward delivering easy-to-use and easy-to-deploy servers, Sequent will preintegrate its custom-configured SMP WinServer® systems with the Microsoft® Windows NT™ Advanced Server operating system and database and applications software. For the first time, customers will be able to deploy complex, high-performance application servers with an ease approaching that of PCs.

The expansion of the relationship includes the following:

- Sequent will preinstall and preconfigure Windows NT Advanced Server as well as leading database and applications software on all models of its new WinServer family. Sequent will work with customers to custom-configure their hardware, operating system, networking, database and applications software to deliver servers that are ready to deploy. Future plans include the licensing of other Microsoft products, including connectivity and system management tools, for the WinServer series.

- more -

Figure 11.8 **This press release illustrates many of the content ideas described in this section, including an embargo date, subhead, and quotes from both companies involved in the announcement.**
Source: Sequent Computer Systems, Inc. Reproduced by permission.

for an existing product; price changes (especially if the price is reduced).

- **Company information.** Announcement of new customers and alliances; acquisitions and divestitures; organizational

- Sequent is a Microsoft Solutions Channel Partner. The field sales divisions of both companies, together with Sequent® Professional Services, will collaborate to assess customers' business requirements and to configure and deliver integrated client-server solutions on WinServer systems.

- Sequent and Microsoft service engineers will work together to quickly diagnose and correct customer problems to maximize system availability for customers running mission-critical applications. Sequent will have ready access to Microsoft's extensive technical information and resources to ensure the appropriate and immediate action for WinServer customers.

- The agreement extends the SMP optimization activities with additional shared engineering projects. For example, Sequent engineers have been working closely with the Microsoft SQL Server and Windows NT development groups to assure scalability and performance on large-scale SMP systems. Since mid-1992, Sequent has demonstrated the industry's most powerful, high-end SMP systems combining up to 16 microprocessors running Windows NT. Microsoft will demonstrate Windows NT scalability on WinServers at the series debut at Database Expo and at Windows World in May.

"Sequent is a world leader in SMP servers for large-scale client-server environments," said Dwayne Walker, director of Windows NT and networking products at Microsoft. "This relationship will allow Sequent to bring the benefits of Windows on high-performance SMP platforms to all types of organizations by delivering complete, easy-to-deploy Windows NT servers throughout the enterprise — from workgroups to departments and data centers."

"Combining the enterprise-capable Windows NT with our scalable SMP technology gives customers a powerful new tool in deploying business-critical, client-server applications," said Casey Powell, Sequent president and CEO. "Our cooperative work with Microsoft reflects our mutual commitment to make these benefits available to customers in an easy-to-use solution."

Sequent Computer Systems, Inc. (NASDAQ: SQNT) is a leading architect of open systems solutions for commercial OLTP and decision support applications. Sequent develops and markets scalable SMP computing systems that support enterprise-wide applications and information services. Since the launch of its symmetric multiprocessor systems in 1984, Sequent has installed more than 4,500 large-scale systems worldwide.

###

Figure 11.8 *continued*

changes; new facilities or expansion into new market areas. (Remember to describe the benefits from a customer's or prospect's perspective.)

· **Event information.** Notice of demonstrations at trade shows; reports on user-group meetings related to your product; announcement of event sponsorships by your company. For a media alert, all facts related to the event: date and time, location, type of activity, a description of what will be announced or demonstrated at the event, names of key participants. Description of facilities or services that will be available to attending journalists, such as the opportunity for individual interviews with customers or company executives. Instructions on how to register for the event (if necessary).

Press releases follow a standard format that incorporates the elements listed below. For detailed instructions and examples, refer to *The Associated Press Stylebook and Libel Manual* (see Bibliography).

- **Release date.** The date when the information in the press release can be published. Stated either as *For Immediate Release* or as an embargo date *Hold Until:* (date and time). The release date may or may not be the same as the date of the actual announcement or event.
- **Editorial contacts.** Always list the person from your company an editor can call for more information. List a contact person from each company involved if you are making a joint announcement with a customer, alliance partner, or other company. List the contact at your public relations agency if appropriate and in-country contacts for releases that are distributed internationally. For each contact person, give the full name; office, home, cellular, and fax phone numbers (if appropriate); and e-mail address if accessible from one of the public services such as the Internet or MCI Mail.
- **Headline.** The headline should be a summary of the most essential news in the release. An alternative to a headline is a summary box at the beginning of the release. This box presents the most essential facts in bullet list or brief narrative form. Also consider placing summary statements or key facts in the left margin of the release for quick reference by an editor.
- **Dateline.** The date and place of the announcement: *Bellevue, WA May 1, 1994—*. The place may be a trade show or press conference if the announcement is being made there. The date on the dateline may or may not be the same as the release date when the press release is issued.
- **Opener.** State the 5Ws (Who, What, When, Where and Why) as the opening sentence or paragraph. Get to the point immediately; avoid prepositional and participial phrases as the lead

in the opening sentence.[11] (See the section on "Openers" in Chapter 5.)

- **Body.** Follow the standards of news writing when writing the body copy for the release. Present an overview of the whole story and the most important facts in the first paragraph, then use the remaining paragraphs for supporting information. Write the body copy so an editor can end the story after any paragraph without losing important information. Include the title and affiliation for any persons quoted in the release (see the section "Citing Sources" in Chapter 6). Use trademark symbols where appropriate in the text and include trademark acknowledgments at the end of the release.
- **Customer contact.** Include information on how a reader can contact your company in the body of the release. This may be a different person than the editorial contacts listed on the release.
- **Company boilerplate.** A press release usually ends with a paragraph of general information about your company. This includes the ticker symbol and exchange if the company's stock is publicly traded.
- **Formatting Elements.** The standard format for press releases includes double-spaced text, printed single-side, at least a one-inch margin on all sides, and notations that indicate the continuation (*–more–*) and end of the release (*–30–*, *###, –end–*)

Q & A DOCUMENT

A question-and-answer document does just what its name implies. It presents answers to the questions most commonly asked about a product or company. This document helps journalists understand user interests and thus write more effectively targeted articles (Figure 11.9).

Content Ideas:

- Include information that is not presented in other materials in the press kit because it is very detailed or secondary to the announcement or other news.
- Include a question for every key message in your announcement.

PANLABS

Panlabs Q&A

1. What is Panlabs?

Panlabs is a privately owned contract research laboratory that provides science services for the pharmaceutical industry, specializing in identifying therapeutic leads and improving products and processes. Panlabs takes an interdisciplinary team approach, providing affordable innovation on novel projects, and reliable solutions to routine projects. Founded in 1970 and headquartered in Bothell, Wash., Panlabs employs more than 330 people, has laboratory facilities in Bothell, Wash., Taipei, Taiwan, and representatives in the United Kingdom, France, Japan and Australia.

2. What is the scope of the pharmaceutical industry, and how do contract research firms fit within that arena?

The pharmaceutical industry is a global one. According to SCRIP, a newsletter covering the industry, the U.S. has a 30 percent market for pharmaceuticals sold; Europe has 30 percent, followed by Japan at 18 percent. The budget for pre-clinical research in the pharmaceutical industry is estimated at approximately 15 percent of pharmaceutical companies' annual research and development budget.

According to a recent article in *Medical Marketing News*, the market for contract research is growing faster than the total R&D budget of pharmaceutical companies, which averages 14 percent of sales. The reason for this growth is that many companies are contracting out more of their research because it requires resources and expertise often not available in-house due to headcount and budgetary restraints. The use of contract research firms such as Panlabs can help bring drugs to market faster, and every day saved in this process can add to a company's profits.

3. Who uses Panlabs, and for what sort of projects?

Panlabs has completed projects ranging from new drug discovery, bioconversion and classical fermentation to compound profiling, synthesis, isolation and analysis. Many of the world's prominent companies such as Sterling, Merck, CIBA-Geigy, Astra, Hindustan Antibiotics, Toyo Jozo and Yoshitomi have taken advantage of Panlabs' expertise and experience, and Panlabs believes it has one of the highest repeat contract rates in the industry.

Panlabs Incorporated
11804 North Creek Parkway South
Bothell, WA 98011-8805 U.S.A.
(206) 487-8200   FAX: (206) 487-3787   Telex: 517335 (PAN LABS SEA)

Figure 11.9   A question and answer document provides responses to the questions asked most frequently about a product or company.
Source: Panlabs, Inc. Reproduced by permission.

4. *What is the advantage of using a contract science research firm instead of in-house teams?*

    In the current competitive market, staff constraints and overhead costs keep in-house teams from being able to tackle all the projects that companies must accomplish in order to bring new drugs to the market. By using a contract research firm such as Panlabs, in-house scientists are free to work on other projects that help to bring new drugs to the market and contribute to profit margins.

5. *How is Panlabs different than other contract research firms?*

    Panlabs' strength as a biotechnology contract research firm is that it offers a strong service orientation and provides timely results. Panlabs functions as a strategic partner with clients, typically charging a fixed fee for services, so that clients know the cost of a project from the beginning. This is unlike most university contract research teams, which often require expensive licensing arrangements, and also unlike other biotechnology companies, which often don't give client projects the same priority as in-house projects.

    Panlabs has also mastered the art of interdisciplinary teams, integrating its chemistry, molecular biology, microbiology, pharmacology and natural products sciences to achieve research goals as quickly as possible. This means that instead of taking a linear approach and trying solutions one at a time, Panlabs' teams of experts look at the problem from more than one scientific perspective. Panlabs functions as a strategic research partner with clients, often delivering research goals more cost effectively than in-house research groups.

6. *What problems currently facing the pharmaceutical industry can Panlabs help clients solve?*

    Two challenging problems facing the pharmaceutical industry today are finding new drug leads and creating cost effective ways to screen them. Panlabs can help clients solve these problems through the pharmacology, discovery and profiling and natural products services it offers.

    For more than five years, Panlabs has been discovering new chemical structures and novel biological activities using natural products as the source material. If clients have natural or synthetic compounds that need to be evaluated, Panlabs offers some of the most comprehensive assay programs available. Services include profiling of selected leads and high throughput screening for discovery of new leads. In addition to these programs, Panlabs also offers services designed to improve microbial strains in terms of potency or yield, and improve manufacturing processes.

Page 2

Figure 11.9 *continued*

EXERCISES

1. Request an editorial calendar and writer's guidelines from a key trade publication for your company. Write a document plan for an article you might submit to that publication.
2. Take an existing press kit and compare its materials to those described in this chapter. Does it contain additional materials not described here? How would you change the content of the press kit for different publications?
3. Plan a press kit for a product launch and one for a first-ever user's conference. Describe the materials you would include in each kit and the target recipients.

CHAPTER 12

Alliance Materials

Reaching Dealers and Partners

For every product there is a salesperson, probably a distributor, dealer, or retail store, perhaps a solutions developer or other marketing partner. All of these sales people need information that will help them sell your product successfully.

This chapter describes the types of marketing materials commonly used to attract, educate, and motivate sales people, dealers, and alliance partners.

APPLICATION GUIDE

The more complex your product, the more you probably need an application guide to help your sales force explain it and your prospects understand it. This type of guide is especially valuable for products that truly involve an "application sell," where a salesperson shows how multiple products or features can be combined to solve a prospect's unique problem (Figure 12.1).

An application guide is a booklet or reference that presents information about potential product uses, often categorized according to customer type or industry. It is a guide for choosing among products, models, or configurations within a product line to meet a specific need. An application guide also can suggest applications for a product when they may not be obvious from an initial assessment of the product's features.

Application guides can be organized by product, by market or industry, or by application type. Some companies produce application guides for use only by the sales staff or dealers, while others develop guides that also are suitable for distribution to potential buyers.

NetMaker XA Solutions for Managing the Network Life Cycle

	REAL-TIME REACTIVE						LONG-TERM STRATEGIC PLANNING
	HOURLY	HOURLY	DAILY	MONTHLY	QUARTERLY	YEARLY	
NETWORK MANAGEMENT CYCLES	Real-Time Ops	Demand Change	Configuration Change	Topology Change	Device/Vendor Change	Technology Change	
NETMAKER XA TOOLS		Interpreter Visualizer	Analyzer Planner Accountant	Designer			
JOB FUNCTION	Network Operations	Project Manager System Administrator	Analyst Engineer	Planner Designer	Network Manager	Strategic Planner	

© 1994 Make Systems Inc.

Figure 12.1 This application guide, in the form of a matrix, shows the match of product modules to a user's activities and job functions.

Source: © 1994, Make Systems, Inc. Reproduced by permission.

Readers should be able to understand the organization of the guide quickly and find specific information easily. This means presenting similar information or content types consistently and clearly identifying optional or configuration-specific items.

Content Ideas:

An application guide can accommodate many of the document elements and content types described in Chapters 5 and 6. In addition, application guides often include:

- A table of contents and indexes by product name, model or part number; cross-references to options or accessory products.
- Charts, checklists, or worksheets to show the match between products and applications.
- Design or configuration diagrams.
- Guidelines for planning an application.
- A list of product-selection criteria.
- A glossary of product, technical, or industry terminology.
- Company information.
- Ordering information or a reply card to request additional product information.

PARTNERS PROGRAM BROCHURE

If your company sells extensively through dealers, marketing partners, or third-party developers, you may develop a complete set of marcom materials targeted to this group. A partners program brochure is the most common of these materials. It describes the benefits of working with your company, the market opportunities addressed by your products, and the programs, services, and support offered to partners (Figure 12.2).

Content Ideas:

A partners program brochure can incorporate many of the content types described in Chapter 6 for sales, services, and company information. More specifically, materials targeted to alliance partners usually describe:

- Benefits of becoming an alliance partner.
- Programs, materials, training, support, incentives, and other services and information offered to alliance partners.
- Requirements from candidates and procedures for acceptance into the partners program.

Figure 12.2   This brochure promotes a company's partnership program for external developers.

Source: © 1991, Dialogic Corporation. Reproduced by permission.

POINT-OF-SALE MATERIAL

If your product is sold in retail stores, you may write copy for small brochures, flyers, signs, or other pieces displayed in the area where a customer actually purchases your product. Called point-

The TECHNOLOGY DEVELOPER PROGRAM,™ part of the Open Development Program™ (OPEN™), provides you an opportunity to work with Dialogic and sell to a wide, established voice processing customer base. The Open Platform Environment™ brings technology users and you, the technology vendor, closer together by providing an accessible, flexible, industry-accepted architecture for your product development.

WHY SHOULD YOU BECOME A TECHNOLOGY DEVELOPER?

As a Dialogic TECHNOLOGY DEVELOPER, you have a way of integrating your products and services into the large installed base of Dialogic call processing equipment users. When you license a Design Package from Dialogic, you get the technical information you need to build extensions to your product. Dialogic Design Packages contain detailed specifications for Dialogic hardware and software components that allow you to develop products that are compatible with Dialogic's product architectures.

In addition to getting the in-depth product information provided in the Design Packages, membership in the TECHNOLOGY DEVELOPER PROGRAM means that you are eligible to receive qualified leads from Dialogic that supplement your own sales efforts.

WHAT'S A LEAD?

A sales lead is anyone who expresses an interest in your product. Someone who wants to buy your product immediately or someone who'll make a purchase sometime in the future. It's anyone who's interested in finding out more about your product.

HOW DOES DIALOGIC GENERATE LEADS FOR YOU?

You benefit from our advertising. Dialogic advertises in a wide range of publications in the voice processing, telephony, computing, and data communications industries. We run general purpose ads as well as targeting more select audiences. When we get inquiries from customers interested in purchasing a collateral technology that Dialogic does not provide, we want to pass these leads to you.

HOW DOES DIALOGIC INSURE SALES LEAD QUALITY?

When Dialogic receives a lead from a customer interested in the technology you provide, a Sales Engineer contacts that person by telephone to further qualify the opportunity. We track the publications in which we advertise and periodically evaluate the effectiveness of our placements.

WHAT ARE OTHER BENEFITS OF BEING A TECHNOLOGY DEVELOPER?

Because you are receiving leads generated from Dialogic's advertising, the scope of your own Sales and Marketing efforts is extended. Since we do advance qualification for you, your sales cycle is shortened. We supplement your resources by initially qualifying leads over the telephone and by mailing potential customers your sales and marketing literature.

Besides sales lead referrals and access to a large voice processing market of Dialogic product users, other benefits of being a TECHNOLOGY DEVELOPER include the following:

○ **Shorter development time.** Design Package documentation and Technical Support (a fee is charged for Design Package-related support) means that you spend less time developing the Dialogic-related parts of your product.

○ **Access to business opportunities.** Through participation in Open Development Seminars, you can become acquainted with Value Added Resellers and Original Equipment Manufacturers who are interested in incorporating your technology into their products. This includes access to the engineering layers of companies as well as top management.

○ **Joint design reviews.** Dialogic offers special design reviews for the Dialogic-related parts of your products under development (this is a fee-charged service).

○ **An avenue for productization.** The TECHNOLOGY DEVELOPERS PROGRAM provides a platform for discussing how Dialogic may license your technology for use in its own products.

We also contact you each quarter and evaluate the Program with you to make sure you are receiving the kinds of properly qualified leads you can turn into sales. You can always contact us with your questions or comments. Your input helps us refine the TECHNOLOGY DEVELOPER PROGRAM so it works better for you.

Figure 12.2 *continued*

of-sale (POS) or point-of-purchase materials, they may appear on shelves, kiosks, aisle ends, and cash-register counters (Figure 12.3).

The primary objective of these materials is to catch the attention of a browsing shopper and encourage him to read the product's package for more information or make an impulse purchase. POS materials can announce special offers such as a sale price,

PS/1® Essential
Model 2133-16E
33 MHz
486SX

IBM® PS/1

POWER MADE EASY

Complete computing: *power, performance and quality at a price you can afford, in a system so easy to use you'll be up and running in minutes!*

Hardware

Intel® 486SX™/33 MHz Processor	*Enjoy fast, powerful computing*
243 MB (DoubleSpace installed) **170 MB Hard Drive**	*Store and use thousands of files*
4 MB Memory (Expandable to 64 MB)	*Run multiple programs at once*
Local Bus SVGA Video (Max. resolution 1024 x 768)	*Run Windows™ faster with 512 KB video memory*
EXCLUSIVE **Smart Energy System™**	*Conserve time and money*
Combo Diskette Drive	*Run both 3.5" & 5.25" diskettes*
8 KB Cache	*Speed tasks: no-wait processing*
2400 bps Modem	*Send files and access online clubs*
EXCLUSIVE **Selectric Touch® Keyboard and Mouse**	

Expandability

3 AT® Slots and 3 Drive Bays	*Add industry-standard options*
Ready for OverDrive™	*Change your 486SX computer into a fast 486DX2™ machine!*

Over $600 Pre-Installed Software Value

MS-DOS® 6	*Includes DoubleSpace and MemMaker*
Windows 3.1	*Run multiple programs at once*
Works for Windows™	*Work productively with word processor, spreadsheet and database, all in one*
EXCLUSIVE **Software Preview™**	*Test-drive programs—then select one of four titles*
EXCLUSIVE **PS/1 Tutorial™**	*Learn Windows and pre-loaded software quickly and easily*
EXCLUSIVE **PS/1 Fitness™**	*Use IBM-exclusive utilities to personalize and expand your system*
EXCLUSIVE **PS/1 Index**	*Find shortcuts for virtually every task*

Figure 12.3 **This point-of-sale flier, placed in a retail store, gives a prospect the essential features and benefits of a product.**

Source: IBM Corporation. Reproduced by permission.

competitive upgrades, or special product package. They also can support promotional activity by a retailer.

Content Ideas:

POS materials typically focus on product information (see Chapter 6). They can use many of the text techniques described in Chapter 7. However, because you may be working with a small size and your message must attract attention at a glance, limit each piece to one high-impact message.

The following are the types of information most frequently presented in POS materials:

- Highlights of product features or a new version.
- Information on special prices or sales incentive offers.
- Quotes from product reviews or customer testimonials.
- Guarantee or warranty statements.

SALES GUIDE OR KIT

A sales guide is a book or package of information that helps a salesperson learn about a product and how to sell it. No matter how great you think your product is, your salespeople or dealers may not share your enthusiasm at first. You need to sell them on the idea of selling the product, especially if they have many other products competing for their time, mind share, or shelf space. A sales guide can help you with this education and motivation process (Figure 12.4).

Whether it is a single booklet or a packaged kit with many materials, a sales guide educates sales personnel about a product, its target market, and customer needs. It describes the selling process and customer environment. It also provides information on competitive products and tips on how to sell against the competition. Where appropriate, it describes contests and other sales incentive programs. It should contain material that is specifically targeted to the sales staff, not customer material that has been slightly modified to address the dealer.

Content Ideas:

A sales guide can incorporate many of the content types, document elements, and text techniques described in Chapters 5 through 7. More specifically, a sales guide usually includes:

- A table of contents or instructions on finding and using the information, especially if the material is packaged in a binder or box.

May 1993

Internetworking
Products

Figure 12.4   This sales guide introduces a major product upgrade to the direct sales force and dealers.

Source: © 1993, Novell, Inc. All rights reserved. Novell, The N design, and Netware are registered trademarks and Netware MultiProtocol Router is a trademark of Novell, Inc. All other product names are the trademarks of their respective companies. Reproduced by permission.

- Description of the dealer program and policies, training, and support services provided by your company.
- Market analysis: information on the needs, buying factors, and other characteristics of prospects.
- Description of the typical sales process and techniques for effective selling; key selling points for the product and advice on how to overcome prospect objections.
- Information on strengths and weaknesses of competitive products.

Target Customers

Novell internetworking products are ideal for customers in any vertical market. In general, the most promising prospective customers for these products will be people who are:

- Installing new LANs, or expanding LAN internetworks
- Extending LANs to include remote locations
- Operating in multivendor and multiprotocol environments
- Currently invested in IBM's Token Ring Network Bridge PC hardware, but migrating from a bridging environment to one that requires concurrent bridging and routing

Prospects who use routers will have a networking environment with some of the following attributes:

- Multiple LAN media, such as shielded and unshielded twisted-pair wire
- Multiple LAN types, such as Ethernet and token-ring
- A LAN which has exceeded its maximum for distance, hop count, or node restrictions
- Broadcast storms, and too much traffic on a single segment
- Mission critical applications on LAN
- Multiple sites (campus and remote/branch offices)

Prospects who use source-route bridges will have a networking environment with some of the following attributes:

- IBM SNA or IBM NetBIOS traffic on the network
- Networks that require WAN connections
- NetWare for SAA and/or IBM equipment installed on token-ring networks
- IBM source-route bridges that must interoperate with new bridge/routers
- NetWare for SAA installed in remote sites communicating with corporate backbone
- Networks with IBM 8209 and Token Ring Network Bridges (both are limited to two LAN or 1-LAN/1-WAN connections)
- Networks that exceed the seven hop token-ring bridging limit[1]
- LAN Network Manager, RS6000 Network Management, or NetView

MIS departments specifically want:

- Single-vendor solutions
- Combined bridging and routing of different protocols on the same interface
- Mixed bridging and routing of the same protocol on different interfaces
- Standards-based network operations
- Decentralized network management systems that can report events to a central management console
- Ease of installation, management, and support
- Leverage network training
- Redundant paths at a low cost
- Preserve hardware investments

Service companies (resellers and distributors) want:

- To extend their service offerings to include—
  - System administration
  - Continuous monitoring
  - Troubleshooting
  - Network planning
  - E-mail communication
  - Disaster recovery
  - Electronic updates
  - Color printing services
  - Security audit
  - Standby storage capacity
  - FAX services
  - Backup service
  - IPX Internet
- To offer a complete line of services, including internetworking software, hubs, and network management
- Products that are easy to install and maintain

---

1. Although the NetWare MultiProtocol Routers support up to 13 hops, the current hardware does not support more than seven hops. Watch CompuServe for updates from the Network Management and Internetworking Products Division on this issue.

4

Figure 12.4 *continued*

- Plans for advertising, publicity, seminars, and trade-show activity by your company.
- Sales tools such as presentation slides with separate speaker notes, product demonstration guidelines or a demo script, and an application guide or configuration worksheets.
- Product line catalogs or a complete set of product literature, press clippings, and case studies. Company information such as a capabilities overview, annual report, or corporate backgrounder.
- Reproducible masters for ads, brochures, and other materials that can be customized with the dealer's name and contact information.
- Sales bulletins or newsletters produced on a monthly or quarterly basis to reinforce the salesperson's interest in your product, provide information on new product capabilities or applications, and offer selling tips.
- Price lists showing dealer pricing and suggested retail prices.
- Ordering information and forms for products, sales collateral, and other dealer materials or services.

SALES PRESENTATION

Sales presentation materials are overhead transparencies or slides that a salesperson can use in a face-to-face meeting with a prospect or in a standup presentation for a group.

A presentation can be made to sell a product, describe the capabilities of your company, offer viewpoints on industry trends or issues, or provide a tutorial about a technology or application.

A sales presentation has three major parts: the opener, the body, and the close. Each of these parts can comprise multiple slides. The opener should present a complete overview of the topic or primary arguments in your presentation. The body of the presentation expands on the topic and presents supporting evidence. The closer summarizes and reinforces the presentation and may include a call to action. The closer also should give the audience a signal that your presentation is about to end.

Preparing a presentation usually involves creating two sets of materials: the overhead transparencies or slides, and a script or set of speaker's notes. Many software programs for producing slides offer the capability to create speaker's notes that are automatically appended to the corresponding slide on the printout.

Content Ideas:

While they can accommodate any subject matter, presentation overheads and slides do have limits on the structure and format of information they present. The following are guidelines for accommodating these limitations:

- Present only one major topic or message per slide.
- Make your statements in phrases; complete sentences are not necessary.
- Convey substantive information in all text, including titles. Use phrases that convey action, benefits, or news such as *Performance more than doubles,* not "Performance Improvements."
- Use callouts to highlight key information on a chart or graphic.
- Format text into bullet points; minimize the line length and number of bullets on each slide. For most slide formats, this means a maximum of seven words per line and seven lines per slide.
- Use a subtitle to expand your message, especially for a slide that has a graphic as the major element.
- Use abbreviations and acronyms only when they are known by the audience.

SPEECH

A speech is a spoken presentation made by a company representative. It may be accompanied by visual aids such as slides, video, or a software demonstration, but it is primarily read from a text written in advance. A speech can be made on almost any topic, but it typically provides information or a viewpoint on industry trends and issues.

In addition to the promotional value of the actual speech presentation, copies of the speech can be distributed as handouts, included in a press kit, or adapted for a magazine article.

Writing a speech involves the special challenge of matching the speaker's personality and speaking skills. Work with the speaker to match her speech patterns, preferred expressions, and delivery style. As a speechwriter, you must also provide the bridge between the speaker's information and the audience's understanding.

It is absolutely essential that you read a draft speech aloud yourself. Better yet, ask the speaker to practice delivering the speech. In this rehearsal, verify that the speaker can read the text easily, without stumbles, running out of breath, or misplaced pauses. Based on this practice delivery, you can work with the speaker to revise the structure, specific words, or pacing of the speech.

In addition to the speech text itself, you may want to prepare two other documents for each speech. The first is a biographical paragraph the event host can read when introducing the speaker. The second is a list of anticipated questions (and their answers) to guide the speaker if a question period will follow the speech.

Content Ideas:

A speech can accommodate many of the content types covered in Chapter 6 and the text techniques in Chapter 7. In addition, consider these items for every speech:

- The speech title should clearly convey the topic or viewpoint discussed in the speech.
- A single theme or message should be carried through the entire speech. The end of the speech should summarize the messages or tie back into the theme, and give the audience a signal that the speaker is drawing to a close.
- Use short, declarative sentences and repeat nouns instead of using pronouns.
- Any use of humor, imagery, and anecdotes must be appropriate to the topic, as well as understandable and acceptable to the audience.

EXERCISES

1. Identify the alliance materials you have developed (or that you could develop) for your product. How would you use any of the other document types described in this chapter?
2. Apply the exercises listed in Chapter 10 for sales materials to your alliance materials.

CHAPTER 13

Marketing Communication in Electronic Media

Expanding Your Horizon

There is a growing trend toward delivering product and press information in a variety of electronic media such as demo disks, multimedia, fax, online services, and video. For the purposes of this chapter, electronic media also includes interactive voice response and closed-circuit television broadcast technology.

Working with these media offers the opportunity to learn new skills, especially those involved in visual communication. This chapter covers marcom projects for electronic media and describes the adjustments you will need to make in your writing techniques.

ELECTRONIC MEDIA FOR MARCOM

Electronic media is an attractive form of high-tech marketing for several reasons:

- It is fast and always available to prospects.
- It is an efficient way to handle a large volume of information that changes frequently.
- It can deliver a high-impact message with higher retention by prospects.
- It is a way of demonstrating the capabilities of your product if it involves electronic media.

One of the key benefits of electronic media—especially online services, fax, and voice response—is that it gives prospects information just at the moment they need it, no matter where they are located. Because the prospect does not need to wait for information to arrive in the mail, the sales cycle can be substantially shorter. In addition, if the prospect first becomes aware of your product when making an online search of its category, you have connected with someone who may not have been reachable by your other marketing methods such as direct mail.

In most cases, companies use electronic media to supplement printed materials. For example, a brochure may be used as the initial fulfillment piece for inquirers, but it will include a reply card for obtaining a demo disk or video. Because of their high production costs, companies want to limit expensive multimedia disks and videos for distribution only to qualified prospects.

Integrating Printed and Electronic Materials

You should determine if an electronic format is really the best medium for the information you want to present and the audience you want to reach. Don't choose electronic media just because it is sexy and new; it must fit with your overall communication strategy and be accessible to the audience you want to reach. For example, you might want to put your very large product catalog onto a compact disc, but this won't be effective if your customers and prospects don't have CD-ROM drives.

No matter what type of electronic media information you offer, publicize it in your advertisements, newsletters, brochures, and other printed materials. This promotion is especially effective for generating calls to voice response or faxback systems.

Copywriting Techniques for Electronic Media

When planning any marcom document, consider how you will accommodate the different capabilities of each medium:

- **Print.** Offers the most flexibility and creativity for content and presentation.
- **Fax.** Content and presentation may be the same as print, depending on the capabilities of your publishing and fax software.
- **Online.** Content and presentation will vary the most from printed materials. Placement of a document online will probably mean a substantial restructure of your information. In addition, you may not be able to use certain document elements such as sidebars, or the capabilities supported will vary substantially from one medium or platform to another. One production consideration for electronic media projects is to develop elements—text, images, sound and video recordings—that can be used across multiple projects.

Different types of electronic media will involve different writing and creative skills and different constraints on the nature of materials you can produce. Faxback and online materials may be the easiest transition, since they can incorporate much of the same text as printed materials. In comparison, multimedia, videos, and demo disks require an understanding of how to communicate visually as well as with words.

Besides collaboration with designers, multimedia projects require an interaction between film and video producers, musicians, sound engineers, animators, instructional design experts, software engineers, and scriptwriters. The Bibliography lists several references for electronic media projects.

In any form of electronic media, the text must be highly related to any images, sound, and video that are included. You don't want to lose sight of your message in the temptation to put a lot of flashy effects or visuals in your demo disk or electronic brochure.

On the other hand, don't force your prospect to read through long, dense blocks of text that essentially make the computer an electronic page-turning device. Horton notes, "Because multimedia productions use fewer words and the words must compete with other media, writing for multimedia must be concise, clear, and potent. Think quality not quantity."[144] In the same article, Horton also advises writers to "overcome your bias for words. . . . Do not let your proficiency and familiarity with words lead you to use them when a picture or sound effect would better tell the story."

You should understand the other limitations of writing for the screen. First is the limited amount of space in which to present your message—even if it is carried across several screens. Second is that prospects don't expect to read the screen for long periods of time, as they would with a printed piece.

BROADCASTS

Videoconference or satellite broadcasts are used by some high-tech companies to announce new products to the press or customers. To view the broadcast, the audience must gather in a facility that has the necessary equipment. A videotape of the broadcast may be made at that time for later distribution. Broadcasts also may be used for live demonstrations of products, conducted at a remote site but broadcast at a conference or trade show.

From a copywriter's perspective, a broadcast may combine aspects of a sales presentation, speech, and demo script. Supporting materials are often given to members of the audience, such as an agenda, copies of presentation slides, Q&A sheets, press kits, or other product materials. See the sections for these materials in Chapters 10 through 12 for more information.

DEMO DISK

A demonstration (demo) disk is a software-based presentation that shows a product's capabilities, applications, and benefits. It can be a fulfillment piece for inquiries generated by advertising, direct-mail campaigns, or publicity. A demo program also may run on a salesperson's notebook computer for use in a group presentation or other personal selling situation. Demo disks also can be included in press kits.

Although demo disks are used extensively to market software products, they also can be an electronic "brochure" for other types of products. Some software companies offer "working model" or limited versions of the actual product instead of a demo disk. Regardless of the form, a demo disk should give the prospect a good understanding of how the product works and its benefits.

Some companies are experimenting with CD-ROM as a distribution medium for product demos. They may publish their own CD or include their demos in a collection published by another company. While CD-ROMs offer the advantage of significantly greater storage than disks, your prospects may not have access to a CD-ROM drive. Even for demo disks, you must consider whether the prospect will have the right computer configuration to run the demo.

A demo disk is usually sent in a package that includes a variety of print materials to provide more detailed information on the product or further motivate a purchase decision (Figure 13.1).

Content Ideas:

Disk

The content of a demo disk will vary depending on whether it is in a "brochure" or "working model" form. Where possible, follow these guidelines:

- State the system requirements and instructions for running the demo on the disk label. For a PC-compatible demo, don't assume the prospect will use Drive A: to run or install the demo.
- Use a title screen to present your primary marketing message, instructions for running the demo, and a list of any special keys that control the program.

EXTRA!® Tools for Microsoft® Office Professional lets you seamlessly
integrate host data into Microsoft Word, Excel, Access® and PowerPoint®
with the touch of a button!

EXTRA! Tools for Microsoft Office Professional was designed specifically
for the Microsoft Office suite of products to work with Attachmate's
EXTRA! for Windows, the world's leading desktop-to-host connectivity
software. Together, they help end users and developers create more
dynamic documents and applications than ever thought possible.

To find out more, call us toll-free at
1-800-426-6283

Attachmate.® Applying intelligence to connectivity.

INNOVATIVE END USER FEATURES

IntelliCopy for Word: Automatically copies and pastes multiple-page Word documents to or
from a host.

IntelliCopy for Excel: Automatically copies and pastes data from the host to Microsoft Excel
worksheets in a snap.

IntelliSend: Lets you copy and send complete documents and files to other host e-mail users
without leaving your Microsoft application.

POWERFUL DEVELOPMENT TOOLS

Create your own custom applications with this comprehensive suite of intelligent developer tools.
We even include cut-and-paste macros and sample code to help get you started.

EXTRA! Tools for Microsoft Office Professional lets you do all this and more
from the graphical, user-friendly environment of your Windows applications!

Figure 13.1 The packaging for a demo disk can provide product information and promote an inquiry or sale.

Source: Attachmate Corporation. Reproduced by permission.

- Use a closing screen to present a call to action or contact information, or to restate your key marketing message.
- Present an overview of the product before you present detailed feature information. This introduction section should be brief, as prospects will be anxious to get into the "meat" of the demo quickly.
- Make sure the prospect will be able to distinguish between the text in your demo messages and any text that appears in the product demonstrated.
- Organize your demo around a presentation of features or show a typical user session for your product. However, verify that the on-screen copy presents benefits as well as feature information.
- Show the same examples and messages in the printed materials that accompany the demo disk.
- If the demo software supports this capability, include product literature or a purchase discount coupon that the prospect can print while viewing the demo.
- Put hidden payoffs in the demo such as displaying a screen with a toll-free number the recipient can call to take advantage of a special offer. In the printed material that accompanies the disk, include information about this incentive as a way to encourage the recipient to watch the entire demo.[121]

Materials in the Disk Package

Many demo disks are accompanied by a brochure or other printed material. Here are several ideas for these materials:

- Cover letter to encourage viewing of the demo program: state the key marketing messages and provide a call to action and contact information.
- Product brochure or data sheet for the main product as well as accessory products.
- Instruction booklet for a "test drive" or "working model" demo.
- Samples of printed output if the demo or working model does not offer a printing capability.
- Specially designed mailing envelope or box for the demo disk and its accompanying materials.
- Order form and information on pricing and options if the objective of the demo is to motivate a purchase of the product.

ELECTRONIC MAIL, BULLETIN BOARDS, AND ONLINE SERVICES

Offering product literature, press materials, demo programs, and other marcom information through some form of online access is becoming increasingly common as more personal computers are connected to network services. Even specialized "e-zines" (electronic magazines) are appearing on the most popular online services.

Access to this material can be offered through electronic mail (e-mail), an in-house bulletin board system (BBS), or public online service such as CompuServe, Prodigy, or the Internet. In addition, some trade publications are offering access to demo programs from multiple companies through their own BBS servers. Other alternatives include providing information through specialized products such as a Lotus Notes database or an Apple Macintosh Hypercard stack.[145,19]

You have more flexibility in the type and content of materials you post if the BBS is operated by your company. Examples of these materials include brochures, press releases, and case studies that would be of interest to prospects and journalists, as well as proposal samples, selling points, application worksheets, and other selling tools for sales people and dealers.

With any of the public network services you need to distinguish between paid advertisements and nonpromotional information or participation in discussion groups for educational purposes. Users resent blatantly promotional messages by vendors who participate in discussion groups or post information onto network servers. Instead, the information you provide in these areas should be more general and educational in nature.[146] Most online services offer areas where you can purchase electronic advertising "space."

Participating in an online service offers two-way communication. In addition to posting your materials, you can use these services to gather information about prospect perceptions of the market, your product, and your company. As Kirk notes, "It's like having a virtual focus group at one's disposal."[143] You can conduct customer surveys or simply monitor messages posted by BBS users that describe problems, needs, and issues. But always be honest about your identity and purpose when participating in these discussion groups.

Electronic mail offers fast, convenient distribution of brief information to multiple customers, sales people, or dealers. However, especially when communicating with customers, don't use e-mail as another form of unsolicited direct mail. Make sure you are controlling the list so that only requesting parties will receive the information.

Content Ideas:
Many of the materials described in Chapters 10 through 12 are suitable for posting or adaptation for online services. However, when preparing these materials for online access, remember they will appear as a straight text file with very limited formatting. You may need to add subheads or modify the text in other ways in order to overcome these limitations.

FAX MATERIALS

Fax technology offers many effective and timely applications for distribution of marcom materials. These include automated faxback systems, broadcast fax, and receiving product inquiries by fax.

A fax-on-demand service allows a caller to use any phone to request one or more documents to be sent to a designated fax machine. The caller selects documents by code number, using a menu system or an index that can be faxed in the first call.

Many types of materials can be made available on a fax-on-demand service, but they are typically used to provide data sheets, dealer lists, and case studies to prospects and press releases, white papers, and backgrounders to journalists. Companies publicize their fax service by including the telephone number and access instructions in advertisements, brochures, press kits, and newsletters.

Your documents may need to be redesigned to accommodate the graphical limitations of fax. However, it is possible to create fax documents that are visually appealing as well as legible. For best results, use fax software to generate the fax document directly from a computer file. Don't scan a printed piece into your fax server and expect it to have acceptable quality when it is transmitted as a fax.

Another use of fax technology is broadcast fax. This capability automatically distributes fax documents to multiple recipients from a centralized computer or fax service bureau. Companies typically use broadcast fax to quickly deliver updated product literature, price lists, and other information to sales people and dealers. Broadcast fax also may be suitable for distributing surveys to customers, encouraging a quick response.

Some companies are using fax forms as a new type of reply card. This allows prospects to request information via fax, receiving it more quickly than would be possible if they mailed the reply card.

Content Ideas:

Develop an index to all the documents available on your fax system. Include the telephone number and complete instructions on how to access the fax system on this index.

MULTIMEDIA/COMPACT DISC

Publishing on compact disc (CD) is an emerging trend in high-tech marketing communication. It offers several benefits, including large storage capacity, high perceived value by recipients, inexpensive unit production and distribution costs, and ability to update information quickly and easily as compared with printed materials. In addition, CD-ROM drives are becoming more affordable and more widely installed, meaning that more recipients are able to actually use a CD.

You do not necessarily need to produce your own CD just for your marketing information. Software vendors are increasingly distributing their products on CD and using the leftover space for marketing information on other products or services. Many of these vendors are also selling advertising and demo space on their CDs to vendors of compatible or accessory products. Another source is trade publications, which are offering their editorial content on CDs along with product literature and demo programs from multiple companies.

Among the types of materials suitable for CD publishing are multimedia brochures and presentations, lengthy catalogs and price lists for multiple products, and product demonstrations. They also can be used for speaker support at speeches and presentations.

Content Ideas:

- **Hardware demonstration.** A CD with a multimedia program is often the only practical medium for presenting demonstrations of hardware products. This is especially true in the case where an evaluation unit is too expensive or impractical to offer to every prospect, or when it would be impossible to set up a live demonstration. By using multimedia techniques on a CD, you can show live operation in a lab or customer setting, or provide a simulation that incorporates product images or video clips of the hardware unit's operation.

- **Sales force education and support.** The large amount of information that can be stored on a CD can help sales people and dealers understand an extensive product line that has constant changes, additions, and deletions. If a demo program is included on the CD, it can help to ensure the consistency of demos among sales people.
- **Demonstration kiosks.** When kiosks are placed in a trade show or retail environment, you can build a tracking capability into the demo software that measures the number of people who access the demo and what they do with it. You can also ask questions and record responses from the demo users in a database.

VIDEO

A sales or news video can promote a product or company. Videos are commonly used to introduce a new product or upgrade by providing information and a demonstration; present customer case studies; present capabilities information about the company; or record a speech, presentation, user-group meeting, or other event.

Content Ideas:

The Bibliography lists several books on writing video scripts, which is a unique and specific form of marketing writing. Here are general guidelines for using copy in a video:

- The opener and closer of the video should work together in terms of both messages and visuals.
- Present a call to action and show contact information at the end of the video.
- Place a marketing message on the tape box and label. This may be in the form of a teaser to encourage viewing.
- For any text that appears on-screen, keep it brief and use phrases instead of complete sentences.
- Use text to identify people interviewed for the tape; show name, title, company or organization.
- If the tape includes a product demonstration, make a statement at the beginning about what will be covered in the demonstration.

VOICE RESPONSE

Interactive voice response (IVR) is a technology that allows you to play a wide variety of prerecorded information to telephone callers. It is sometimes called an information line. An IVR system also can be coordinated with a faxback system, allowing the caller to request printed material on the topic or product described in an IVR message.

Content Ideas:

- Record a menu of brief product descriptions.
- Provide dealer locations matched to the caller's area code or postal code.
- Present announcements of sale prices or other promotional offers.

EXERCISES

1. Which forms of electronic media are currently used by your company to market products? How do these materials compare with the ideas and guidelines presented in this chapter?
2. Access one of the online services and explore its information offerings and discussion groups. What type of information or materials would you post on this service? What research information could you gain about the market and audience for your products?
3. Collect examples of electronic media materials from a variety of sources. Analyze their objective, purpose, elements, organization, and style. Compare this analysis to the ideas presented in this chapter and in Chapters 5 through 7.

Copywriting Checklist

This checklist will give you a quick reference for reviewing your marcom documents. You may want to create a similar checklist of your own, with questions and items that are specific to your projects and company standards.

Overall Document

- Has the right document type been selected, based on the message, objective, purpose, and audience? Does this document fit well with other pieces in the set?
- Does the document follow the guidelines and strategies established by the marcom plan, creative platform, and document plan?
- Is the amount, type, and structure of the copy appropriate for the messages, objective, purpose, layout, and audience for the document? Is the copy grammatically correct and does it follow the principles of good writing? Does the text adhere to all legal constraints on content and presentation?
- Is the document inviting and does it encourage readership? Will the document reflect positively on your company for both its content and its presentation? Is the correct viewpoint conveyed in the writing (the prospect's or the company's)?
- Is the tone and style of the copy appropriate for the medium, the objective, the purpose, and the audience? Does the tone and style conform to company guidelines?

- Are the key messages presented clearly? Can the reader recognize the unique selling proposition for the product or service? Are your claims honest and believable?
- Does the information flow logically from one section or paragraph to the next? Is the copy easy to read and understand?
- Is all important information included? Is the amount of detail appropriate? Does the document contain extraneous information that could be eliminated?
- Could the reader be misled by any statement in the copy? Have all quotes, statistics, and other reference information been verified?
- Do the words and images support each other in delivering their intended messages?
- Does the document contain the correct document number, revision number, publication or release date?
- Does the document contain the correct contact information? Company address, telephone number, fax number; for headquarters, sales offices, or dealers.

Document Elements

- Are the different document elements being used effectively? Could the clarity and impact of the text be improved by using other document elements?
- Will the headlines capture the reader's interest? Do the headlines and subheads present all of the key messages or selling points for the skimming reader? Do the subheads guide the reader through the piece? Is there a good match between a headline and the body copy that follows?
- Is the opener strong and engaging? Does it identify the target audience? Do the opening sentences or paragraphs deliver key messages or information quickly and effectively?
- Is the supporting evidence presented adequately and appropriately? Is the information sufficient for the reader to make a decision or take the next step? Do your captions, pull quotes, and other document elements reinforce your message?
- Does the closer fit well with the rest of the document? Does it bring the topic or discussion to a graceful conclusion?
- Is the call to action stated clearly? Does it include all information needed by the reader to take the next step?

Content Types

- Does the document contain the correct content types given its objective and purpose? Is the information presented for each content type complete and appropriate?
- Are feature and benefit statements presented clearly? Are comparisons presented fairly and backed by verifiable evidence?
- Are quotes presented accurately and the source cited correctly? Are paraphrases a fair representation of the original?

Text Techniques

- Are text techniques used appropriately given the writing style, tone, content, and audience?
- If using any form of imagery, do the text and visuals work together to support the image? Will readers understand the imagery? Does the use of imagery enhance the message or will it distract or confuse the reader?
- If using humor, is it appropriate to the content and audience for the document?
- Does the text contain any of the mistakes described in Chapter 7?

Legal and Ethical Considerations

- Does the text comply with all legal and regulatory requirements? Has the document been reviewed by the company attorney?
- Are all claims about product features and performance based on actual capabilities and verifiable evidence? Are all comparisons with competitive products fair and accurate?
- Do endorsement quotes reflect actual and recent usage by the endorser? Is the source cited correctly for quotes taken from surveys or research studies?
- Does the use of text and images produced by external resources comply with the terms of the usage rights purchased? Have proper releases been obtained from all people who appear in photos, illustrations, and video footage?
- Does any information violate the privacy rights of an individual or company? Does the text reveal any confidential information?
- Are trademark symbols used correctly on product names in the text and do trademark acknowledgments appear at the end of the document? Is a copyright notice included? Are information disclaimer statements and other legal boilerplate presented correctly?

Glossary

Ad Slick   Reproducible masters for advertisements that are created by the product manufacturer and distributed to dealers or resellers for their use in promoting a product. Ad slicks usually include a blank area for the dealer to add information on location, hours, and telephone numbers for the store or office.

Advertisement   A paid message from a company that appears in a print or broadcast medium. Print ads can range from two-line listings in the classified section to a multipage, four-color spread. Most advertisements for high-tech products appear in trade, business, or consumer magazines, local or national newspapers, distributor catalogs, and card decks. Advertising can generate inquiries about the product (called product or brand advertising) or build a company's image in the market (called image advertising). In the case of products that have a low price or involve low risk in making a purchase decision, advertising can generate an immediate order by the customer (called direct-response advertising).

Advertorial   An *advert*isement that is written and designed to resemble the edit*orial* content in a magazine or newspaper. Often written in the form of an article, an advertorial is developed and paid for by the sponsoring company. Advertorials may be placed on one or more pages in the publication, or bound in as an insert. Most publications require that an advertorial be labeled explicitly as advertising and use a different type style or layout to distinguish it from the editorial content.

AIDA   *A*ttention, *I*nterest, *D*esire, *A*ction. The process described in traditional marketing that is followed by a reader in response to a specific advertisement or sales brochure.

Application Guide   A booklet or reference document that presents information about potential product applications, often categorized according to customer type or problem. An application guide helps a salesperson understand the requirements of prospects and helps in choosing the best product to meet a customer need.

Article   An essay, report, or other material contributed to a trade publication or professional journal under the byline of a person who is not on the editorial staff. Sometimes articles are ghostwritten for a company executive or customer. Article types include: case study, editorial, how-to guide, news, profile of a company or person, product selection guide, research report, technical paper, or issues analysis.

Backgrounder   An essay style document that provides detailed information about a product, technology, or company. Often included in press kits.

Bingo Card   In a trade publication, a postcard that enables readers to request information from vendors by circling the number specified in the vendor's advertisement. Also called a Reader Service Card.

Blurb   A slang term for boilerplate language.

Body Copy   The main text of any marcom document.

Boilerplate   A standard paragraph or section of text that describes a company or product and is used in many marketing and PR materials.

Brochure   A multipage booklet that describes a product, service, or company. A brochure may take many formats and reflect different levels of production expense. Brochures are used primarily for direct-mail campaigns, sales presentations, and inquiry fulfillment.

BRC (Business Reply Card)   See Reply Card.

Business-to-Business   Products sold primarily to businesses instead of individual consumers.

Bylined Article   An article or other material contributed to a trade publication under the byline of a person who is not on the editorial staff. Also used sometimes as a label for articles that are ghostwritten for a company executive or customer.

Call to Action   A sentence or phrase, usually at the end of a marketing piece, that motivates the reader to buy the product, contact a dealer, request more information, or take another action in the sales process.

Callout   A line of text that points to a detail in a diagram, illustration, or photograph.

Campaign   A series of planned marketing activities that can include multiple advertisements, direct-mail packages, or other forms of communication with prospects or customers. Campaigns can be organized around activities such as the introduction of a new product or to encourage attendance at a meeting, conference, or trade show.

Capabilities Overview   A document that describes a company's expertise, services, resources, and experience. Usually in the form of a brochure, a capabilities overview typically markets a company's services. This document also can show "the company behind the product" for high-cost, high-commitment products.

Card Deck   A direct-mail package comprised of multiple reply cards that advertise individual products from many different vendors. Card decks are often sponsored by trade publications as a service for their advertisers.

Case Study   An article that describes how a particular customer uses a product. Sometimes called a profile or application note.

Catalog   A booklet that presents a collection of products offered for sale through mail or phone order, or through a retail store.

Collateral   A general term for any type of printed marketing material, including brochures, data sheets, catalogs, and newsletters.

Creative Platform   A document that describes the strategy, messages, and guidelines for the visual and written elements of a marketing piece. A creative platform also may include a description of acceptable style and word usage. Sometimes called a creative brief or copy plan (if describing the copy only).

Data Sheet   Usually a single-page document that presents detailed information about a specific product, service, option, or application. A data sheet often supplements a more extensive, glossy product brochure and can have many of the same attributes, uses, and distribution methods.

Dealer   A company that sells a manufacturer's product. A dealer may be a consultant, a systems-integration company, or a retail store. Some high-tech companies sell their products only through dealers, while others use a combination of dealers and a direct sales force.

Direct Mailer   A brochure or package that is mailed to a prospect for the purpose of generating inquiries or to directly sell a product. Direct mailers can be used in a product launch campaign or as a key ongoing marketing method. A direct-mail package usually includes a cover letter, a brochure, a lift note, a reply card or order form, and an envelope. A variation on this package is the self-mailer, a brochure with a built-in address area that allows it to be mailed without an envelope.

Editorial Copy   The articles, news reports, columns, and other nonadvertising material in a magazine or newspaper.

Fact Sheet   A single page of key information about a product, event, or company that is usually distributed in a press kit. Fact sheets help reporters find the most commonly requested data quickly.

Feedback Device   A reply card, survey, comment form, or other document that enables a reader to provide advice, suggestions, or market research data to the product's developer or manufacturer. Sometimes called an action device, response device, or bounceback.

Formatting Device   Changes in type style, use of a different color, use of punctuation, or changes in copy layout that are made to highlight key messages in the text.

Fulfillment Piece   A brochure, white paper, article reprint, or other marcom document that is sent in response to a reader's request for more information about a product.

Insert   A separate page or brochure that is inserted into a trade publication. It may be bound into the publication (the most common method is called "tip-in"), inserted loose, or placed with the publication in an envelope or wrapper.

Involvement Device   A checklist, quiz, worksheet, or other text element that prompts a reader to pause and "become involved" with the document.

Johnson Box   An introductory paragraph at the top of a sales letter that describes the offer or provides a teaser to entice the reader into the body of the letter. Usually appears in an indented, boxed format.

Leave-Behind   Marketing materials that are left with the prospect by a salesperson after a meeting.

Lift Note   A brief letter included in a direct-mail package to convince recipients who need additional motivation before buying the product. A lift note attempts to overcome a recipient's objections to the offer that is presented in the direct-mail package.

Logotype   The graphical image of a company name, usually printed in a specified color and typeface. The logotype may be separate from the company's logo symbol, or may itself serve as the logo.

Marketing Mix   The combination of marketing activities (such as advertising and dealer materials) and publicity activities (such as press tours and article placement) that will be used to promote a product or service. Also called promotion mix.

Masthead   A box that lists contact information for a periodical's publishing and editorial staff. Contrast with nameplate, which is the title area of the publication.

Media Kit   A package of information that a publication uses to sell advertising space. A media kit typically includes data about the publication's circulation, target readership, advertising rates, production services, and mechanical specifications. Compare with Press Kit.

MSRP   Manufacturer's Suggested Retail Price. The price at which the manufacturer offers a product directly to customers and which it recommends to dealers. However, manufacturers cannot specify or control the price at which a dealer will sell the product, so a customer may find different prices for the product offered by different sources.

Multimedia   Historically, the term *multimedia* describes a marcom or advertising campaign that is placed in several media (e.g., print and radio ads). Today, the more common definition of multimedia is an electronic form of marketing communication that combines audio, image, text, and video elements.

Newsletter   A news-oriented publication that is targeted to a limited, often highly-specific group of employees, customers, or other readers. Internal newsletters are also called house organs.

OEM   An Original Equipment Manufacturer is a company that buys a generic product, then customizes or labels it for sale under its own brand name.

Offer   The buying terms for a product or service, including price, payment options, delivery terms, time limitations, and purchase incentives.

Overline   A line of text that appears over a main headline to serve as a lead-in. An overline is an alternative way to present a secondary idea in a headline (the other way is to state the secondary idea after the main headline). Sometimes called an eyebrow.

Package Insert   Catalogs, brochures, or other marketing materials that are placed in product packaging. These materials typically promote add-on products, other products from the same company, or service plans.

Pitch Letter   A letter written to an editor proposing an article idea or other coverage opportunity. A pitch letter often includes an outline or synopsis of the proposed article and information on the author's expertise.

Point-of-Sale (POS) Materials   Brochures, flyers, signs, or other pieces for display in the area where a customer actually purchases the product. POS materials are used extensively in retail stores for display on shelves, kiosks, aisle ends, or near cash registers. Also called point-of-purchase materials.

Positioning   The market perception of a product, service, or company; often a statement of the perception that the company wants to create.

Press Kit   A collection of press releases, fact sheets, backgrounders, photos, diagrams, and other materials that give a reporter or analyst complete information about a product, service, event or company. A press kit is usually packaged in a presentation folder. Contrast with Media Kit.

Press Release   A document that is intended to generate publicity by announcing current news about a company, product, service, or event. Usually developed as a printed piece, but also may be produced in a video form. Also called a news release.

Press Tour   A set of individual interviews with publication editors and industry analysts, held in their offices (hence "tour"). From the company's side, a press tour usually involves a company executive, product manager, or technical expert, with coordination and participation by a public relations specialist.

Profile   An article that describes a person or company. Profiles are often produced in a question-and-answer format.

Publicity   Materials and activities designed to generate favorable news coverage about a product, service, event, or company. Publicity is considered to be just one element of a public relations program.

Pull Quote   A statement or quotation that appears in a boxed area within the body of a brochure or article. A pull quote is a technique for emphasizing a very positive quotation or key message, especially for readers who only skim the text.

Qualifying Questions   Multiple-choice questions on a reply card or feedback device that collect information about a prospect's interest level, budget, decision-making authority, environment, and purchasing plans for a product or service.

Question-and-Answer Sheet   A document that presents answers to the questions most commonly asked about a product or company to help journalists understand user interests.

Reply Card   A card that is included in an ad, brochure, or direct-mail package to encourage the reader to order a product or request more information. Most companies use a postal permit that allow prospects to mail the reply card postage-free. Also called a BRC (business reply card).

Reseller   A company that resells a manufacturer's product, often as part of a package with other products to offer the customer a complete solution. In this case, this company is often called a Value-Added Reseller. This term is often synonymous with dealer.

Sales Guide   A book, kit, or other package of information that helps a salesperson understand and sell a product. A sales guide typically includes detailed product materials, market and application information, a description of features and benefits, comparison with competitive products, a description of the selling process or environment, and key selling messages.

Self-Mailer A brochure designed with an address area that allows it to be mailed without an envelope. A self-mailer is commonly used for direct mail.

Shelf Talker A small card or sign designed for placement on the shelf where the product is displayed. A shelf talker often includes excerpts from positive product reviews, or sales-motivating words such as "New," "Special Price," or "Limited-Time Offer." Also called a flagger.

Tag Line A single line of copy that presents a key product or company message. Also called a slogan. A tag line is usually placed at the end of an advertisement or printed underneath the company logo.

Teaser Most commonly a phrase that appears on the outside of a direct-mail envelope to entice the recipient to open the package. Sometimes called corner copy. A teaser also can be advertising that provides limited information at the beginning of a multistage advertising campaign to entice the reader to watch for follow-on ads.

Testimonial A quote, case study, or other information from a customer that endorses a product, service, or company.

Trade Publication A magazine or newspaper that is targeted to a specialized industry or market.

Unique Selling Proposition (USP) The USP is intended to define the key differentiating factor for a product. This factor may become the key marketing message.

Vertical Market An industry or other market segment with customers that have similar characteristics or similar needs for a class of products. Many high-tech companies develop product lines or positioning strategies that are based on the needs of selected vertical markets.

White Paper An essay-style document that provides in-depth explanation of a product, technology, issue, trend, or application. A white paper also can present a company's viewpoint on industry strategies and directions.

Bibliography and Resources

GENERAL HIGH-TECH MARKETING

Barry, John A.: *Technobabble*. Cambridge, MA: MIT Press, 1991. A thorough, enjoyable examination of the development of technical jargon.

Berry, Leonard L. and Parasuraman, A.: *Marketing Services: Competing Through Quality*. New York: Free Press, 1991. An overview of all factors related to marketing a services company, but primarily focused on traditional service industries such as banking and travel. Includes some discussion of marketing communication issues and techniques.

Congram, Carole A. and Friedman, Margaret L., editors: *The AMA Handbook of Marketing for the Service Industries*. New York: AMACOM, 1991. A hefty handbook on all aspects of marketing services. Includes chapters on both internal and external marketing communication.

Katsaros, John: *Selling High Tech, High Ticket*. Chicago, IL: Probus, 1993. A useful guide to relationship selling strategies as they apply to high-tech products.

Kawasaki, Guy: *Selling the Dream*. New York: HarperCollins, 1991. The appendix includes the complete product plan for the first Apple Macintosh computer; it is a useful example of how a company defines the positioning and marketing messages for a product.

Kiamy, Dee, editor: *The High-Tech Marketing Companion*. Reading, MA: Addison-Wesley, 1993. A collection of articles from an Apple Computer publication. While focused on software, much of the information is applicable to any high-tech product.

Marcus, Bruce W.: *Competing for Clients in the 90s*. Chicago, IL: Probus, 1992. Describes marketing techniques for professional-services firms such as accounting and law firms. May offer some useful ideas for technology-services companies.

McKenna, Regis: *The Regis Touch*. Reading, MA: Addison Wesley, 1986. Describes how to position a high-technology company or product.

McKenna, Regis: *Relationship Marketing: Successful Strategies for the Age of the Customer*. Reading, MA: Addison Wesley, 1991. Updates *The Regis Touch* and extends many of the concepts presented in that book to a broad range of industries.

Moore, Geoffrey A.: *Crossing the Chasm: Marketing and Selling Technology Products to Mainstream Customers*. New York: HarperBusiness, 1991. Describes how new high-tech products are adopted by the marketplace. Particularly useful for startup companies or those introducing products into completely new markets.

Ries, Al and Trout, Jack: *Positioning: The Battle for Your Mind*. New York: Warner Books, 1986. A general overview of positioning in advertising.

GENERAL MARKETING COMMUNICATION

Ljungren, Roy G.: *The Business-to-Business Direct Marketing Handbook*. New York: American Management Association, 1989. A professional reference book that presents an overview of direct marketing to business customers.

Patti, Charles H., Hartley, Steven W., and Kennedy, Susan L.: *Business to Business Advertising: A Marketing Management Approach*. Lincolnwood, IL: NTC Business Books, 1991. A collection of articles on business advertising theory and practice.

Schultz, Don E., Tannenbaum, Stanley I., and Lauterborn, Robert F.: *Integrated Marketing Communications*. Lincolnwood, IL: NTC Business Books, 1993. Describes the philosophy of integrating advertising with other forms of marketing communication, although from the perspective of consumer-products companies.

GENERAL WRITING SKILLS

Bayan, Richard: *Words That Sell*. Chicago, IL: Contemporary Books, 1984. A very useful thesaurus of words for marketing materials. Organized by product characteristics and document element.

Bender, Hy: *Essential Software for Writers*. Cincinnati, OH: Writer's Digest Books, 1994. A review of software tools that support writers who work on IBM-compatible personal computers.

Fryxell, David: *How to Write Fast (While Writing Well)*. Cincinnati, OH: Writer's Digest Books, 1992. A good book to turn to when you are feeling stuck or burned out on a project, and need to find a way out of this situation *fast*. Targeted to freelance magazine writers.

Gunning, Robert: *The Technique of Clear Writing*. New York: McGraw Hill, 1968. Read the chapter "Readability Yardsticks," which describes the Gunning Fog Index—a widely used method for measuring the readability of text.

McDowell, Earl E.: *Interviewing Practices for Technical Writers*. Amityville, NY: Baywood Publishing, 1991. Presents a detailed analysis of different types of interviews. Somewhat scholarly in its focus, but it may provide good ideas on phrasing questions for very formal interviews.

Miller, Casey and Swift, Kate: *The Handbook of Non-Sexist Writing*. New York: Harper & Row, 1988. A useful guide, especially the chapter on alternatives to gender-specific pronouns.

Rees Cheney, Theodore A.: *Getting the Words Right: How to Revise, Edit & Rewrite*. Cincinnati, OH: Writer's Digest Books, 1983. An excellent guide to improving the clarity and impact of your writing.

Rubens, Philip, editor: *Science and Technical Writing: A Manual of Style*. New York: Henry Holt, 1992. Although it is targeted primarily to writers who produce documentation, it is a useful reference for the issues related to any type of material on technical subjects.

Schumacher, Michael: *Creative Conversations*. Cincinnati, OH: Writer's Digest Books, 1990. Covers interview techniques for book authors and writers of general-interest magazine articles. Contains some useful information on structuring interviews, working with quotes, and legal considerations for using information gained from an interview.

ADVERTISING

Burton, Philip Ward: *Advertising Copywriting*, 6th edition, Lincolnwood, IL: NTC Business Books, 1990. A college-level textbook on copywriting techniques for both consumer and business advertising. Covers print and broadcast media with many examples and guidelines for writing.

Gregory, James R. and Wiechmann, Jack G.: *Marketing Corporate Image*. Lincolnwood, IL: NTC Business Books, 1991. Describes advertising that is designed to establish a specific image for a corporation, not its products.

Lewis, Herschell Gordon: *Power Copywriting*. Chicago: Dartnell Corporation, 1992. A word-usage guide that is geared primarily to advertising, but is also useful for any type of marketing communication.

Marra, James L.: *Advertising Creativity: Techniques for Generating Ideas*. New York: Prentice-Hall, 1990. Presents a helpful discussion of the creative process that faces any copywriter, and gives techniques for developing concepts that can be applied to many types of marketing materials.

DIRECT MAIL

Jones, Susan K.: *Creative Strategy in Direct Marketing*. Lincolnwood, IL: NTC Business Books, 1991. A thorough reference book on all aspects of direct-mail selling.

ELECTRONIC MEDIA

Burger, Jeff: *Desktop Multimedia Bible.* Reading, MA: Addison-Wesley, 1993. A good overview of the equipment, software, and other resources you will need to produce multimedia projects.

Cronin, Mary J.: *Doing Business on the Internet.* New York: Van Nostrand Reinhold, 1993. A discussion directed to companies that want to use the Internet for internal communication as well as information distribution.

Hoge, Cecil C.: *The Electronic Marketing Manual.* New York: McGraw-Hill, 1993. An extensive guide to marketing activities that can be conducted through all forms of electronic media.

Horton, William K.: *Illustrating Computer Documentation,* New York: Wiley, 1991. A valuable guide to working with visuals for any technical material, both printed and online.

Horton, William K.: *Designing and Writing Online Documentation,* 2nd edition. New York: Wiley, 1994. A useful guide for adapting any type of written material for online display.

INTERNATIONAL

Adams, Loretta, Adams-Esquivel, Henry, and Harris, Philip: *Transcultural Marketing: Global Strategies for Diverse Consumers.* Gulf Publishing, 1991. Geared primarily to consumer-product companies, but contains useful information.

Atkinson, Toby: *Merriam-Webster Guide to International Business Communication.* New York: Merriam-Webster, 1994. Presents information for each country on address formats, salutations, and other standards for communication.

Baines, Adam: *Handbook of International Direct Marketing.* London: Kogan-Page, 1992. A high-level overview of international direct marketing practices, with details on specific marketing factors to consider for individual countries. Published in conjunction with the European Direct Marketing Association.

Ferraro, Gary P.: *The Cultural Dimension of International Business.* Englewood Cliffs, NJ: Prentice-Hall, 1990. An overview of the issues around cross-cultural communication in business. Somewhat academic, but presents useful background information.

Hall, Edward T. and Hall, Mildred Reed: *Understanding Cultural Differences.* Portland, ME: Intercultural Press, 1990. Any of Hall's books are excellent background for understanding cross-cultural communication. This book examines cultural differences between Americans, Germans, and the French, with a discussion of how these differences impact business practices and communication.

Hoft, Nancy L.: *International Technical Communication.* New York: Wiley (forthcoming 1995). A comprehensive book on the issues of localiza-

tion. Although geared primarily for documentation and user interfaces for software products, it contains information that is useful for
marcom materials.

Ricks, David A.: *Blunders in International Business.* Cambridge, MA:
Blackwell Business, 1993. A very humorous guide to mistakes made
by American companies engaged in international business. Includes
many examples for marcom, although largely from consumer-
product companies.

Taylor, Dave: *Global Software: Developing Applications for the International
Market.* New York: Springer-Verlag, 1992. Describes issues related to
localization of software products.

Todd, Loreto and Hancock, Ian: *International English Usage.* New York: NYU
Press, 1987. An extensive guide to the subtle variations of the English
language as it is spoken and written in different parts of the world.

Uren, Emmanuel, Howard, Robert, and Perinotti, Tiziana: *Software
Internationalization and Localization: An Introduction.* New York:
Van Nostrand Reinhold, 1993.

Victor, David A.: *International Business Communication.* New York:
HarperCollins, 1992.

LEGAL ISSUES

What Every Account Executive Should Know About the Law and Advertising.
New York: American Association of Advertising Agencies, 1990. A
brief but useful booklet on legal considerations specifically for advertising, but applicable to all types of marcom materials. Available
directly from the Association.

Baker, Lee W.: *The Credibility Factor: Putting Ethics to Work in Public
Relations.* Homewood, IL: Business One–Irwin, 1993. A valuable
examination of ethical dilemmas and considerations for marketing
and public relations professionals, especially those dealing with
journalists and the general public.

Fueroghne, Dean Keith: *"But the People in Legal Said . . .".* Homewood, IL:
Dow Jones–Irwin, 1989. A thorough and useful guide to legal issues
around advertising, but also relevant to all forms of marketing
communication.

Meyerowitz, Steven A.: *An Ounce of Prevention: Marketing, Sales, and
Advertising Law for Non-Lawyers.* Detroit: Visible Ink Press, 1993.
Covers a broad range of legal issues, but includes useful information
on warranty concerns in marcom, trademark usage, and using
endorsements.

Nash, Laura L: *Good Intentions Aside: A Managers Guide to Resolving
Ethical Problems.* Boston: Harvard Business School Press, 1993.
Covers a wide range of issues, including ethical concerns around
marketing communication.

NEWSLETTERS

Floyd, Elaine: *Marketing With Newsletters*. New Orleans, LA: EF Communications, 1991. Describes promotional newsletters for a wide variety of organizations, although with an emphasis on small business and nonprofits.

PRESENTATIONS

Wilder, Claudyne: *The Presentations Kit*. New York: Wiley, 1990. A practical and thorough guide to presentation materials and skills. Includes a variety of examples and checklists.

PROPOSALS

Bowman, Joel P. and Branchaw, Bernadine P: *How to Write Proposals That Produce*. Phoenix, AZ: Oryx Press, 1992. A comprehensive, highly useful guide for preparing technical proposals.

PUBLIC RELATIONS

Aronson, Merry and Spetner, Don: *The Public Relations Writer's Handbook*. New York: Lexington Books, 1993. A broad overview of all public relations writing projects. Includes guidelines and examples from a range of industries, although focused on consumer products. Primarily useful for writers who are new to public relations materials.

Blundell, William E.: *The Art and Craft of Feature Writing*. New York: Plume, 1988. Based on a *Wall Street Journal* guide for writing newspaper articles. Presents some useful techniques for handling the elements of a feature story.

Cappon, Rene J.: *The Associated Press Guide to News Writing*. New York: Prentice-Hall, 1991. Presents advanced-level information on writing news and feature articles.

French, Christopher, editor: *The Associated Press Stylebook and Libel Manual*. Reading, MA: Addison-Wesley, 1992. The definitive guidebook for journalists and public relations writers.

Kessler, Lauren and McDonald, Duncan: *Mastering the Message: Media Writing with Substance and Style*. Belmont, CA: Wadsworth Publishing, 1989. A college-level textbook for aspiring journalists, it contains useful techniques for persuasive writing.

Wilcox, Dennis L. and Nolte, Lawrence W.: *Public Relations Writing and Media Techniques*. New York: Harper Collins, 1990. A solid introductory textbook on writing the full range of press materials. Includes tips on working with reporters. Examples are from general business and nonprofit organizations.

SPEECHES

Cook, Jeff Scott: *The Elements of Speechwriting and Public Speaking.*
    New York: Macmillan, 1989. A complete, useful guide for writing
    speeches.
Filson, Brent: *Executive Speeches.* Williamstown, MA: Williamstown
    Publishing, 1991. Based on interviews with executive speechmakers.
    Includes several chapters on specific writing techniques for speeches.

VIDEOS

Hampe, Barry: *Video Scriptwriting.* New York: Plume, 1993. A beginner's
    guide to planning and writing a video script. Also includes a brief
    discussion of the production process. Primarily targeted to freelance
    writers who want to add scriptwriting to their list of services.

OTHER BOOKS OF INTEREST

Tufte, Edward R.: *The Visual Display of Quantitative Information.* Cheshire,
    CT: Graphics Press, 1983. An excellent, highly illustrated guide to
    presenting data in table, chart, or graph form.

PERIODICALS

Business Marketing, Crain Communications Inc., 740 N. Rush St., Chicago,
    IL 60611, 312/649-5260. A monthly tabloid publication on business-
    to-business marketing issues, with many examples drawn from
    high-tech companies.
Marketing Computers, 1515 Broadway, New York, NY 10036, 800/722-6658.
    A monthly discussion of issues and tactics for marketing computer
    hardware and software. Often contains information that is useful for
    marketing any high-tech product.
New Media, 901 Mariner's Island Blvd. Suite 365, San Mateo, CA 94404,
    415/573-5170. A hands-on guide to the technologies and activities in
    producing multimedia projects.
Sales and Marketing Management, 355 Park Ave. South, New York, NY
    10010, 212/592-6412. A monthly guide to sales techniques and issues.

ORGANIZATIONS

American Marketing Association, 250 S. Wacker Dr., Suite 200, Chicago, IL
    60606, 312/648-0536. A large organization focused on high-level
    marketing issues. Offers many publications and events.
Business Marketing Association, 150 N. Wacker Dr., Suite 1760, Chicago, IL
    60606, 312/409-4262. Members in this organization focus on market-
    ing communication for business-to-business products. Offers several

publications, local chapters, and an annual conference.

Direct Marketing Association, 11 W. 42nd St., New York, NY 10036, 212/689-4977. A professional organization for anyone involved in direct marketing. Offers many publications, training seminars, and events.

International Association of Business Communicators, One Hallidie Plaza, Suite 600, San Francisco, CA 94102, 415/433-3400. Primarily targeted to communication professionals who focus on internal or employee communications. Produces a monthly magazine with some useful information, local chapters, and an annual conference.

Public Relations Society of America, Technology Interest Group, 33 Irving Place, New York, NY 10003, 212/995-2230. An organization targeted only to professionals who work full-time in public relations. Produces useful publications, training programs, and an annual conference.

Society for Technical Communication, 901 N. Stuart St., Arlington, VA 22203, 703/522-4114. Historically an organization for technical writers who produce documentation, STC has broadened its focus to include a *Marketing Communication Professional Interest Committee* and a useful quarterly journal.

References

1. Karls, John B. and Szymanski, Ronald: *The Writer's Handbook: A Guide to the Essentials of Good Writing*, 2nd edition. Lincolnwood IL: NTC Books, 1990.
2. Jones, Susan K.: *Creative Strategy in Direct Marketing*. Lincolnwood, IL: NTC Business Books, 1991.
3. Provost, Gary: *Beyond Style: Mastering the Finer Points of Writing*. Cincinatti, OH: Writer's Digest Books, 1988.
4. Kaplan, Burton: *Strategic Communication*. New York: Harper Business, 1991.
5. Kessler, Lauren and McDonald, Duncan: *Mastering the Message: Media Writing with Substance and Style*. Belmont, CA: Wadsworth, 1989.
6. Winters, Elaine: "Preparing Materials for Use by the Entire World," *Technical Communication*, Third Quarter 1993, p. 502.
7. Klein, Erica Levy: *Write Great Ads: A Step-by-Step Approach*. New York: Wiley, 1990.
8. Lewis, Herschell Gordon: *On the Art of Writing Copy*. Chicago: Dartnell Corporation, 1986.
9. Schumacher, Michael: *Creative Conversations*. Cincinnati: Writer's Digest Books, 1990.
10. Marra, James L.: *Advertising Creativity: Techniques for Generating Ideas*. New York: Prentice-Hall, 1990.
11. Wilcox, Dennis L. and Nolte, Lawrence W.: *Public Relations Writing and Media Techniques*. New York: Harper Collins, 1990.
12. Customer case study, ADC Kentrox.
13. Product ad, Symantec Corp.

14. Burton, Philip Ward: *Advertising Copywriting*, 6th edition. Lincoln-wood IL: NTC Business Books, 1990.
15. Product brochure, Walker, Richer & Quinn, Inc.
16. Blundell, William E.: *The Art and Craft of Feature Writing*. New York: Plume, 1988.
17. Smith, Ruth Ann: "Inferential Processes in Consumer Response to Marketing Communications: Review and Directions for Research," in *Marketing Communications: Theory and Research*, Houston, Michael J. and Lutz, Richard J., editors. Chicago: American Marketing Association, 1985.
18. Barry, John A.: *Technobabble*. Cambridge, MA: MIT Press, 1991.
19. Kiamy, Dee, editor: *The High-Tech Marketing Companion*. Reading, MA: Addison-Wesley, 1993.
20. Bendinger, Bruce: *The Copy Workshop Workbook*. Chicago: Copy Workshop, 1988.
21. Rees Cheney, Theodore A.: *Getting the Words Right: How to Revise, Edit & Rewrite*. Cincinnati, OH: Writer's Digest Books, 1983.
22. Cappon, Rene J.: *The Associated Press Guide to News Writing*. New York: Prentice-Hall, 1991.
23. Nadziejka, David E.: Term Talk. *Technical Communication*, Second Quarter 1992, p. 250.
24. Victor, David A.: *International Business Communication*. San Francisco, CA: HarperCollins, 1992.
25. Patti, Charles H., Hartley, Steven W., and Kennedy, Susan L.: *Business to Business Advertising: A Marketing Management Approach*. Lincolnwood, IL: NTC Business Books, 1991.
26. Ad-Vantage. *Marketing Computers*, December 1992, p. 29.
27. McKenna, Regis: *The Regis Touch*. Reading, MA: Addison Wesley, 1986.
28. Product ad, Mitsubishi Electronics America, Inc.
29. Product brochure, Digital Equipment Corp.
30. Product brochure, Banyan Corp.
31. Vögele, Siegfried: *Handbook of Direct Mail*. New York: Prentice-Hall, 1992.
32. Product data sheet, Symantec Corp.
33. Product booklet, ADC Fibermux.
34. Product brochure, Radish Systems, Inc.
35. Product ad, ICOM Simulations, Inc.
36. Product catalog, Central Point Software, Inc.
37. Product ad, Apple Computer, Inc.
38. Product line ad, Dallas Semiconductor.
39. Product line ad, CORE International.
40. Product ad, Macromedia, Inc.
41. Corporate image ad, Hyundai Computers.

42. Product ad, Symantec Corp.
43. Kirk, John: Reaching Users Through the Network. *OEM Magazine*, October 1993, p. 76.
44. Product catalog, Central Point Software, Inc.
45. Article in customer newsletter, Digital Systems International, Inc.
46. Training program brochure, Aldus Corp.
47. Direct-mail letter, Saber Software Corp.
48. Product brochure, Digital Systems International, Inc.
49. Product ad, Lotus Development Corp.
50. Product ad, Harley Systems.
51. Product ad, AT&T Corp.
52. Product line ad, Silicon Systems, Inc.
53. Product ad, IBM Corp.
54. Product ad, MediaVision, Inc.
55. Product ad, Motorola, Inc.
56. Product ad, MainLan, Inc.
57. Company brochure, Prep Publishing.
58. Corporate image ad, Kenworth Truck Co.
59. Ad, NAB Multimedia World Conference.
60. Article in *Network World,* 11/1/93.
61. Product ad, Northern Telecom, Inc.
62. Simpson, Bill: Sleepless in Seattle. *TE&M Magazine*, December 1, 1993, p. 54.
63. Product ad, NEC Corp.
64. Product ad, Alcatel Network Systems.
65. Service ad, Bell Atlantic Corp.
66. Product brochure, British Telecom Ltd.
67. Product ad, Samsung Information Systems America, Inc.
68. Corporate image ad, Sanofi Diagnostics Pasteur, Inc.
69. Product booklet, Telco Systems, Inc.
70. Product line ad, Motorola, Inc.
71. Corporate image ad, Continuum, Inc.
72. Totally XLNT FDDI Mgm't. *Communication Week,* March 15, 1993, p. 42.
73. Product ad, Amoco Corp.
74. Product ad, AMBRA Computer Corp.
75. Product line brochure, Wellfleet Communications, Inc.
76. Corporate image ad, Fujitsu Network Switching of America, Inc.
77. Can you put that in English? *San Jose Business Journal,* May 3, 1993, p. 14.
78. Corporate brochure, Brooktrout Technology, Inc.
79. Product brochure, Aldus Corp.
80. Product line brochure, Compaq Computer Corp.
81. Product ad, Computer Associates International, Inc.

82. Product ad, Contact Software International.
83. Product ad, MainLan, Inc.
84. King, Janice: A Guide to Planning a Wide-Area Network. *NetWare Technical Journal*, October–November 1993, p. 45.
85. Product brochure, Apple Computer, Inc.
86. Press release, ADC Kentrox.
87. Article in customer newsletter, Texas Instruments, Inc.
88. Product brochure, Microsoft Corp.
89. Customer case study, Microsoft Corp.
90. Product ad, Analog Devices Corp.
91. Product brochure, Adobe Systems, Inc.
92. Product brochure, Attachmate Corp.
93. Product brochure, Northern Telecom, Inc.
94. Product brochure, WordPerfect Corp.
95. Product brochure, John Fluke Manufacturing Co., Inc.
96. Press release, Digital Systems International, Inc.
97. Customer case study, Digital Systems International, Inc.
98. Product data sheet, Networx, Inc.
99. Press release, Wall Data, Inc.
100. Direct mail brochure, Digital Equipment Corp.
101. Direct mail letter, Aldus Corp.
102. Product ad, Borland International, Inc.
103. Product ad, Compaq Computer Corp.
104. Product booklet, Tektronix, Inc.
105. Direct mail brochure, Stac Electronics.
106. Press release, Andrew Corp.
107. Product ad, Oracle Corp.
108. White paper, Microsoft Corp.
109. Product brochure, TeleSciences, Inc.
110. Customer newsletter, Wellfleet Communications, Inc.
111. Product brochure, Intuit.
112. Cole, Bernard C.: The Art of Blending Video and Graphics. *IABC Communication World*, December 1993, p. 32.
113. Product ad, Micropolis Corp.
114. Product brochure, US WEST NewVector Group, Inc.
115. Product ad, InFocus Systems, Inc.
116. Product brochure, Renaissance GRX.
117. Corporate backgrounder, Dialogic Corp.
118. Vick, James: Changing Channels of Reader Response. *Business Marketing*, April 1992, p. 75.
119. Product ad, Perception Technology, Inc.
120. Product ad, Boole & Babbage, Inc.
121. Thornswood, Lance, presentation at High-Tech Direct conference, 2/28/94.

122. Vogel, Al: Model aids in cost-effective communications. *Public Relations Journal*, February 1994, p. 8.

123. Fryer, Bronwyn: Client-Proofing Your Concepts. *Marketing Computers*, July 1993, p. 32.

124. Schultz, Don E., Tannenbaum, Stanley I., Lauterborn, Robert F.: *Integrated Marketing Communications*. Lincolnwood IL: NTC Business Books, 1993.

125. The New Marketing. *Marketing Computers*, November 1993, p. 46.

126. Berry, Leonard L. and Parasuraman, A.: *Marketing Services: Competing Through Quality*. New York: Free Press, 1991.

127. Ad, Berlitz Translation Services.

128. Ott, Richard: *Creating Demand: Powerful Tips and Tactics for Marketing Your Product or Service*. Homewood, IL: Business One–Irwin, 1992.

129. Product brochure, Racal-Datacom, Inc.

130. Bowman, Joel P. and Branchaw, Bernadine P.: *How to Write Proposals That Produce*. Phoenix, AZ: Oryx Press, 1992.

131. Moore, Geoffrey A.: *Crossing the Chasm: Marketing and Selling Technology Products to Mainstream Customers*. New York: HarperBusiness, 1991.

132. Meyerowitz, Steven A.: *An Ounce of Prevention: Marketing, Sales, and Advertising Law for Non-Lawyers*. Detroit, MI: Visible Ink Press, 1993.

133. Burriss, Richard S.: Ads can be a legal problem when they tell the truth, but not the whole truth. *San Jose Business Journal*, November 22, 1993, p. 22.

134. Direct-mail package, Phoenix Technologies Ltd.

135. Copy Chasers. *Business Marketing*, June 1992, p. 40.

136. Kadanoff, Marcia: High-tech marketing should give up technical approach. *San Jose Business Journal*, October 12, 1993, p. 7.

137. Hoft, Nancy L.: *International Technical Communication*. New York: Wiley (forthcoming 1995).

138. Hall, Edward T. and Hall, Mildred Reed: *Understanding Cultural Differences*. Portland, ME: Intercultural Press, 1990.

139. Farinelli, Jean L.: Technology Respects No Boundaries, Why do We? *Mass High Tech*, June 14, 1993, p. 1.

140. Elmore, Laura L.: The Global Product Launch: Part III. *Export Today*, January 1991, p. 35.

141. Chapter in Baines, Adam: *Handbook of International Direct Marketing*. London: Kogan-Page, 1992.

142. Freivalds, John: Creating a Verbal Identity. *IABC Communication World*, December 1993, p. 36.

143. Article in *OEM Magazine*, 3/94.

144. Horton, William: New Media Literacy. *Technical Communication*, Fourth Quarter 1993, p. 794.

145. Lisker, Peter: Start-up launches Notes-based information service. *Network World*, November 8, 1993, p. 62.

146. Locke, Christopher: Advertising on the Internet? Try Somethng
     Else! *Network Computing*, January 15, 1994, p. 62.
147. Newsletter, Walker, Richer & Quinn, Inc.
148. CompuServe message, Howard J. Sewell.
149. Product catalog, ADC Kentrox.
150. Trademark usage guide, Microsoft Corp.
151. Trademark usage guide, Tandem Computers, Inc.
152. Direct-mail package, Intuit.
153. Fueroghne, Dean Keith: *"But the People in Legal Said . . ."*
     Homewood, IL: Dow Jones–Irwin, 1989.
154. Product ad, CBIS, Inc.
155. Product brochure, Aldus Corporation.
156. Direct mail letter, Citadel Computer Systems, Inc.

Index

A

acronyms, 83–84, 156
action objective, 35
active voice, 111
adaptation
  See localization
advertising, 160
  comparative, 99–100, 140–141
  deceptive, 130
  international, 155
advertorials, 165
agenda, setting, 14
agreement, nondisclosure, 139
AIDA Model, 4
alliance, 225–236
  announcements, 90
  partners, as an audience, 24
alliteration, 107
allusion, 115
altering images, 142
analogy, 114
analysts, as an audience, 31
anecdotes, 103
announcements:
  alliance, 90
  product, 67, 77
  upgrade, 85–86
applications:
  digest, 195
  guide, 225
  images, 70
  information, 85
  messages, 43
  product, 171
arguments, presenting, 42
articles, 185, 199–200, 204
  concepts, 54
  technology primer, 13
assignments, 20, 22

attorneys, working with, 128–129
attracting readers, 106
attribution, 142
audience, 23–34
  forgetting, 124
  in creative platform, 16–17
  in document plans, 19, 21
  messages, 47
awareness, creating, 14

B

background information, 85
  See also supporting evidence
backgrounder, 204
benefits, 43, 79–81
blah, blah, blah syndrome, 120
body copy, 69, 82
boilerplate, 158, 221
box, product, 188
broadcasts, 239
brochures, 165, 167, 172, 184
budgets, 10
bullet lists, 71, 82
bulletin board system
  (BBS) 31, 243
business reply cards (BRC)
  See reply cards
buying concerns, 26

C

call to action, 74, 120
  international, 157
callouts, 70, 82
campaign themes, 17–18
capabilities statements, 89, 167
captions, 70, 82
card decks, 172
case studies, 13, 91, 201, 210
catalogs, 174
CD-ROM, 245
celebrities, 140

certifications, 79
charts
    See visuals
citing sources, 96
claims, product, 130
clarity, 121–122
closers, 72–73
communications cycle, 2–7, 37
company:
    backgrounders, 205
    fact sheets, 211
    information, 78, 88, 172, 218
    messages, 43
    personality, 57
    privacy, 140
    reputation, 27
    trademarks, 136, 138
comparative advertising, 140–141
comparisons, 98–99, 172
competitive:
    activity, 9, 12, 16
    information, 86
    positioning, 90
concepts, 53–56, 61
    creative, 16
    international, 148–149
concerns, customer, 26–28
confidential information, 138–139
confused messages, 48–49
conjunctions, 117
consents, 131
constraints, 17–18
consumer market, 29
content types, 77–104
    in document plans, 20–21
    international, 156
contests, 131
contractions, 117
contrasting semantics, 114
copy:
    reason-why, 101
copyright, 134–135
    international, 148
copywriting guidelines, 20–21
corporate market, 29
creating awareness, 14
creating quotes, 95
creative platforms, 15–18
credibility, 41
customers:
    as an audience, 23, 26, 29
    information, 90, 172, 210
    research, 30–32

D
data sheets, 13, 175
dateline, 220
dealers, 23–24, 30–32
    education, 3
    materials, 225
    sustained communication, 7
    See also sales staff
deceptive advertising, 130
definitions, in openers, 67
demo disks, 168, 240, 242
design, electronic media, 239

designers, 20, 61
developer brochures, 227
diagrams, 70
    See visuals
dialects, 151
direct mail, 167, 180–185
    international, 147
    packages, 175
disclaimers, 133
distrust, audience, 28
document elements, 64–77, 113
    in document plans, 20–21
document plans, 19–21, 53, 58
documents:
    audience-targeted, 32
    evaluation methods, 34
    in marcom plans, 9, 13
    objective, 36
    purpose, 39
    review process, 16
    types, 19, 21
E
editing quotes, 95
editorial, 201
    contacts, 220
    coverage, 14
    information, 188
education, 3
electronic mail, 243
electronic media, 237–247
    brochures, 168
elements, document
    See document elements
emotion, 42, 107
emphasis, 60, 109
employees, as an audience, 23, 25
endorsements, 131
    See also case studies
envelopes, direct mail, 183
errors, 125
ethics, 141–144
evaluation methods, 9
    creative platform, 17–18
    marcom plans, 12, 14
    messages, 51
event information, 91, 219
evidence
    See supporting evidence
evocative language, 106
examples, as a content type, 103
excessive hype, 118
extrapolation, 54
F
fact sheets, 211
fair-trade laws
    See trade laws
false advertising
    See deceptive advertising
fax, 244
fear, uncertainty, and doubt
    (FUD) 49, 108
features, 43, 79–81
featuritis, 124
Federal Trade Commission
    (FTC) 129, 131

fictitious names, 140
financial:
    information, 89, 100
    regulations, 133
five Ws, 66
focus groups, 31
forgetting to sell, 120
formal style, 58
formatting devices, 109, 142
G
getting attention, 106
glossary, translation, 153
government market, 29
graphic designer
    See designers
guarantees, 131–132
guidelines:
    comparative advertising, 99
        100
    copywriting, 20–21
Gunning Fog index, 122
H
headlines, 64–65
home office market, 29
humor, 116
hype, 118–119
I
ideas, judging, 55–56
idiom, 117, 156
illustrations
    See visuals
imagery, 114–116, 157
images, altering, 142
implementation issues, 27
impression objective, 35
in-country reviewers, 148, 153
inappropriate interpretation, 142
individual privacy, 139
industry trend overview, 195
informal style, 59
information, 84–91
    company, 78, 88, 172, 218
    comparative, 98–99
    confidential, 138–139
    customer, 90, 172, 210
    event, 91, 219
    offers, 98
    ordering, 172
    pricing, 87, 172
    problem/solution, 100
    product, 77, 86, 89, 217
    purpose, 38, 40
infrastructure education, 3
inspiration, 110
integrated marketing communica-
        tion, 7
interactive voice response, 247
international, 146–159
    dealers, 31
    market, 29, 147, 155
    messages, 46, 149
    See also localization
Internet, 243
interviews, 143, 201
investors, as an audience, 23–24

involvement devices, 72
irrelevancies, 124
issues, 101–102
    analysis, 197
    audience for, 25
J
jargon, 82–83, 122, 155
Johnson Box, 183
journalists, as an audience, 23,
        31–32
K
kiosks, 246
L
language, 106
Lanham Act, 129–130, 141
launch, product
    See product introduction
laws, trade, 129
legal, 128–145
    direct mail, 180
    international, 148, 155, 157
    requirements, in document
        plans, 20, 22
letters, sales, 183
lift notes, 184
localization, 54, 146–151
    See also international
logos, company, 136
M
magazine articles
    See articles
Magnuson-Moss Act, 132
management discussion, 196
marcom plans, 8–15
market, 29–33
    international, 29, 31, 147
    leadership message, 43
    new, 14
market information, 16, 86, 88
    in marcom plans, 9, 11
    international, 155
masthead, 188
material, source, 20–21
materials:
    audience for, 25
    customized to market, 33
    product introduction, 3–4
    staging, 14–15
    sustained communication, 6
measuring results, 14
media buying, 10
media kits, 213
messages, 35–51
    closers, 73
    consistency, 15
    in creative platform, 16–17
    in document plans, 20–21
    in openers, 66
    international, 46, 149
    negative, 40, 49, 123
metaphor, 114
misrepresentation, 141–142
mistakes, 118–127
modifiers, 119
modifying images, 142

motivation purpose, 38–39
multilingual documents, 151
multimedia
    See electronic media
N
nameplate, 188
narrator's voice, 118
negative messages, 40, 49
negativism, 123, 155
new business announcement, 91
newsletters, 185
nondisclosure, 138–139
notation, 134–137, 157
numbered lists, 71
numbers, 92–93
O
objectives, 35–37
    in document plans, 20–21
    in marcom plans, 14
offers, 97–98, 131, 180
    in document plans, 20–21
online services, 243
    See also electronic media
onomatopoetic language, 107
openers, 66–68
opinion article, 201
order form, 184, 188
organizational history, 89
overimportance, 123
overlines, 66
overstatement, 141
overview documents, 167
P
packaging, 188, 242
paradox, 116
parallelism, 112
paraphrasing quotes, 96, 142
partners program brochures, 227
passive voice, 111, 121
patents, 89, 138
permissions, 134
personality, company, 57
personification, 115
persuasion purpose, 38, 41
photographs
    See visuals
plagiarism, 143
planning guide, 195
plans, 2–22
    articles, 201
    international, 147–148
platforms, creative, 15–17
point-of-sale material, 228
positioning, 14–17
    images, 70
postal regulations, 133
postpublication survey, 34
power words, 106
premiums, 131
presentations, sales, 234–235
press kits, 13, 213, 216–217
press materials, 54, 199–224
press releases, 217, 220–221
pricing information, 43, 87, 131, 172

primary messages, 47
privacy rights, 139–140
problems, describing, 67, 100
product:
    announcements, 3–4, 77
    applications, 171
    background information,
        84–86
    backgrounders, 205
    claims, 130
    fact sheets, 211
    images, 70
    maintenance, 27
    mentions, 201
    misrepresentation, 141
    overviews, 167
    preference, 14
    prospect concerns, 27
    safety warnings, 133
    sales information, 31
    selection guides, 200
    selling factors, 30
    specifications, 82
    support, 27
profile articles, 201
profile, audience, 16
progression, 54
projection, 54
promotion plans, 87
proofreading, 125
proposals, 32, 141, 189
proprietary information, 138
prospects, as an audience, 23,
        26–27, 29
public relations plans, 10
publication:
    style, 201
    style guide, 57
    type, 19, 21
puffing, 131
pull quotes, 70
purchase:
    factors, 27
    information, 43
    offer, 97
purpose, 36–41
    and writing style, 57
    emphasis, 61
    exercises, 52
    in document plans, 20–21
    tone, 59
Q
Q & A documents, 221
qualifiers, 106
qualifying questions, 193
questions, 113
    ethical, 144
    in openers, 67
quotes, 78, 94–97, 131
    in closers, 73
    in openers, 67
    international, 157
R
reason-why copy, 41, 101

recyclable copy, 15
regulations, 133
release date, 220
relevance, 108
reply cards, 172, 184, 188–189
request for proposal
    (RFP) 32, 189
research, 31–32, 200
resistance, audience, 28
results:
    as a content type, 100
    measuring, 14
retail materials, 228
review process, 16, 20, 22
reviewers, in-country, 148, 153
rhythm, 110–112
rights:
    privacy, 139
    usage, 135
risk aversion, audience, 28
S
safety warnings, 133
sales:
    guides, 231, 234
    information, 86, 89, 120
    kits, 86
    letters, 183, 193
    presentations, 234–235
sales cycle, 4–5, 29
sales materials: 54, 160–198
sales staff:
    as an audience, 23–24, 30
    education, 3
    sustained communication, 7
schedules, 10, 22
secondary audience, 23
secondary messages, 46–47
self-mailers, 185
selling factors, 30
semantics, 114
sentences, 111
service information, 87–88
service marks, 136
setting the agenda, 14
sidebars, 71
situation analysis, 9, 11
slang, 117
SOHO market, 29
solutions, 26, 100
source material, 20–21
sources, 96–131
specifications, product, 82, 172
speech, 235–236
staging materials, 14–15
statistics, 92–93, 142
strategy, 8, 12, 89
structure, defined in style, 58
style, 56–62
    in creative platform, 17–18
    international, 155
style guides, 57, 153–154
subheads, 64, 82
submission requirements, 201
supporting evidence, 92

surveys, 131
sustained communication, 6
synthesis, 54
T
tactics, 9, 12
technical support
    See service information
technology:
    briefings, 195
    leadership, 43
    primers, 13, 200
test results, 93
testimonials
    See endorsements
testing messages, 51
text techniques, 105–127
tone, 17–18, 59
trade laws, 129
trade secrets, 138–139
trademarks, 79, 117, 136–137, 157
        international, 148
translation, 148–154
trends, as a content type, 102, 201
trendy words, 120
truth-in-advertising
    See deceptive advertising
U
unique selling proposition
    (USP) 44
upgrades, 27, 85–86
usage:
    international, 155–156
    rights, 135
    trademarks, 137
user groups, 31
V
vagueness
    See clarity
varied sentences, 111
videos, 168, 246
viewpoint switching, 54
visuals, 69, 172
    international, 148, 157
voice response, 247
W
warnings, safety, 133
warranties, 131–132
weak quotes, 94
weaving messages, 47
white papers, 195, 197
word charts, 70, 81
word usage, 155
wordplay, 111
work for hire, 135
writers, assignments, 20
writing:
    creative platforms, 18
    document plans, 19
    electronic media, 238–239
    ideas, 53, 55–56
    international, 154
    marcom plans, 15
    style, 3, 56, 155
    techniques, 105–127